# The Bible of Amiens

Proust by Way of Ruskin

By the same author in the same series

*Sesame and Lilies*

To Jennifer

## Translator's Introduction

John Ruskin (1819-1900) wrote *The Bible of Amiens* in 1882 when he was sixty-three. Six years after Ruskin's death, Marcel Proust (1871-1922) published his translation *La Bible d'Amiens* at the age of thirty-five. This is the first translation into English of Proust's work which, in addition to the translation, includes a long preface and copious notes. The text on which this translation is based was published by *Éditions Payot & Rivages* in 2011. I am grateful to Hazel Hale for encouraging me during the three years I have been working on the series *Proust by Way of Ruskin*.

R A Goodlake Lowen
Grimsby, Lincolnshire
August 2014

**BELL & CLEWS**

Published in the United States of America

ISBN : 978-1-4937-7148-6

To the memory
of my father
Struck down at work on 24 November 1903
Died on 26 November
This translation
is tenderly dedicated
M P

'Then comes the time of work ... then the time of death, which in happy lives is very short.'

John Ruskin

The preface and Proust's translation
were published in 1906, by *Mercure de France*.

## Table of Contents

## Preface by Marcel Proust

| | | |
|---|---|---|
| I | Foreword | 9 |
| II | Notre-Dame d'Amiens according to Ruskin | 14 |
| III | John Ruskin | 35 |
| IV | Postscript | 57 |

## The Bible of Amiens

| | | |
|---|---|---|
| Preface | | 72 |
| I | By the Rivers of Waters | 75 |
| | *Notes to Chapter I* | 97 |
| II | Under the Drachenfels | 104 |
| III | The Lion Tamer | 136 |
| IV | Interpretations | 168 |

Appendix I  Chronological list of the main
events referred to in *The Bible of Amiens*  219

Appendix II  General plan of *Our Fathers Have
Told Us*  221

Notes  223

## I

# Foreword

I offer here a translation of *The Bible of Amiens*, by John Ruskin. But it seems to me that this is not enough for the reader. To read only one book by an author is to see this author but once. Now, in talking to someone once, one can discern in him special traits. But it is only by their repetition, in various circumstances, that one can recognise them as characteristic and essential. For a writer, for a musician or for a painter, this variation of circumstances which permits one to discern, by a sort of experimentation, permanent character traits, is the variety of their works. We find again, in a second book, in another painting, the distinctive features which we might have thought the first time belonged to the subject matter as much as to the writer or the painter himself. And by comparing different works we distinguish common traits which, taken together, reveal the moral character of the artist. When several portraits painted by Rembrandt, using different models, are brought together in a room, we are immediately struck by what is common to all of them and what makes up the characteristic features of a Rembrandt face. By inserting a footnote to the text* of *The Bible of Amiens*, each time this text evoked by even remote analogies the memory of other works by Ruskin, and by translating in the note the passage which had thus come to mind, I have tried to put the reader in the situation of someone who would not find

---

*In our edition, we have chosen to regroup all the notes at the end of the work.

himself in Ruskin's presence for the first time but who, having already had previous conversations with him, would be able to recognise in his words what is permanent and fundamental in him. Thus I have tried to provide the reader with something akin to a makeshift memory in which I have arranged memories of other books by Ruskin, a kind of sounding board against which the words of *The Bible of Amiens* would resonate more deeply by awakening fraternal echoes. But these echoes will no doubt not correspond to the words of *The Bible of Amiens*, as they evoke a memory which is itself composed of distant horizons generally hidden from our view and whose various distances our life itself has measured day by day. In order to come into focus with the present word whose resemblance evoked them, these echoes will not have to traverse the gentle resistance of this interposed atmosphere which is the span of our life itself and all the poetry of memory.

Fundamentally, helping the reader to be impressed by these special traits, drawing his attention to similar traits that permit him to recognise them as the essential traits of the genius of a writer, these things must be the first part of every critic's task.

If he has felt that, and helped others to feel it, his job is almost done. And if he has not felt it, he could write all the books in the world on Ruskin: the Man, the Writer, the Scope of his Effort, the Errors of his Doctrine, all of these works may perhaps reach a very high level, but be beside the point; they may praise to the skies the critic's literary status but, as regards the understanding of the work, they would be of less value than the exact perception of a correct nuance, however insignificant it may appear.

I am conscious though that the critic should go even further. He should try to reconstruct what the unique spiritual life of a writer haunted by such special realities could have been, his inspiration being the measure of his vision of these realities, his talent the measure of his ability to recreate them in his work, his morality finally, the instinct which, making him consider them under an aspect of eternity (however particular these realities appear to us), impelled him to sacrifice to the need of perceiving them and to the necessity of reproducing them, in order to ensure their durable and clear vision, all his pleasures, all his duties and even his own life, which has no purpose except as the only possible way of entering into contact with these realities, and has no value except that which an instrument indispensable to his experiments may have for a physician. I need not say that I have not attempted to fulfil this second part of the job of the critic with regard to Ruskin. That could be the goal of subsequent efforts. This is only a translation and, for the notes, most of the time I have contented myself with quotations that seemed to me appropriate without adding commentaries. Some notes however are more developed. Those might have been better placed if, instead of leaving them here and there as footnotes, I had incorporated them into the body of my preface, which they complete and rectify on several points. But I did not want to do that because this preface, except for the foreword and a more recent postscript, simply reproduces articles that I had given to the *Mercure de France* and the *Gazette des Beaux-Arts* at the time of Ruskin's death.

Other notes have a different character. Those in Chapter IV are mainly archaeological. In effect, every time that Ruskin by way of quotation, but more often by way of allusion, incorporates into the structure of his sentences something from the Bible, as the Venetians inserted in their monuments the saved sculptures and precious stones they brought from the East, I have always looked up the exact reference so that the reader might see what changes Ruskin would make to a verse before using it, and thus might better realise the mysterious yet unchanging chemistry of his mind, the original and specific way his mind worked. Seeking the references, I could trust neither the index to *The Bible of Amiens* nor the Misses Gibbs' book *The Bible References of Ruskin*, which are excellent but far too incomplete. So I used the Bible itself.

The text translated here is *The Bible of Amiens* in extenso. Despite the various suggestions I received and which I should perhaps have followed, I have not omitted a single word of it. But having taken this line, so that the reader could have a complete version of *The Bible of Amiens*, I must confess that there are many tedious passages in this book, as in all those Ruskin wrote towards the end of his life. Furthermore, in this period of his life, Ruskin lost all respect for syntax and all concern for clarity, more so than the reader will often be prepared to believe. He will then very unjustly blame defects on the translator.

For the same reasons, I have given all the appendices, except for the *Alphabetical Index* and the *List of Photographs of the Cathedral* by Mr Kaltenbacher, photographs which one could formerly buy with *The Bible of Amiens*. Finally, the English edition includes four engravings which are not reproduced here, *The Dynasties of France*, *Cimabue's Madonna*, *Amiens on All Souls' Day* (I describe this engraving later on pages 47 and 48), and *The Northern Porch before Restoration*. Since photographs were sold with the book, one understands why Ruskin chose for his engravings subjects related only by a sort of allusion to the descriptions he gives of the cathedral and why he did not use the photographs as well. But those who are familiar with the books of Ruskin will more readily see in the somewhat singular choice of the subjects of these engravings an effect of the original, one might almost say humorous, disposition of his mind – which in a sense always led him to avoid what was expected, to put opposite a description of the Baptism of Christ by Giotto, an engraving representing the baptism of Christ, not by Giotto, but as one might see in an old psalter, or else, in a study of the church of St Mark, not to describe any of its important features but to devote numerous pages to the description of a bas-relief which one would never notice, or would distinguish with difficulty, and which besides is of no interest; but these are defects of Ruskin's mind which his admirers recognise with pleasure when encountering them because they know that, even though these are mannerisms, they are an integral part of the particular physiognomy of a great writer.

It remains for me to express my most particular gratitude, from among so many people whose advice has been precious to me, to Mr Alfred Vallette, who has given this edition infinitely intelligent and generous attention that does him the greatest honour; to Mr Charles Ephrussi, always so good to me, who has facilitated all my research by putting at my disposal the library of the *Gazette des Beaux-Arts*, and to Mr Robert d'Humières. When I was given pause by a difficult form of language, I would consult the remarkable translator of Kipling, and he would immediately resolve the problem with his astonishing understanding of English texts into which his intuition as much as his knowledge enters. Thus he was often and tirelessly helpful to me. I offer him here my affectionate thanks.

II

# Notre-Dame d'Amiens
## according to Ruskin[1]

I would like to give the reader the desire and the means to spend a day in Amiens on a sort of Ruskinian pilgrimage. It is not worth the trouble to begin by asking him to go to Florence or Venice when Ruskin has written a whole book on Amiens.[2] And on the other hand, it seems to me that it is thus that the 'cult of Heroes' should be celebrated, I mean in spirit and in truth. We visit the place where a great man was born and the place where he died; but did he not inhabit even more the places that he admired above all others, whose beauty is the very thing we love in his books?

We honour with a fetishism that is no more than an illusion a tomb in which the only part remaining of Ruskin was not himself, and we would not go to kneel before the stones of Amiens, to which he came seeking ideas and which keep them still, similar to a tomb in England where only the heart remains of a poet whose body was consumed – snatched from the flames in a sublime and tender gesture by another poet.[3]

Without doubt snobbery, which makes everything it touches seem reasonable, has not yet reached these aesthetic excursions (for the French at least) and has thereby saved them from ridicule. Say that you are going to Bayreuth to hear an opera by Wagner, to Amsterdam to visit an exhibition, and people will be sorry they cannot accompany you. But if you admit that you are going to see a storm at the Pointe du Raz, apple trees in bloom in Normandy, or a statue beloved of Ruskin at Amiens, people would not be able to conceal a smile. I hope nevertheless that you will go to Amiens after reading this.

When we work to please others we may not succeed, but the things we have done to satisfy ourselves always have a chance of interesting someone else. It is impossible that there should be nobody who takes any pleasure in what has given me so much. For nobody is unique, and fortunately for the sympathy and understanding which are such great pleasures in our life, it is in a universal framework that our individualities are formulated. If we could analyse the soul as we analyse matter, we would see that, under the apparent diversity of minds as well as of things, there are only a few simple substances and irreducible elements, and that into the composition of what we believe to be our personality enter elements that are quite common and that are discovered to some degree everywhere in the universe.

The indications that writers give us in their works of the places they have loved are often so vague that the pilgrimages we attempt there have something uncertain and hesitant about them, as if we were afraid of being deceived. Like Edmond de Goncourt's character searching for a tomb unmarked by a cross, we are reduced to making our devotions haphazardly. This is a kind of disappointment you will not have to fear with Ruskin, particularly at Amiens; you will not have to run the risk of coming to spend the afternoon there without knowing how to find him in the cathedral: he has come to fetch you at the railway station. He will find out not only how well equipped you are to appreciate the beauties of the cathedral, but also how much time the train you plan to take for your return trip will allow you to devote to them. He will not only show you the way which leads to Notre-Dame but will also show you alternative routes according to whether or not you are pressed for time. And as he wants you to follow him in the carefree frame of mind which comes with physical comfort, perhaps also in order to show you that in the manner of the saints whom he prefers he is not contemptuous of 'honest'[4] pleasures, before taking you to the church he will lead you to the pastry shop. Stopping at Amiens for aesthetic reasons you are already welcome, for many do not do as you do: 'The intelligent English traveller in this fortunate age knows that, half way between Boulogne and Paris, there is an important railway station in which his train, slowing down, takes him with many more than the average number of bangs and bumps expected on entering every great French station, so as to startle the sleepy or distracted passenger into a sense of his situation. He probably also remembers that at this stop in the middle of his journey there is a well-stocked buffet at which he has the privilege of a ten minute wait. He is not however as clearly conscious that this ten minute wait is granted him within not so many minutes' walk from the main square of a town which was once the Venice of France. Leaving aside the lagoon islands, the "Queen of the Waters" of France was almost as large as Venice herself.'

But enough has been said of the traveller for whom Amiens is only a station stop compared to you who are coming to see the cathedral and who deserve that someone see to it that your time is well spent; you will be led to Notre-Dame, but by which route?

'I have never been able to decide which was really the best way to approach the cathedral for the first time. If you have plenty of leisure and it is a fine day,[5] the best thing would be to walk down the main street of the old town, cross the river and go all the way out to the chalk hill on which the citadel is built. From there you will understand the real height of the towers and how they are built up over the rest of the town, then returning, find your way by any of the narrow streets; take the bridges that you find on your way; the more winding and dirty the streets, the better; and whether you come first upon the west front[6] or the apse, you will think them worth all the trouble you have had to reach them.

'But if it is a gloomy day, as can sometimes happen, even in France, or if you cannot or will not walk, which can also happen because of all our athletic sports and lawn tennis, or if you must really go to Paris this afternoon, and only want to see what you can in an hour or two, I am supposing that, despite these weaknesses, you are still a nice sort of person for whom it is of some consequence which way you come upon a pretty thing and begin to look at it. So I think the best way is to walk up the *rue des Trois Cailloux*. Stop for a moment along the way so as to get into a good mood, and buy some of the tarts and sweets in one of the charming little pastry shops on the left. Just past them ask for the theatre, and go straight up to the south transept which has really something about it to please everybody. Everybody must like the transparent fretwork of the spire on top of it, which seems to bend to the west wind, even though it does not – at least its bending is a long habit gradually adopted with growing grace and submissiveness over these last three hundred years – and coming right up to the porch, everybody must like the pretty little French Madonna in the middle of it, with her head a little to one side, and her halo a little to one side too, like a hat that suits her. She is a decadent Madonna despite, or rather because of, her prettiness and her gay flirt's smile; and she has no business there either, because this is St Honoré's porch, not hers. St Honoré used to stand there and receive you, rough and grey; he is now banished to the north porch where nobody ever goes in. This was done long ago, in the fourteenth century, when the people first began to find Christianity too serious, devised a merrier faith for France and wanted to have everywhere a flirtatious Madonna with bright glances, letting their own dark-eyed Joan of Arc be burned for a witch; and since then things went their merry way, straight on, 'ça allait, ça ira', to the merriest days of the guillotine. But they still knew how to sculpt in the fourteenth century, and the Madonna and her hawthorn blossom lintel are worth looking at, and even more the sculptures above, just as delicate and more calm, which tell St Honoré's own story, little talked of now in the faubourg in Paris that bears his name.

'But you must be impatient to go into the cathedral. First put a penny in the box of every beggar who stands there. It is none of your business to know if they should or should not be there nor whether they deserve to have a penny. Know only if you yourself deserve to have it to give and give it prettily and not as if it burned your fingers.'[7]

It is this second itinerary, the simplest one and, I suppose, the one you will prefer, that I followed the first time I went to Amiens; and the moment I caught sight of the south portal, I saw in front of me, on the left, at the same place Ruskin indicated, the beggars he talks about, and so old they were perhaps still the same ones. Happy to be able to start following Ruskinian directions so quickly, I went straight over to give them alms, under the illusion, into which entered some of this fetishism I was blaming just now, that I was performing a lofty act of piety towards Ruskin. Associated with my charity, with a half share in my offering, I thought I felt him directing my gesture. I knew and at less expense the state of mind of Frédéric Moreau in *L'Éducation sentimentale*, when on the boat, in front of Mme Arnoux, he extends his closed hand towards the cap of the harpist and 'opening it bashfully' drops a gold sovereign into it. 'It was not,' says Flaubert,'vanity that drove him to give these alms in front of her, but a thought of benediction with which he associated her, an almost religious impulse of the heart.'

Then, being too close to the portal to see its overall effect, I retraced my steps and, having arrived at the distance I considered appropriate, only then did I look. The day was splendid and I had arrived at the hour when the sun, at this time of year, pays its daily visit to the virgin once gilded and which it alone gilds today when it restores to her, on the days when it shines, a different, fugitive and sweeter brilliance. Besides, there is no saint the sun does not visit, giving to the shoulders of this one a coat of warmth, to the forehead of that one a halo of light. It never ends its day without having gone all around the immense cathedral. It was the hour of its visit to the virgin, and it was to its momentary caress that she seemed to address her centuries-old smile, this smile which Ruskin considers, as you have seen, that of a flirt to which he prefers the queens, with a more unaffected and more serious art, of the royal porch of Chartres. Here I refer the reader to the pages of *The Two Paths* which I have given later in note 190 and in which Ruskin compares the Gilded Virgin to the queens of Chartres. If I allude to it here it is because *The Two Paths* dating from 1858 and *The Bible of Amiens* from 1885, a comparison of the texts and the dates shows how much *The Bible of Amiens* differs from the kinds of books we write on matters we have studied in order to talk about them (supposing we have even taken this trouble) instead of talking about things which we have long been studying to satisfy a disinterested taste, and without thinking that they could later be the subject of a book. I thought that you would prefer *The Bible of Amiens*, feeling that as you leafed through it you were finding here things upon which Ruskin meditated continually, things which therefore express most profoundly his thought; that the present he was giving you was one of those which are most precious to those who love, and which consist of objects one has used a long time oneself, and only for oneself, with no intention of ever giving them away. In writing his book, Ruskin did not have to labour for you, he had to do nothing but publish his memoir and open his heart to you. I thought that the Gilded Virgin would have some importance in your eyes when you saw that almost thirty years before *The Bible of Amiens* she had a place in Ruskin's memory where, when he needed to give an example to his listeners, he knew he could find her, full of grace and charged with these serious thoughts that he often conjured up in her presence. Even then she already counted among these manifestations of beauty which not only gave to his sensitive eyes a more vivid delight than he had ever known, but in which Nature, in giving him this aesthetic sense, had predestined him to go and look for, as in the most touching expression, all that can be gathered on earth of the True and Divine.

Without doubt if, as has been said, Ruskin's mind wandered in extreme old age, as with the mysterious bird which in Gustave Moreau's famous painting does not wait for the arrival of death to flee the house, among the familiar forms which still ran through the confused reverie of the old man without his being able to reflect on them as they passed, the Gilded Virgin must surely have been there. Having become maternal again, as the sculptor of Amiens portrayed her, holding the divine infant in her arms, she must have been like the muse who alone is allowed to remain at the bedside, having rocked the cradle for so long. And, as in contact with familiar furniture, in tasting familiar dishes, old people experience their last joys almost without realising it, being recognisable only by the often fatal suffering their deprivation would cause, so Ruskin must have felt an obscure pleasure at seeing a casting of the Gilded Virgin, lowered by the invincible force of time from the heights of his thought and the predilections of his taste into the depth of his unconscious life and the satisfactions of habit.

There, with her special smile, which not only makes the Virgin a person, but an individual work of art of the statue, she seems to reject this portal she leans out of as being merely the museum we have to go to when we want to see her, as foreigners are obliged to go to the Louvre to see the Mona Lisa. But if the cathedrals, as has been said, are the museums of religious art of the Middle Ages, they are living museums to which Mr André Hallays could find no fault. They were not built to house works of art, but it is they – however individual they may be – that were made for them and could not without sacrilege (I simply speak here of aesthetic sacrilege) be located anywhere else. There with her so special smile, how I love the Gilded Virgin, with her smile of the mistress of the house of heaven; how I love her welcome at this door of the cathedral in her exquisite and simple garb of hawthorns. Like the rose bushes, the lilies and the fig trees of another porch, these sculpted hawthorns are still in bloom. But this mediaeval spring, prolonged for so long, will not be eternal and the wind of the centuries has already stripped from the front of the church, as on the solemn day of a Corpus-Christi without fragrance, some of its stone roses. No doubt one day the smile of the Gilded Virgin (which has already, however, lasted longer than our faith)[8] will also disappear, through the erosion of the stones which it dismisses graciously, to spread beauty for our children as it once poured out courage for our believing fathers. I feel I was wrong to call it a work of art: a statue that is thus forever part of a particular place on earth, of a particular town, that is to say a thing that has a name as a person has, that is an individual, the like of which we will never see again on the face of the continents, of which the railway employees at the place where we must inevitably come to find it, in announcing its name seem to tell us without realising it: 'Love that which you will only see this once', such a statue perhaps has something less universal than a work of art; it holds us at any rate by a bond stronger than that of the work of art itself, one of these bonds such as persons and countries hold us by. The Mona Lisa is the Mona Lisa of da Vinci. Without wishing to offend Mr Hallays, what does it matter to us where she was born, what does it even matter to us that she is naturalised French? She is rather like a wonderful 'stateless' person. Nowhere that thoughtful looks meet hers could she ever be considered a 'displaced' person. We cannot say as much of her smiling and sculpted sister, the Gilded Virgin (need we say moreover how inferior she is?). Coming no doubt from the quarries near Amiens, having made only one journey in her youth to come to the St Honoré porch, not having moved since, having been little by little weathered by the damp wind of the Venice of the North which has bent the spire above her, gazing for so many centuries on the inhabitants of this town of whom she is the oldest and most sedentary,[9] she is truly an Amiénoise. She is not a work of art. She is a beautiful friend we must leave in the melancholy provincial square that no one has ever succeeded in taking her from and where, for other eyes than ours, she will continue to receive the full force of the wind and sun of Amiens in her face, and to let the little sparrows settle with a sure instinct for decoration in the palm of her welcoming hand, or pick at the stone stamens of the antique hawthorn that has been her young garb for so many centuries. In my room a photograph of the Mona Lisa retains only the beauty of a masterpiece. Near her a photograph of the Gilded Virgin takes on the sadness of a keepsake. But let us not wait until, followed by its countless processions of rays and shadows resting on the relief of the stone, the sun has ceased to silver the greyness of the ancient porch, at once sparkling and tarnished. It has been too long since we lost sight of Ruskin. We had left him at the feet of this same virgin before whom his indulgence will have waited patiently for us to address our personal homage to her in our own way. Let us enter the cathedral with him.

'We cannot enter it to better advantage than by this south door, for all cathedrals of any importance produce nearly the same effect when you enter by the west door, but I know of no other which reveals its nobility at this point when seen from the south transept. The opposite rose is exquisite and splendid and the pillars of the transept aisles form with those of the choir and nave a wonderful group. From there also the apse shows its height better, as it opens to you as you advance little by little from the transept to the central nave. Seen from the west end of the nave, however, an irreverent person could almost believe that it is not the apse that is high, but the nave that is narrow. If besides you do not feel yourself filled with admiration for the choir and the circle of light that surrounds it, when you lift your eyes up towards it from the centre of the cross, you have no need to continue to travel further in search of cathedrals, for the waiting room of any railway station is a place that would suit you a lot better. But if, on the contrary, it amazes and delights you at first, then, the more you know of it, the more it will amaze, for it is not possible for imagination and mathematics together to achieve anything more powerful or nobler than this procession of windows marrying glass with stone, nor anything that appears grander.

'Whatever you see or are forced to leave unseen at Amiens, if the overwhelming responsibilities of your existence and the inevitable necessities of precipitate locomotion leave you just a quarter of an hour – without being out of breath – for the contemplation of the capital of Picardy, give it wholly to the woodwork of the cathedral choir. The portals, the lancet windows, the roses, you can see elsewhere as well as here, but such a masterpiece of carpenter's work, you cannot. It is fully developed flamboyant right at the end of the fifteenth century. You will see there the union of Flemish solidity with the charming flame of the French style: sculpting with wood was Picardy's joy; and so far as I know, there is nothing else so marvellous cut from any of the trees of any country anywhere. It is a sweet young-grained wood: oak chosen and fashioned for such work and resonating now in the same way as four hundred years since. Under the sculptor's hand, it seems to be modelled like clay, to be folded like silk, to have grown like living branches, to have leapt like living flame, … and it shoots, wreathes and branches out into an enchanted clearing, inextricable, imperishable, with a fuller foliage than any forest and a fuller story than any book.'[10]

Now famous the world over, represented in museums by castings that the attendants keep from being touched, these choir stalls, so old, so illustrious and so beautiful continue to exercise in Amiens their modest function of stalls – as they have been doing for several centuries to the great satisfaction of the Amiénois – like those artists who, having achieved glory, continue nevertheless to hold down a small job or give lessons. These functions consist in supporting the body, even before instructing the soul, and it is to this end that, turned down for each service and showing their backs, they are modestly useful.

Through continual rubbing, the wood has little by little taken on, or rather revealed, the dark purple at its heart which the eye, once enchanted by it, prefers to all else, to the point even that it can no longer look at the colours of paintings, finding these coarse by comparison. It is then a sort of intoxication to experience the glow of that wood, ever more vivid, which is like the sap of the tree, overflowing as time passes. The simplicity of the figures sculpted here takes from the material in which they live some quality of the doubly natural. And as for 'these fruits, these flowers, these leaves and these branches', all motifs taken from the local vegetation and which the Amiénois sculptor has sculpted in the wood of Amiens, the diversity of the planes having resulted in different patinas, one sees some wonderful contrasts of colours, where a leaf stands out in a shade other than that of its stem, making one think of these noble accents that Mr Gallé knew how to draw from the harmonious heart of oak trees.

But it is time to arrive at what Ruskin calls more particularly the Bible of Amiens, the west porch. Bible is taken here in its literal sense, not the figurative sense. The porch of Amiens is not only, in the vague sense in which Victor Hugo[11] would have understood it, a stone book: it is 'the Bible' in stone. No doubt, before knowing it, when you see the western front of Amiens for the first time, blue in the mist, brilliant in the morning, sun-soaked and sumptuously gilded in the afternoon, pink and already softly nocturnal at sunset, at whatever hour its bells ring out in the sky and as Claude Monet has captured them in his sublime canvases,[12] where the life of this man-made thing reveals itself, but which nature has reclaimed by enveloping it, a cathedral, and whose life like that of the earth in its double revolution unfolds down the centuries, while renewing itself and maturing daily – then, if you release it from the changing colours in which nature clothes it, you will feel again in front of this façade a confused but powerful impression. In seeing this monumental and lace-like swarming of human figures in stone which rise skyward, holding their crosses in their hands, their banderoles or sceptres, this world of saints, these generations of prophets, this succession of apostles, this host of kings, this line of sinners, this assembly of judges, this flight of angels, side by side, one above the other, standing near the door, looking at the town from the high recesses or from the ledge of the even higher galleries, receiving only the vague and dazzled looks of the men at the foot of the towers and in the ringing of the bells, no doubt in the heat of your emotion you feel that this magnificent pile, motionless and thrilling, is a stirring sight. But a cathedral is not only a beauty to be felt. Even if it is for you no longer a teaching to be followed, it is at least a book to be understood. The portal of a Gothic cathedral, and more particularly the portal of Amiens, the Gothic cathedral par excellence, is the Bible. Before explaining it to you I would like, with the help of a quotation from Ruskin, to make you understand that, whatever your beliefs may be, the Bible is something real, of the present, and we have to find in it something other than the savour of its archaism and the entertainment of our curiosity.

'The first, eighth, twelfth, fifteenth, nineteenth, twenty-third and twenty-fourth psalms, well learned and believed, are enough for all personal guidance and have in them the law and prophecy of all righteous government, and every real triumph of natural science is anticipated in the one hundred and fourth. Consider what other group of historical and didactic literature has a range comparable with that of the Bible.

'Think if you can compare its table of contents, I do not say to any other book, but to any other literature. Try, so far as it is possible for any of us – whether defender of the faith or its adversary – to extricate his intelligence from the habit and association of moral sentiment based upon the Bible, and ask what literature could have taken its place or fulfilled its function, even if all the libraries in the universe had remained intact. I am no despiser of profane literature, so far from it that I believe no interpretation of Greek religion so reverent, as those which will be found at the base of my art teaching, and running through the entire body of my works. But it was from the Bible that I learned the symbols of Homer and the faith of Horace. The duty imposed on me from my early youth, while reading every word of the gospels and prophesies, of penetrating conviction that they were written by the hand of God, gave me the habit of awed attention which afterwards made many passages of profane literature, frivolous to an irreligious reader, deeply serious for me. That there is a sacred classic literature, parallel with that of the Hebrews and merging with the symbolic legends of mediaeval Christianity, is a fact that appears in the most tender and impressive way by the independent yet similar influence of Virgil on Dante, and on Bishop Gawaine Douglas. And the story of the Nemean Lion conquered with the help of Athena is the real root of the legend of St Jerome's companion, conquered by the healing gentleness of the spirit of life. I call it a legend only. Whether Heracles ever killed or St Jerome ever cared for the wild or wounded creature is of no importance for us. But the legend of St Jerome takes up the prophecy of the millennium and predicts with the Cumaean Sybil, and with Isaiah, a day when the fear of man will cease to be a hatred for creatures of a lower order but will be spread over them as a blessing, when there shall be no hurt or destruction in all the holy mountain, and the peace of the earth will be as far removed from its present sorrow as the present gloriously animate universe from the nascent desert, whose deeps were the places of dragons, and its mountains domes of fire. Of that day no man knows, but the kingdom of God is already come to those who have tamed in their own hearts what was rampant of the lower nature and have learned to cherish what is charming and human in the wandering children of the clouds and fields.'[13]

And perhaps now you would like to follow the summary that I am going to try and give you, according to Ruskin, of the Bible written at the west porch of Amiens.

In the middle is the statue of Christ which is, not in the figurative but in the literal sense, the cornerstone of the structure. To his left (that is, to the right for us who are facing the Christ as we look at the porch, but we will use the terms left and right with regard to the statue of Christ), six apostles: near him Peter, then some distance from him James the Greater, John, Matthew, Simon. On his right Paul, then James the bishop, Philip, Bartholomew, Thomas and Jude.[14] Following the apostles are the four major prophets. After Simon, Isaiah and Jeremiah; after Jude, Ezekiel and Daniel; then, on the piers of the entire west front come the twelve minor prophets; three on each of the four piers, and beginning with the left-most pier: Hosea, Joel, Amos, Micah, Jonah, Obadiah, Nahum, Habakkuk, Zephaniah, Haggai, Zechaniah, Malachi. So that the cathedral, always in the literal sense, rests on Christ and on the prophets who foretold him as well as on the apostles who proclaimed him. The prophets of Christ and not those of God the Father:

'The voice of the entire building is that which came from heaven at the moment of the Transfiguration: This is my beloved son, listen to him.' Though Moses was an apostle not of Christ but of God, though Elijah was a prophet not of Christ but of God, they are not here. But, exclaims Ruskin, there is another great prophet who seems at first not to be here. Will the people enter the temple singing: 'Hosanna to the son of David,' and see no image of his father? Has Christ himself not declared: 'I am the root and the offspring of David,' and does not the root have near it no trace of the earth that nourished it? Not so; David and his son are together. David is the pedestal of the statue of Christ. He holds his sceptre in his right hand, a scroll in his left.

'Of the statue of Christ itself I will not speak, as no statue could or ought to satisfy the hope of any loving soul that has learned to believe in him. But at this time it exceeded anything that had ever been attained up to that point in sculpted tenderness. And it was known far and near as the "Beau Dieu d'Amiens". Yet it was only a sign, a symbol of the divine presence and not an idol, in our sense of the word. However, everyone conceived of it as the living spirit, coming to welcome him at the gate of the temple, the word of life, the King of glory, the Lord of hosts. "Lord of Virtues", Dominus Virtutum is the best rendering of the idea conveyed to a well-taught disciple of the thirteenth century in the words of the twenty-fourth psalm.'

We cannot stop at each of the statues of the west porch. Ruskin will explain to you the meaning of the bas-reliefs placed below them (two quatrefoil bas-reliefs, one under the other below each of them), the upper one under each apostle representing the virtue he taught or practised, the lower one, the opposite vice. Under the prophets the bas-reliefs represent their prophecies.[15]

Under St Peter is Courage with a leopard on its shield; under Courage, Cowardice is depicted as a man who, frightened by an animal, drops his sword while a bird sings on: 'The coward has not the courage of a thrush.' Under St Andrew is Patience whose shield bears a bull (never retreating).

Under Patience, Anger: a woman stabbing a man with a sword (Anger, an essentially feminine vice which has no connection to indignation). Under St James, Gentleness whose shield bears a lamb, and Coarseness: a woman giving her cupbearer a kick in the pants, 'the forms of ultimate French coarseness being the gestures of the cancan'.

Under St John, Love, divine Love, not human love: 'I in them and you in me.' Its shield bears a tree with branches grafted on to a cut off trunk. 'In those days the Messiah will be cut off, but not for himself.' Underneath Love, Discord: a man and a woman quarrelling; she has dropped her distaff. Under St Matthew, Obedience. On his shield, a camel: 'Today it is the most disobedient and obnoxious of beasts,' says Ruskin, 'but the northern sculptor knew little of its character. As in spite of everything it spends its life in the most painful of services, I think he has chosen it as the symbol of passive obedience experiencing neither joy nor sympathy, such as the horse, and on the other hand incapable of doing harm like the bull. It is true that its bite is dangerous enough, but at Amiens, it is very probable that it was not known, even by the Crusaders, who would ride their horses only, or nothing.'

Under Obedience, Rebellion, a man snapping his fingers in front of his bishop ('as Henry VIII in front of the Pope and the English and French cockney in front of every kind of priest').

Under St Simon, Perseverance caresses a lion and holds its crown. 'Hold tight to what you have so that no one takes your crown.' Below, Atheism leaves its shoes at the church door. The infidel fool is always represented, in the twelfth and thirteenth centuries, barefoot, Christ having his feet shod with the preparation of the gospel of Peace. 'How beautiful your feet are with shoes, O Prince's daughter!'

Under St Paul is Faith. Under Faith is Idolatry worshipping a monster. Under St James the bishop is Hope which holds a standard with a cross. Under Hope, Despair, which stabs herself.

Under St Philip is Charity which gives its cloak to a naked beggar.

Under St Bartholomew, Chastity with the phoenix, and under her, Lust, represented by a young man kissing a woman who is holding a sceptre and a mirror. Under St Thomas, Wisdom (a shield with an edible root signifying temperance, beginning with wisdom). Under her, Folly, the type used in all the early psalters of a glutton armed with a club: 'The fool has said in his heart: "There is no God, he devours my people as a piece of bread."' (Psalm 53, quoted by Mr Mâle.) Under St Jude, Humility which bears a shield with a dove, and Pride which is falling off its horse.

'Note,' says Ruskin 'that the apostles are all serene, nearly all with a book, some with a cross, but all with the same message: "That peace be in this house and if the Son of Peace is born", etc.; but the prophets, all seeking, or pensive, or tormented, or wondering, or praying, except Daniel. The most tormented of all is Isaiah. No scene of his martyrdom is depicted, but the bas-relief under him shows him seeing the Lord in his temple, and yet he has the feeling that his lips are unclean. Jeremiah also carries his cross, but more serenely.'

Unfortunately, we cannot stop at the bas-reliefs under the prophets which depict the verses of their main prophecies: Ezekiel seated before two wheels,[16] Daniel holding a book supported by lions,[17] then sitting at Belshazzar's feast, the fig tree and the vine without leaves, the sun and the moon without light as prophesied by Joel,[18] Amos gathering the leaves of the vine without fruit to feed the sheep which find no grass,[19] Jonah escaping from the waves, then seated under a gourd, Habakkuk whom an angel holds by the hair to visit Daniel, who strokes a young lion,[20] the prophesies of Zephaniah, the beasts of Nineveh, the Lord with a lantern in each hand, the hedgehog and the bittern,[21] etc.

I do not have the time to lead you to the two secondary doors of the west porch, the one of the Virgin[22] (which contains, besides the statue of the Virgin: to the left of the Virgin, the statues of the angel Gabriel, the Virgin Annunciate, the Virgin Visitant, St Elizabeth, the Virgin presenting the Child, St Simeon, and to the right the three Magi Kings, Herod, Solomon and the Queen of Sheba, each statue having under it, as under those of the main porch, bas-reliefs whose subjects relate to each) – and the door of St Firmin which contains the statues of the saints of the Diocese. No doubt it is because of this, because they are 'friends of the Amiénois', that the bas-reliefs under them represent the signs of the Zodiac and the labours of the months, bas-reliefs that Ruskin admires above all. You will find in the Museum of the Trocadéro the castings of these bas-reliefs of the porch of St Firmin[23] and in Mr Mâle's book charming commentaries on the local and climatic truths of these little genre scenes.

'I do not intend to study here,' says Ruskin again, 'the art of these bas-reliefs. They were never meant to serve as more than guides to thought. And if the reader follows this guidance quietly, he will be free to create for himself more beautiful pictures in his heart; and at all events, he may recognise the following truths affirmed by the entire grouping.

'First, throughout this sermon on the Amiens mount, Christ is never depicted as crucified, never for a moment thought of as dead: but appears as the Incarnate Word – as the present Friend – as the Prince of Peace on the earth – as the Eternal King in heaven. What his life *is*, what his commandments *are*, what his judgement *will be*, are the things taught here, not what he once did, not what he once suffered, but what he is doing now, and what he orders us to do. Such is the pure, joyous and beautiful lesson of Christianity; and the fall from this faith, and the corruption of a dissolute practice can be attributed to our habit of contemplating Christ's death instead of his life, and substituting his past suffering for our present duty.

'Then secondly, though Christ does not bear his cross, the mourning prophets, the persecuted apostles, the martyred disciples do bear theirs. For just as it is well for you to remember what your immortal creator has done for you, it is no less well to remember what mortal men, our fellow creatures, have done too. You can at your pleasure deny or defy Christ, but the martyr you can only forget; deny him you cannot. Every stone of this building has been cemented with his blood. Keeping then these things in your heart, look back now towards the central statue of Christ; hear his message and understand it. He holds the book of the eternal Law in his left hand; with his right he blesses, but blesses on condition: "Do this and you will live" or rather in a stricter, more rigorous sense: "Be this, and you will live". Showing mercy is nothing, your soul must be full of mercy; to be pure in deed is nothing, you must also be pure in heart.

'And with this word of the unabolished law: "If you do not do this, if you are not this, you will die." – Die – whatever meaning you would give the word – totally and irrevocably.

'The gospel and its power are written entirely in the great works of the true believers: in Normandy and Sicily, on the river islets of France, in the river valleys of England, on the rocks of Orvieto, by the sands of the Arno. But the teaching that is at the same time the simplest and most complete, which speaks with the greatest authority to the active mind of northern Europe, is this on the foundation stones of Amiens.

'All human creatures, in all times and places of the world, who have had warm affections, common sense and self-control, have been and are naturally moral. The knowledge and enforcement of these things have nothing to do with religion.

'But if, loving creatures who are like yourself, you feel that you would love more dearly creatures better than yourself if they were revealed to you, if, striving with all your might to improve what is bad near you and around you, you would like to think of the day when the judge of all the earth will wholly do right and the little hills will rejoice on every side, if, separating yourself from the companions who have given you all the best joy you have had on the earth, you desire ever to meet their eyes again and clasp their hands – where eyes will no more mist over or hands fail, if, preparing yourself to lie down beneath the grass in silence and loneliness seeing no more beauty, feeling no more joy, you would worry about the promise to you of a time when you would see God's light again, and know the things you have longed to know, and walk in the peace of eternal love – then the hope of these things to you is religion; their substance in your life is faith. And in their virtue it is promised to us that the kingdoms of this world will one day become the kingdoms of our Lord and his Christ.'[24]

Here ends the teaching that the men of the thirteenth century came to seek at the cathedral and which, through a useless and bizarre luxury, it continues to offer in a kind of open book, written in a solemn language where each character is a work of art, and which nobody understands any more. Giving it a meaning less literally religious than during the Middle Ages or even an aesthetic meaning only, you have been able nevertheless to relate it to one of these feelings that appear to us as the true reality beyond our lives, to one of 'these stars to which it is best to hitch our wagon'. Not appreciating until then the scope of religious art in the Middle Ages, I had told myself in my fervour for Ruskin: He will teach me, for he too, in some portion at least, is he not the truth? He will make my spirit enter where it had no access, for he is the door. He will purify me, for his inspiration is like the lily of the valley. He will intoxicate me and give me life, for he is the vine and the life. And I have felt in effect that the mystic perfume of the rose trees of Sharon has not vanished for ever, since we breathe it still, at least in his words. And now indeed the stones have for me taken on the dignity of the stones of Venice, and almost the grandeur the Bible had, when it was still the truth in the hearts of men and grave beauty in their works. *The Bible of Amiens* was intended by Ruskin to be but the first book of a series entitled *Our Fathers Have Told Us*; and in effect if the old prophets of the porch of Amiens were sacred to Ruskin, it is because the soul of the thirteenth century artists was still in them. Even before knowing if I would find it, it was the soul of Ruskin I went to seek there which he imprinted on the stones of Amiens as deeply as their sculptors had imprinted theirs, for the words of genius can give as well as the chisel an immortal form to them. Literature too is a 'lamp of sacrifice' which consumes itself to light future generations. I was complying unconsciously with the spirit of the title *Our Fathers Have Told Us*, when I went to Amiens with these thoughts and with the desire to read the Bible of Ruskin there. For Ruskin, having believed in these men of former times because in them was faith and beauty, also happened to write his Bible as they had written theirs, believing in the prophets and the apostles. For Ruskin, the statues of Jeremiah, Ezekiel and Amos perhaps no longer had the same meaning as they had for the sculptors of the past; yet they were at least works full of instruction from great artists and men of faith, and the eternal meaning of forgotten prophecies. For us, if the work of these artists and the meaning of these words are no longer sufficient to make them precious, let them for us at least be the things in which Ruskin found this spirit, the brother of his own and father of ours. Before we arrived at the cathedral, was it not for us above all the one he had loved? And did we not feel that there were such things as Holy Scriptures, since we were reverently looking for Truth in his books? And now we stop in vain in front of the statues of Isaiah, Jeremiah, Ezekiel and Daniel, saying to ourselves: 'Here are the four great prophets, after come the minor prophets, but there are only four great prophets,' there is one more who is not there and of whom, moreover, we cannot say that he is absent, for we see him everywhere. It is Ruskin: if his statue is not at the door of the cathedral,[25] it is at the entrance to our heart. That prophet's voice is no longer heard. But it is because he has finished uttering his words. It is for the coming generations to take them up again in chorus.

## III

# John Ruskin

Like 'the Muses leaving Apollo their father to enlighten the world',[26] one by one the ideas of Ruskin had left the divine head that had carried them and, incarnated in living books, had gone forth to teach the people of the world. Ruskin had retired into the solitude where prophetic beings often go until it pleases God to call to himself the cenobite or ascetic whose superhuman task is finished. And one can only guess, through the veil held by pious hands, the mystery that was being accomplished, the slow destruction of a perishable brain that had sheltered an immortal legacy.

Today death has let humanity take possession of the immense heritage left by Ruskin. For the man of genius cannot give birth to immortal works except by creating them in the image, not of his mortal being, but of the humanity he bears within himself. His thoughts are in a way lent to him during his life, for which they are the companions. At his death, they return to humanity and teach it. It is like this august and familiar dwelling on the *rue de la Rochefoucauld* that was called Gustave Moreau's house while he was alive and that is called, since he died, the Gustave Moreau Museum.

For a long time there has been a John Ruskin Museum.[27] Its catalogue seems to be a summary of all the arts and all the sciences. Photographs of paintings by masters rub shoulders with collections of minerals, as in Goethe's house. Like the Ruskin Museum, the work of Ruskin is universal. He sought the truth, and found beauty even in chronological tables and social laws. But the logicians having given the 'Fine Arts'[28] a definition that excludes mineralogy as well as political economy, it is only of the part of Ruskin's work that relates to the 'Fine Arts' as generally understood, of Ruskin the aesthetician and art critic that I shall have to speak here.

At first he was called a realist. And, in effect, he often repeated that the artist must insist on the pure imitation of nature 'without rejecting, without despising, without choosing anything'.

But it was also said that he was an intellectual because he wrote that the best picture was the one that contained the loftiest thoughts. Speaking of the group of children who, in the foreground of Turner's *Construction of Carthage*, are playing with toy boats, he concluded: 'The exquisite choice of this episode, as a means of indicating the maritime genius from which the future grandeur of the new city was to come, is a thought which had lost nothing by being written, which has nothing to do with the techniques of art. A few words would have conveyed it to the spirit as completely as the greatest achievements of the brush. Such a thought is something above all art; it is epic poetry of the highest order.' 'Likewise,' adds Milsand[29] who quotes this passage in analysing the *Holy Family* by Tintoretto 'the features which allowed Ruskin to recognise the great master are a ruined wall and the beginning of a new structure, by which the artist symbolically makes us understand that the birth of Christ was the end of the Jewish order and the coming of the new covenant.' In a composition by the same Venetian, the *Crucifixion*, Ruskin sees a masterpiece of painting because the author, by means of the apparently insignificant incident of an ass feeding on palm leaves in the background of Calvary, knew how to assent to the profound idea that 'it was Jewish materialism, with its expectation of a wholly temporal Messiah and with the confounding of its hopes at the time of the entry into Jerusalem, that had been the cause of the hatred unleashed against the Saviour and hence of his death.'

It has been said that he suppressed the role of imagination in art by giving too large a share to science. Did he not say that 'every class of rock, every variety of soil, every kind of cloud must be studied and rendered with a geological and meteorological precision? ... Every geological formation has features entirely peculiar to itself, definite lines of fracture which give rise to constant forms in earth and rocks, particular vegetations, among which still further distinctions are wrought by elevation and temperature. The painter observes in the plant all characters of form and colour ... seizes on its lines of rigidity or repose ... observes its local habits, its love or fear of particular places, the conditions which nourish its life or make it die. He associates it ... with all the characteristics of the places it inhabits ... He must render the fine fissure and the descending curve and the undulating shadow of the mouldering soil with a finger as light as the touch of rain itself ... A picture is admirable by reason of the number and the importance of the lessons it provides on the realities.'

It has been said on the other hand that he ruined science by giving imagination too large a part in it. And, in fact, one cannot help but think of the naïve finalism of Bernardin de Saint-Pierre saying that God had divided melons into segments so that men could eat them more easily, when one reads such pages as this: 'God has used colour in his creation as the accompaniment of all that is pure and precious, while he has reserved common colours for things of an only material utility or harmful things. Look at a dove's neck and compare it with the grey back of a viper. The crocodile is grey, the innocent lizard is of a splendid green.'

If it has been said that he reduced art to be a mere vassal of science, as he put forth the theory that the work of art should be considered as teaching on the nature of things so far as to declare that 'a Turner discovers more on the nature of rocks than any academy will ever know', and that 'a Tintoretto has but to let his hand go to reveal on the play of muscles a multitude of truths that will baffle all the anatomists on earth', it has also been said that he humiliated science before art.

Finally, it has been said that he was a pure aesthetician and that his only religion was Beauty, because in fact he loved it all his life.

But, on the other hand, it has been said that he was not even an artist, because he introduced into his appreciation of beauty considerations perhaps superior, but in any case foreign to aesthetics. The first chapter of *The Seven Lamps of Architecture* prescribes to the artist the use of the most precious and durable materials, and makes this duty derive from the sacrifice of Jesus, and permanent conditions for the sacrifice pleasing to God, conditions which must not be considered as abrogated, God never having expressly informed us that they were. And in *Modern Painters*, to settle the question of who is right, the partisans of colour or the adepts of chiaroscuro, here is one of the arguments: 'Take a wider view of nature and compare generally rainbows, sunrises, roses, violets, butterflies, birds, goldfish, rubies, opals and corals, with alligators, hippopotami, sharks, slugs, bones, fungi, fog and the mass of corrupting, stinging, and destroying things in general, and you will feel then how the question stands between the colourists and the chiaroscurists, which of them have nature and life on their side, and which sin and death.'

And since so many contrary things have been said about Ruskin, it has been concluded that he himself was contradictory.

Of so many aspects of Ruskin's character, the one which is most familiar to us, because it is the one of which we possess, if we may put it in this way, the most beautiful portrait, the most studied and most comely, the most striking and the most famous,[30] and in fact thus far the only one,[31] is the Ruskin who during his whole life knew but one religion: that of Beauty.

That the adoration of Beauty was, in effect, the perpetual act of Ruskin's life may be literally true: but I think the aim of this life, its profound, secret and constant intention was something else, and if I say this, it is not to take a position contrary to Mr de la Sizeranne's system, but to prevent it from being depreciated in the minds of the readers by a false but natural and almost inevitable interpretation.

Religion itself was not only Ruskin's principal religion (and I shall return to this point shortly, for it dominates and characterises his aesthetics) but, considering for the moment only the 'Religion of Beauty', we should warn our contemporaries that they cannot use this term correctly with reference to Ruskin unless they rectify the meaning that their aesthetic dilettantism is prone to give it. In fact, for an age of dilettantes and aesthetes, an adorer of Beauty is a man who practises no other cult and who, recognising no other god, spends his life in the voluptuous contemplation of works of art.

Now, for reasons whose metaphysical nature exceeds the bounds of a simple study of art, Beauty cannot be loved fruitfully if it is loved only for the pleasures it gives. And, just as the pursuit of happiness for happiness' sake leads but to boredom, and as in order to find it we must look for something else, so too aesthetic pleasure is given to us in addition if we love Beauty for itself as something real existing outside us and infinitely more important than the joy it gives us. And, far from having been a dilettante or an aesthete, Ruskin was precisely the opposite, one of these men who, like Carlyle, were warned by their genius of the vanity of pleasure and, at the same time, of the presence near them of an eternal reality, intuitively perceived by inspiration. Talent is given to them as a power to relate this reality to the all-powerful and eternal to which, with enthusiasm and as if obeying a command of conscience, they dedicate their ephemeral life in order to give it some value. Such men, attentive and anxious about the universe to be deciphered, are made aware of the parts of reality which their special gifts provide them with a particular understanding of, by a kind of demon which guides them, a voice they hear, the eternal inspiration of men of genius. The special gift for Ruskin was the feeling for beauty, in nature as in art. It was in beauty that his nature led him to seek reality, and his entirely religious life received from it an entirely aesthetic use. But this beauty to which he thus happened to dedicate his life was not conceived of by him as an object of enjoyment made to charm, but as a reality infinitely more important than life, for which he would have given his own life. From that you will see Ruskin's entire aesthetic unfold. First you will understand that the years when he became acquainted with a new school of architecture or of painting were the principal dates of his moral life. He would speak of the years when Gothic art presented itself to him with the same gravity, the same emotional nostalgia, the same serenity with which a Christian speaks of the day the truth was revealed to him. The events of his life are intellectual and the important dates are those when he fully understands a new form of art, the year he understands Abbeville, the year he understands Rouen, the day Titian's painting and the shadows in Titian's painting appear to him as nobler than Rubens' painting and than the shadows in Rubens' painting.

You will then understand that the poet being for Ruskin, as for Carlyle, a sort of scribe writing at nature's dictation a more or less important part of its secret, the artist's first duty is to add nothing of his own to this divine message. From these heights you will see vanish, like low-lying clouds, the accusations of realism as well as of intellectualism levelled against Ruskin. If these objections do not hit home, it is because they are not aimed high enough. There is an error of altitude in these criticisms. The reality that the artist must record is both material and intellectual. Matter is real because it is an expression of the mind. As for simple appearance, no one has ridiculed better than Ruskin those who see in its imitation the goal of art. 'Our enjoyment,' he says, 'of the imitation would be precisely the same, if the accuracy could be equal, whether the subject of it were the hero or his horse. We may consider tears as the result of art or of pain, whichever we please, but not of both at the same time; if we are surprised by them as a masterpiece of mimicry, it is impossible to be moved by them as a sign of suffering.' If he attaches so much importance to the aspect of things, it is because this alone reveals their deep nature. Mr de la Sizeranne has admirably translated a page in which Ruskin shows that the principal lines of a tree reveal which other pernicious trees have pushed it aside, which winds have tormented it, etc. The configuration of an object is not merely the image of its nature, it is the expression of its destiny and the outline of its history.

Another consequence of this conception of art is this: if reality is one and if the man of genius is he who sees it, what does it matter what medium he represents it in, be it in paintings, statues, symphonies, laws or acts? In his *Heroes*, Carlyle does not distinguish between Shakespeare and Cromwell, between Mohammed and Burns. Emerson counts Swedenborg as well as Montaigne among his *Representative Men of Humanity*. The problem with the system is that, because of the unity of the reality expressed, it does not differentiate deeply enough between the various modes of expression. Carlyle says it was inevitable that Boccaccio and Petrarch would make good diplomats, since they were good poets. Ruskin commits the same mistake when he says that 'a painting is beautiful inasmuch as the ideas it translates into images are independent of the language of the images.' It seems to me that if Ruskin's system errs in any direction, it is in this. For painting can attain the unique reality of things, and thus rival literature, only on condition that it is not itself literary.

If Ruskin has laid down that the duty of the artist is to obey scrupulously these 'voices' of genius which tell him what is real and must be transcribed, it is because he has himself experienced what is true in inspiration, infallible in enthusiasm, fruitful in respect. However, although what excites enthusiasm, what commands respect, and what provokes inspiration is different for everyone, each ends up attributing to it a character more privately sacred. One could say that for Ruskin this revelation, this guide, was the Bible: 'I would read every passage of it as if written by the hand of God. And this state of mind, fortified with the years, made many passages of the profane writers, frivolous for an irreligious reader, deeply grave for me. It is from the Bible that I learned the symbols of Homer, and the faith of Horace.'

Let us stop here as at a fixed point, at the centre of gravity of Ruskinian aesthetics. It is thus that his religious feeling directed his aesthetic feeling. And let us first reply to those who might believe that his religious feeling altered his aesthetic feeling, that to the artistic appreciation of monuments, statues and paintings he added religious considerations that had no business there, let us respond that it was quite the contrary. This something of the divine which Ruskin felt was the basis of the feeling which works of art inspired in him was precisely what was profound and original in this feeling and which imposed itself on his taste without being susceptible to modification. And the religious respect with which he expressed this feeling, his fear of distorting it in the slightest degree when translating it, prevented him, contrary to what has often been thought, from ever mixing any artificial reasoning that could be foreign to his impression when confronting works of art. So that those who see in him a moralist and an apostle loving in art what is not art are as mistaken as those who, neglecting the profound essence of his aesthetic feeling, confuse it with a voluptuous dilettantism. So that, in short, his religious fervour, which had been the sign of his aesthetic sincerity, strengthened it further and protected it from all foreign attack. Whether some of these conceptions of his supernatural aesthetics be false is a matter which, in our opinion, is of no importance. All those who have any understanding of the laws governing the development of genius know that its force is measured more by the force of its beliefs than what may be satisfying to common sense in the objects of those beliefs. But, since Ruskin's Christianity resulted from the very essence of his intellectual nature, his artistic preferences, equally profound, must have borne some relation to it. Also, just as the love of Turner's landscapes corresponded in Ruskin to this love of nature which gave him his greatest joys, so too the thoroughly Christian nature of his thinking corresponded to his permanent attraction, which dominates his whole life and work, to what one may call Christian art: French mediaeval architecture and sculpture, Italian mediaeval architecture, sculpture and painting. You need not look in his life for traces of the disinterested passion with which he loved these works, you will find the proof of it in his books. His experience was so vast, that very often the most profound knowledge of which he provides evidence in one work is neither used nor mentioned, even by a simple allusion, in those of his other books where it would belong. He is so rich that he does not lend us his words; he gives them to us and does not take them back. You know, for instance, that he wrote a book on the cathedral of Amiens. From this you might conclude that this was the cathedral he liked most or which he knew best. Yet in *The Seven Lamps of Architecture*, where the cathedral of Rouen is mentioned forty times as an example, and that of Bayeux nine times, Amiens is not mentioned once. In *Val d'Arno*, he confesses to us that the church which gave him the deepest enthusiasm for the Gothic is Saint-Urbain at Troyes. Now neither in *The Seven Lamps* nor in *The Bible of Amiens* is there a single reference to Saint-Urbain.[32] With regard to the absence of references to Amiens in *The Seven Lamps*, you might think that perhaps he came to know Amiens only at the end of his life. Not so. In 1859, in a lecture given at Kensington, he compares at length the Gilded Virgin of Amiens with the statues of an art less skilful, but of deeper feeling, which seem to support the west porch of Chartres. Now in *The Bible of Amiens*, where we might think he had gathered all his thoughts on Amiens, not once in the pages where he speaks of the Gilded Virgin does he allude to the statues at Chartres. Such is the infinite richness of his love, of his knowledge. Usually with a writer, the recurrence of certain favourite examples, if not even the repetition of certain developments, reminds you that you are dealing with a man who had a particular life, a particular body of knowledge as opposed to another, a limited experience from which he draws all the profit he can. Just consulting the indexes of Ruskin's various works, the perpetual newness of the works cited, and still more the disdain for the information of which he availed himself once and, very often, abandoned forever, give the idea of something more than human, or rather the impression that each book is by a new man, who has a different knowledge, not the same experience, another life.

It was the charming play of his inexhaustible richness to draw from the marvellous jewellery cases of his memory treasures that were always new: one day the precious rose window of Amiens, the next the golden lacework of the porch of Abbeville, to join them with the dazzling jewels of Italy.

He could in fact pass thus from one country to another, for the same soul he had adored in the stones of Pisa was also the one that had given to the stones of Chartres their immortal form. No one has felt as he did the unity of Christian art during the Middle Ages, from the banks of the Somme to those of the Arno, and he realised in our hearts the dream of the great popes of the Middle Ages: 'Christian Europe'. If, as has been said, his name must remain attached to Pre-Raphaelism, one should understand by that not what followed Turner, but what preceded Raphael. We can forget today the services he rendered to Hunt, to Rossetti, to Millais; but what he has done for Giotto, for Carpaccio, for Bellini, we cannot. His divine work was not to resuscitate the living, but to raise the dead.

Does not this unity of Christian art of the Middle Ages constantly appear in the perspective of these pages where his imagination illuminates here and there the stones of France with a magic reflection of Italy? See him telling you in *The Pleasures of England*: 'While the Charity of Giotto at Padua tramples on bags of gold, all the treasures of the earth, gives corn and flowers and presents her blazing heart in her hand to God, at the porch of Amiens the Charity is content to clothe a beggar with a solid mantle of wool from the manufacture of the town.' In *The Nature of Gothic*, see him comparing the manner in which the flames are treated in the Italian Gothic and in the French Gothic, of which the porch of Saint-Maclou at Rouen is taken as an example. And in *The Seven Lamps of Architecture*, see again a little of the colours of Italy playing on the grey stones of this same porch.

'The bas-reliefs of the tympanum of the porch of Saint-Maclou in Rouen represent the Last Judgement, and the part of Hell is treated with a degree of fearful grotesqueness I can only describe as a mingling of the minds of Orcagna and Hogarth. The demons are perhaps even more frightful than Orcagna's; and in certain expressions of debased humanity in its utmost despair, the English painter is at least equalled. Not less wild is the imagination which expresses fury and fear, even in the way the figures are placed. An evil angel, balancing on its wing, drives the troops of the damned from the seat of Judgement; they are urged on by him so furiously that they are driven not merely to the extreme limit of this scene, which the sculptor confined elsewhere within the tympanum, but out of the tympanum and *into the niches* of the vault; while the flames that follow them, activated it seems by the movement of the angels' wings, rush into the niches as well, and burst up through their tracery, the three lowest niches being represented as all on fire while, instead of their usual vaulted and ribbed ceiling, there is a demon on the roof of each, with the wings folded, grimacing out of the black shadow.'

This comparison of the different kinds of arts and of the different countries was not as far as he went. He must have been struck by the similarity of certain religious ideas in pagan and Christian symbols.[33] Mr Ary Renan[34] has commented, with profundity, on what there is of Christ already in Gustave Moreau's *Prometheus*. Ruskin, whose devotion to Christian art never made him contemptuous of paganism,[35] has compared, in an aesthetic and religious manner, the lion of St Jerome to the lion of Nemea, Virgil to Dante, Samson to Hercules, Theseus to the Black Prince, the prophesies of Isaiah to the prophesies of the Cumaean Sibyl. There is no good reason for comparing Ruskin to Gustave Moreau, but one can say that a natural tendency, developed through familiarity with the Primitives, had led them both to proscribe the expression of violent feelings in art and, inasmuch as this was applied to the study of symbols, to proscribe a certain fetishism in the worship of the symbols themselves, not a very dangerous fetishism for minds so attached in reality to the feeling symbolised that they could pass from one symbol to another, without being arrested by superficial diversity. Regarding the systematic prohibition from expressing violent emotion in art, the principle which Mr Ary Renan has called the principle of Beautiful Inertia, where can one find it better defined than in the pages of *Relation between Michaelangelo and Tintoretto*?[36] As for the somewhat exclusive worship of symbols, was not the study of French and Italian mediaeval art inevitably bound to lead to it? And since, through works of art, he was seeking the spirit of an age, the resemblance of these symbols of the porch of Chartres to the frescoes of Pisa would necessarily strike him as proof of the originality typical of the spirit which thus animated the artists, and their differences as evidence of its versatility. In anyone else the aesthetic sensations would have run the risk of being chilled by reasoning. But in him everything was love, and iconography, as he understood it, would better have been called iconolatry. Furthermore, art criticism makes room for a timely way for something possibly greater; it almost has the processes of science, it contributes to history. The appearance of a new element in the porches of cathedrals alerts us to changes no less profound in the history, not only of art, but of civilisation, than those announced to geologists by the appearance of a new species on earth. The stone sculpted by nature is no more instructive than the stone sculpted by the artist, and we do not draw a greater profit from the one which has preserved an ancient monster for us than the one which shows us a new god.

The drawings that accompany the writings of Ruskin are from this point of view very significant. In the same plate you would be able to see the same feature of architecture as it is treated at Lisieux, at Bayeux, at Verona and at Padua, as if it were a matter of variations within the same species of butterfly under different skies. Yet never do these stones he loved so much become abstract examples for him. On each stone you see the nuance of the hour united with the colour of centuries. 'To run to St Wulfram of Abbeville,' he tells us, '*before the sun had left the towers*, was always for me one of these joys to cherish the past for to the end.' He went even further; as in a primitive painting, he did not separate the cathedrals from the background of rivers and valleys where they appear to the traveller who approaches them. One of his most instructive drawings in this respect is the one reproduced as the second engraving of *Our Fathers Have Told Us*, and which is entitled: *Amiens, All Souls' Day*. In these towns of Amiens, Abbeville, Beauvais, Rouen, which a visit from Ruskin consecrated, he would pass his time drawing at times in the churches ('without being disturbed by the verger'), at times in the open air. And the company of draughtsmen and engravers he took with him must have formed a most delightful passing colony in those towns, like the scene Plato shows us of the sophists following Protagoras from town to town, similar also to the swallows, in imitation of which they liked to stop at the old roofs and ancient towers of the cathedrals. Perhaps one might still be able to find some of these disciples of Ruskin who accompanied him to the banks of this newly evangelised Somme, as if the days of St Firmin and St Salve had returned, disciples who, as the new apostle spoke and explained Amiens as a Bible, made drawings instead of taking notes, gracious notes whose collection is no doubt in some English museum, and where I imagine reality has been slightly rearranged, according to Viollet-le-Duc's taste. The engraving *Amiens on All Souls' Day* seems to lie a little with regard to beauty. Is it perspective alone that thus brings the cathedral and the church of Saint-Leu close to the banks of a widened Somme? It is true that Ruskin could answer us, drawing support from the words of Turner which he quoted in *Eagle's Nest* and which Mr de la Sizeranne has translated: 'Turner, in his early life, was sometimes good-natured and would show people what he was doing. He was one day doing a drawing of Plymouth harbour, with some ships at a distance of a mile or two, seen against the light. Having shown this drawing to a naval officer, the latter observed with surprise, and objected with very justifiable indignation, that the ships of the line had no portholes. "No," said Turner, "certainly not. If you climb Mount Edgecumbe and look at the ships against the sunset, you will find that you can't see the portholes." "Well but," said the naval officer, still indignant, "you know the portholes are there." "Yes," said Turner, "I know that well enough; but my business is to draw what I see, and not what I know is there." '

If, being in Amiens, you go in the direction of the slaughterhouse, you will have a view which is no different than the engraving. You will see distance arranging, in the lying but happy manner of the artist, the monuments which, as you approach, will resume their original but wholly different position; you will for instance see inscribed on the front of the cathedral the outline of one of the town's water hydrants making plane geometry out of solid geometry. Should you nevertheless find this landscape, tastefully composed by perspective, a little different from the one that Ruskin's drawing relates, you could blame in particular the changes that have occurred in the aspect of the town during the almost twenty years since Ruskin's stay there and, as he said about another place he loved, 'so many *improvements* have been made since I last composed and meditated there.' [37]

But at least this engraving from *The Bible of Amiens* will have associated in your memory the banks of the Somme with the cathedral, better perhaps than your vision would have done, no matter where in the town you were located. It will prove to you, better than anything I could have said, that Ruskin did not separate the beauty of the cathedrals from the charm of the regions from which they sprang, and which everyone who visits them still enjoys in the particular poetry of the region and in the memory of the misty or golden afternoon he spent there. Not only is the first chapter of *The Bible of Amiens* called *By the Rivers of Waters*, but the book Ruskin intended to write on the cathedral of Chartres was to be entitled *The Sources of the Eure*. So it was not only in his drawings that he set the churches by the river banks and that he associated the grandeur of the Gothic cathedrals with the charm of the French locations.[38] And we would feel more vividly the individual charm of a region if we did not have at our disposal these seven league boots that express trains are, and if, as formerly, to arrive at some particular place we were obliged to pass through countrysides increasingly more like those to which we were heading, like zones of graduated harmony which, by making this harmony less easily penetrable that what differs from it, by protecting it gently and mysteriously from fraternal resemblances, not only envelop it in nature, but also prepare our minds for it.

These stories by Ruskin on Christian art were for him like the verification and proof of his ideas on Christianity and of other ideas we have not been able to mention here, the most famous of which we will let Ruskin define shortly: his horror of mechanisation and industrial art. 'All the beautiful things were made when men of the Middle Ages *believed* the pure, joyous and beautiful lesson of Christianity.' And he saw then art declining with faith, skill taking the place of feeling. Seeing the power of realising beauty, which was the privilege of the ages of faith, his belief in the goodness of faith must have been strengthened. Each volume of his last work *Our Fathers Have Told Us* (only the first was written) was to comprise four chapters, of which the last was to be dedicated to the masterpiece which was the culmination of the faith whose study formed the object of the first three chapters. Thus Christianity, which had cradled Ruskin's aesthetic sense, received from it a supreme consecration. And as he was about to take his Protestant reader to the statue of the Madonna, and after scoffing at her 'who must understand that no cult of the female was ever pernicious to humanity', or to the statue of St Honoré, after deploring that he is so little spoken of 'in the faubourg of Paris that bears his name', he could have said as he did at the end of *Val d'Arno*:

'If you will fix your minds only on what the giver of it demands, "he has shown you, man, what is good, and what does the Lord require of you but to act justly and to love mercy and to walk humbly with your God?", you will find that such obedience is always repaid with a blessing. If you direct your thoughts to the state of forgotten multitudes who laboured in silence and adored humbly, as the snows of Christianity brought the memory of the birth of Christ or the spring sunshine the memory of his resurrection, you will know that the promise of the angel of Bethlehem has been literally fulfilled, and you will pray that your English fields, joyously as the banks of Arno, can still dedicate their pure lilies to St Mary of the Flowers.'

Finally, Ruskin's mediaeval studies confirmed, with his belief in the goodness of faith, his belief in the necessity of free, joyous and personal work without the intervention of mechanisation. In order for you to understand this better, it would be well to transcribe here a very characteristic page of Ruskin. He is speaking of a little figure of a few centimetres in size, lost in the middle of hundreds of such tiny figures, at the Booksellers' porch of Rouen cathedral.

'The fellow is angry and confused in his malice, and his hand is pressed hard on his cheek bone, and the flesh of the cheek is wrinkled under the eye by the pressure. The whole can appear terribly coarse, if it is compared to delicate engravings; but considering it as a mere filling of an interstice on the outside of a cathedral gate and as one of three hundred or more similar figures, it bears witness to the most noble vitality in the art of the time.

'We have certain work to do for our bread, and it must be done strenuously; other work is to be done for our delight, and that is to be done with heart; neither one nor the other should be done by halves or hastily, but with a will; and what is not worth this effort is not to be done at all; perhaps all that we have to do is meant for nothing more than an exercise of the heart and of the will, and is useless in itself; but in any case, the little use it has may be spared if it is not worth putting our hands and our strength to. It does not become our immortality to take an ease inconsistent with its authority, nor to suffer any instruments with which it can dispense, to come between it and the things it rules. There is enough dreaming, enough coarseness and sensuality in human existence without our turning its few brilliant moments into mechanisation; and, since our life – to put things in the best light – must be but a vapour that appears for a little time and then vanishes away, let it at least appear as a cloud in the height of heaven, and not as the thick darkness that broods over the blast furnace and the turnings of the wheel.'

I confess that when I reread this page at the time of Ruskin's death, I was seized with the desire to see the little man he refers to. And I went to Ruskin as if obeying a testamentary thought, and as if Ruskin in dying had in some way entrusted to his readers the poor creature to which he had given life again by speaking of it and which, without knowing it, had just lost forever the person who had done for it as much as the first sculptor. But when I arrived near the immense cathedral in front of the portal where the saints were warming themselves in the sun, I saw, higher up, the galleries where the kings radiated up to these supreme heights of stone I believed uninhabited, and where a sculpted hermit lived in isolation, letting the birds settle on his forehead, while there a gathering of apostles listened to the message of an angel poised near them, folding her wings, under a flight of pigeons spreading theirs and not far from a person who, receiving a child on his back, turned his head in a sudden and secular motion; when I saw, lined up before its porches or leaning over the balconies of its towers, all the stone hosts of the mystic city breathing the sun or the morning shadow, I understood it would be impossible to find a figure of only a few centimetres in the middle of this superhuman multitude. I nevertheless went to the porch of the Booksellers. But how to recognise the little figure among hundreds of others? All of a sudden, a talented and promising young sculptress, Mrs L Yeatman, said to me: 'Here is one that looks like it.' We looked a bit lower, and … there it was. It scarcely measures ten centimetres. It is crumbling, and yet the look is the same, the stone still has the hole that raises the eyeball and gives it this expression that makes me recognise it. The artist who died centuries ago left there, among thousands of others, this little person who dies a little every day, and has been dead for a really long time, forever lost in the middle of the crowd. But he had put it there. One day, a man for whom there is no death, for whom there is no material infinity, no oblivion, a man who, throwing far away from him this nothingness which oppresses us to follow purposes which dominate his life, purposes so numerous that he will not be able to achieve them all, while we seemed to have none, this man came and, in these waves of stone where each lace-like effervescence seemed to resemble the others, seeing there all the laws of life, all the thoughts of the soul, naming them by their names, he said: 'See, it is this, it is that.' As on the Day of Judgement, which is portrayed near by, his words resound like the Archangel's trumpet, and he says: 'Those who have lived, will live. Matter is nothing.' And in fact, like the dead whom, not far away, the tympanum represents awakening at the sound of the Archangel's trumpet, rising up, having recovered their forms, recognisable, alive, the little figure is now alive again and has recovered its look, and the Judge has said: 'You have lived, you will live.' As for him, he is not an immortal judge, his body will die; but what does it matter! As if he were not destined to die he performs his immortal task, unconcerned at the size of the thing that occupies his time and, having but one human life to live, he spends several days in front of one of the ten thousand figures of a church. He drew it. It corresponded for him to these ideas that exercised his mind, indifferent to approaching old age. He drew it, he spoke of it. And the inoffensive and monstrous little figure will have come back to life, against all hope, from this death that seems more total than the others, which is the disappearance into the breast of infinite numbers and under the levelling of similarities, but from which genius also quickly rescues us. Finding the little figure there again, one cannot help but be moved. It seems to live and to gaze, or rather to have been caught by death at the very moment of its gaze, like the Pompeians whose gestures remain interrupted. And it is a thought of the sculptor, in fact, which has been seized here in its gesture by the immobility of the stone. I was moved in finding it there again; nothing therefore dies that has lived, no more the sculptor's thought than Ruskin's thought.

On meeting the little figure there, necessary to Ruskin, who dedicated to it one of the few engravings illustrating his book,[39] because it was an actual and enduring part of his thought, and agreeable to us because his thought is necessary to us, guides ours which met his on the way, our state of mind was closer to that of the artists who carved the Judgement on the tympana and who thought that what is individual, what is most original in a person, in an intention, does not die but persists in the memory of God and will live again. Who is right, the gravedigger or Hamlet, when the one sees but a skull where the other recalls a fantasy? Science can say: the gravedigger; but it has reckoned without Shakespeare, who will make the memory of this fantasy last beyond the dust of the skull. At the call of the angel, each death will be found still there, in its place, when we believed it dust long ago. At the call of Ruskin, we see the smallest figure framing a minuscule quatrefoil resurrected in its form, looking at us with the same look that seems to be contained in just one millimetre of stone. No doubt, poor little monster, I would not have been skilled enough, among the millions of stones of the towns, to find you, to make out your face, to rediscover your personality, to call you, to bring you back to life. But it is not that infinity, that number, that nothingness which oppresses us are very strong; it is that my imagination is not very strong. Certainly, you had nothing of true beauty about you. Your poor face, which I might never have noticed, does not have a very interesting expression, although evidently it has, like any person, an expression nobody else ever had. But since you lived enough to continue gazing with this same sideways glance for Ruskin to notice you and, after he had said your name, for his reader to be able to recognise you, are you living enough now, are you loved enough? And one cannot help thinking of you with tenderness, although you do not seem to be attractive, but because you are a living creature, because through so many centuries you were dead without hope of resurrection, and because you are resurrected. And one of these days perhaps someone else will go to find you at your porch, looking with tenderness at your naughty and sideways resurrected face, because what came from one man's thought can alone one day capture another thought, which in turn has fascinated ours. You were right to stay there, unregarded, crumbling. You could not expect anything from matter where you were except nothingness. But the small have nothing to fear, nor do the dead. For sometimes the spirit visits the earth; at its passing, the dead arise and the little forgotten figures reawaken and capture the attention of the living who, for them, forsake the living who are not alive and go looking for life only where the spirit has revealed it to them, in stones that are already dust and yet still thought.

He who enveloped the old cathedrals in more love and more joy than even the sun bestows on them when it adds its fleeting smile to their secular beauty cannot, if well understood, have been mistaken. It is the same with the world of spirits as with the physical universe, where a jet of water cannot rise above the height of the place from which the water first descended. The great beauties of literature correspond to something, and it is perhaps enthusiasm in art which is the criterion for truth. Suppose that Ruskin sometimes made mistakes, as a critic, in the exact appraisal of the value of a work, the beauty of his erroneous judgement is often more interesting than that of the work being judged and corresponds to something which, in spite of being different, is no less precious. That Ruskin was wrong in saying that the *Beau Dieu* of Amiens 'exceeded in sculpted tenderness what till then had been achieved, though any representation of Christ must eternally disappoint the hope of any loving soul that has learned to put his trust in him,' and that Mr Huysmans was right when he calls this same *Dieu* of Amiens 'a fop with a bovine face', is something that we do not believe, but it matters little that we know it. 'I call it a legend only,' says Ruskin, speaking of the story of St Jerome. 'Whether Heracles killed or St Jerome ever cherished the wild or wounded creature is without importance for us.' As Buffon has said that 'all the intellectual beauties found (in a beautiful style), all the relationships of which it is composed, are so many truths as useful and perhaps more precious for the public mind than those which can form the basis of the subject,' the truths of which the beauty of the pages of the *Bible* on the *Beau Dieu* of Amiens are composed have a value that is independent of this statue, and Ruskin would not have found it if he had spoken of them with contempt, for enthusiasm alone could give him the power to discover them.

To what extent this marvellous soul faithfully reflected the universe, and under what touching and tempting forms falsehood may have crept in spite of everything into the heart of his intellectual sincerity, is something we will perhaps never know, and it is in any case something we cannot look for here. 'How far,' he said, 'my mind has been paralysed by the sorrows and faults of my life, how far short its knowledge may be of what I might have known if I had more faithfully walked in the light I was given, is beyond my conjecture or confession.' At any rate, he would have been one of these 'geniuses' of whom even those among us who were born with the gifts of the fairies have need in order to be initiated into the knowledge and love of a new part of Beauty. Many of the words used by our contemporaries for exchanging ideas bear his mark, as one sees on coins the effigy of the sovereign of the day. Dead, he continues to enlighten us, like these dead stars whose light still reaches us, and one can say of him what he said on the death of Turner: 'It is through these eyes, closed for ever at the bottom of the grave, that generations yet unborn will see nature.'

## IV

# Postscript

'Under what magnificent and tempting forms falsehood may have crept into the heart of his intellectual sincerity ...' Here is what I meant: there is a kind of idolatry that nobody has better defined than Ruskin in a page of *Lectures on Art*: 'It was, I think, not without some admixture of good, as doubtless very great evil brings some good in its wake, such I conceive to have been the nefarious function of art in helping what, whether in pagan or Christian lands, and whether in the mirage of words, or colours or fair forms, is truly, and in the deep sense, to be called idolatry, the serving with the best of our hearts and minds some dear and sad fantasy which we have created for ourselves, while we disobey the present call of the Master, who is not dead, who is now fainting under his cross, but orders us to take up ours.'[40] Now it seems that at the very basis of Ruskin's work, at the root of his talent, is found precisely this idolatry. No doubt he never let it completely smother – even to embellish it – immobilise, paralyse and finally kill, his intellectual and moral sincerity. At every line in his work, as in every moment of his life, one feels this need for sincerity struggling against idolatry, proclaiming its vanity, humiliating beauty before duty, even if it were unaesthetic. I will not take examples of this from his life (which is not like the life of a Racine, a Tolstoy, a

Maeterlinck, aesthetic at first and later moral, but where from the start morality claims its rights within the very heart of aesthetics – never perhaps freeing itself from aesthetics as completely as in the lives of the masters I have just mentioned). It is sufficiently well known that I need not recall the phases, from the first scruples he experiences when drinking tea while looking at Titians to the moment when, having spent the five million his father left him on philanthropic and social works, he decides to sell his Turners. But his is a dilettantism more inward than the dilettantism of action (over which he triumphed), and the true duel between his idolatry and his sincerity took place not at certain hours of his life, not in certain pages of his books, but at every moment, in these deep, secret regions almost unknown to us, where our personality receives images from imagination, ideas from intelligence, words from memory, affirms itself in the continual choices it must make, and in some way incessantly decides the fate of our spiritual and moral life. In those regions, it seems that Ruskin never ceased to commit the sin of idolatry. And at the very moment he was proclaiming sincerity, he was himself lacking in it, not by what he said but by the way in which he said it. The doctrines he professed were moral doctrines and not aesthetic doctrines, and he chose them for their beauty. And because he did not want to present them as beautiful but as true, he was forced to deceive himself about the nature of the reasons that made him adopt them. Hence there was such a continual compromise of conscience, that immoral doctrines sincerely professed would perhaps have been less dangerous for the integrity of the mind than these moral doctrines in which affirmation is not absolutely sincere, as they are dictated by an unavowed aesthetic preference. And the sin was constantly committed, in the very choice of each explanation given for a fact, of each appreciation given of a work, in the very choice of the words he used – and it finally gave a deceitful attitude to the mind ceaselessly addicted to it. To put the reader in a better position to judge the kind of trickery that a page of Ruskin is for each of us and evidently was for Ruskin himself, I am going to quote one of these pages which I find most beautiful and yet in which this defect is at its most flagrant. We will see that, if the beauty in it is *in theory* (that is to say, in appearance, the basis of the writer's thought having always been appearance, and the form, reality) subordinated to moral feeling and truth, in reality truth and moral feeling are there subordinated to aesthetic feelings, and to an aesthetic feeling somewhat falsified by this perpetual compromising. The passage is from the *Causes of the Fall of Venice*.[41]

'It is not in the caprice of wealth, for the pleasure of the eyes and pride of life, that these marbles were hewn into transparent strength, and these arches arrayed in the colours of the iris. A message is written in their colours that was once written in blood; and a sound in the echoes of their vaults, that one day will fill the vault of heaven: "He will return to render judgement and justice." The strength of Venice was given to her as long as she remembered this; and her destruction arrived on the day she forgot this; it came to her irrevocably because she had no excuse for forgetting it. Never had a city a more glorious Bible. Among the nations of the North, a rough and dark sculpture filled their temples with confused and hardly legible imagery; but for her, the art and treasures of the East had gilded every letter and illuminated every page, till the Temple-Book shone from far away like the star of the Magi. In other towns, meetings of the people were often in places far from all religious association, subject to violence and upsets; on the grass of the dangerous rampart, in the dust of the troubled street, there were things done and decisions taken for which we cannot find any justification, but which we can sometimes forgive. But the sins of Venice, committed in her palace or in her piazza, were done with the Bible at her right hand. The walls on which the book of the law was written were separated by only a few inches of marble from those which guarded the secrets of her councils, or held prisoner the victims of her government. And when, in her last hours, she threw off all shame and all restraint, and the great square of the city was filled with the madness of the whole earth, let us recall how much her sin was greater, because it was committed in the face of the house of God, burning with the letters of his law.

'The acrobats and masks laughed their laugh and went their way; and a silence has followed them, not unforetold; for in the middle of all of them, across century after century of gathering vanity and guilt, this white dome of St Mark's had uttered its words in the dead ear of Venice: "Know that for all these things God will call you to judgement".'[42]

Now, if Ruskin had been entirely sincere with himself, he would not have thought that the crimes of the Venetians had been more inexcusable and more severely punished than those of other men because they possessed a multicoloured marble church instead of a limestone cathedral, because the Doge's palace was near St Mark's instead of at the other end of town, and because in Byzantine churches the biblical text, instead of being represented as in the sculpture of the northern churches, is accompanied on the mosaics by letters that form a quotation from the Gospel or the prophecies. It is nevertheless true that this passage from *The Stones of Venice* is of great beauty, rather difficult though it is to give an account of the reasons for this beauty. It seems to us to rest on something false and we feel some scruples on giving in to it.

And yet there must be some truth in it. There is properly speaking no beauty that is entirely deceitful, for aesthetic pleasure is precisely what accompanies the discovery of a truth. To what kind of beauty can the very vivid aesthetic pleasure we experience when reading such a page correspond is rather difficult to say. The page itself is mysterious, full of images both of beauty and of religion, as this same church of St Mark where all the figures of the Old and New Testaments appear against the background of a sort of splendid obscurity and scintillating brilliance. I remember having read it for the first time in St Mark's itself, during an hour of storm and darkness when the mosaics shone only by their own physical light and with an internal, ancient and earthly gold to which the Venetian sun, which sets even the angels of the campaniles ablaze, mingled nothing of its own; the emotion I felt while reading this page there, among all these angels which shone forth from the surrounding darkness, was great but perhaps not very pure. Just as the joy of seeing the beautiful mysterious figures grew, but was altered in some way by the pleasure of erudition that I experienced in understanding the text that had appeared in Byzantine letters around their haloed brows, in the same way the beauty of Ruskin's images was intensified and corrupted by the pride of referring to the sacred text. A sort of egoistic self-reference is inevitable in these joys in which erudition and art mingle and in which aesthetic pleasure can become more acute, but not remain as pure. And perhaps this page of *The Stones of Venice* was more beautiful mainly because it gave me precisely these mingled joys I experienced in St Mark's, this page which like the Byzantine church also had in the style of its mosaic that dazzled in the shadows, next to its images the biblical quotation inscribed nearby. Furthermore, was this page not like these mosaics of St Mark's which set out to teach and cared little about their artistic beauty? Today they give us nothing but pleasure. Yet the pleasure their didacticism gives the erudite is selfish, and the most disinterested is still that given the artist by this beauty, little thought of or even unknown by those who merely set out to teach the people and who in addition give them beauty.

In the last page of *The Bible of Amiens*, truly sublime, the line: 'if you would remember the promise made to you' is an example of the same kind. When, again in *The Bible of Amiens*, Ruskin ends his piece on Egypt by saying: 'She was the Teacher of Moses and the Hostess of Christ',[43] we may grant him 'Teacher of Moses': to educate certain virtues are needed. But, in a reasoned judgement of the qualities of Egyptian genius, can the fact of having been *the hostess* of Christ really be considered relevant, even if it does add to the beauty of the sentence?

It is with my most cherished aesthetic impressions that I have wanted to struggle here, trying to push intellectual sincerity to its utmost and cruellest limits. Need I add that if I make this general reservation, in some sense *in the absolute*, less on the essence of their inspiration and the quality of their beauty, for me he is nevertheless one of the greatest writers of all times and of all countries. I have tried to capture in Ruskin, as in a 'subject' particularly favourable to this observation, an infirmity essential to the human mind, rather than wanting to denounce a personal fault. Once the reader has come to grips with what this 'idolatry' consists of, he will come to understand the excessive importance Ruskin attaches in his studies of art to the literalness of his works (an importance for which I have indicated, in much too summary a fashion, another reason in the preface, see page 46 above) and also this abuse of the words 'irreverent', 'insolent', and 'difficulties which we would be insolent in resolving, a mystery which we are not required to clear up' (*The Bible of Amiens*, p.164), 'Let the artist beware of the spirit of choice, it is an insolent spirit' (*Modern Painters*), 'the nave could almost appear too wide to an irreverent spectator' (*The Bible of Amiens*), etc., etc. – and the state of mind that they reveal. I was thinking about this idolatry (I was thinking also about this pleasure Ruskin feels in balancing his sentences in an equilibrium that seems to impose on the thought rather than receiving from it a symmetrical arrangement)[44] when I said:

'Under what touching and tempting forms lying may have crept, in spite of everything, into the heart of this intellectual sincerity is what I do not have to seek.' But I should instead have sought it and would indeed be guilty of idolatry if I were to take refuge behind this essentially Ruskinian formula of respect.[45] It is not that I am unable to recognise the virtues of respect, it is the very condition of love. But it must never, where love ceases, be substituted for it, allowing us to believe without inquiry and to admire on faith. Ruskin would have been the first to applaud us for not granting to his writings an infallible authority, since he refused it even to the Holy Scriptures. 'There is no form of human language from which error can be prevented from entering' (*The Bible of Amiens*, III, §49). But the attitude of 'reverence' that believes it to be 'insolent to clear up a mystery' pleased him. To have finished with idolatry and to make sure no misunderstanding on this matter remains between the reader and me, I would like here to call upon one of our most justly famous contemporaries (as different, moreover, as one can be from Ruskin!) but who in his conversations, not in his books, shows this defect carried to such an extreme that it is easier to recognise and show it in him without further need to magnify it. When he speaks he is affected – deliciously – with idolatry. Those who have heard him once will consider very crude an 'imitation' where nothing remains of his charm, but they will nevertheless know of whom I speak, whom I take here as an example, when I tell them that he recognises admirably in the material with which a tragic actress drapes herself, the very fabric seen on *Death* in *The Young Man and Death*, by Gustave Moreau, or in the outfit of one of his lady friends, 'the very dress and hairstyle worn by the Princess de Cadignan the day she saw d'Arthez for the first time.' And looking at the actress's costume or at the society lady's dress, touched by the nobility of his memory he exclaims: 'It is truly beautiful!' not because the fabric is beautiful, but because it is the fabric painted by Moreau or described by Balzac and is thus forever sacred … to the idolaters. In his room you will see, alive in a vase or painted in frescoes on the wall by some of his artist friends, bleeding hearts, because it is the very flower that one sees represented at the Madeleine in Vézelay. As for an object that belonged to Baudelaire, to Michelet, to Hugo, he surrounds it with a religious respect. I enjoy too deeply, even to the point of intoxication, the witty improvisations to which a particular kind of pleasure he finds in this veneration leads and inspires our idolater, to want to quarrel with him in the least.

But at the height of my pleasure, I wonder whether the incomparable talker – and the listener who lets him have his way – do not sin equally by insincerity; whether because a flower (the passion flower) partly resembles the instruments of the crucifixion, it is sacrilege to make a present of it to someone of another religion, and whether the fact that a house may have been lived in by Balzac (even if there is in any case nothing left in it that may teach us about him) makes it more beautiful. Must we really, other than to pay her an aesthetic compliment, prefer a person because her name is Bathilde like the heroine of *Lucien Leuwen*?

Mme de Cadignan's dress is a delightful invention of Balzac because it gives us an idea of the art of Mme de Cadignan, because it lets us know what impression she wants to make on d'Arthez and some of her 'secrets'. But once stripped of the spirit that is in it, it is no more than a sign deprived of its meaning, that is to say nothing; and to continue to adore it, to the point of being in ecstasy when encountering it in real life on a woman's body is properly speaking idolatry. It is the favourite intellectual sin of artists and one to which only a very few have not succumbed. *Felix culpa!* one is tempted to say when seeing how very fertile it has been for them in charming inventions. But at least they must not succumb without having struggled. There is not in nature any particular form, no matter how beautiful, that is worth anything other than through the measure of infinite beauty incarnated in it: not even the blossom of the apple tree, not even the blossom of the pink hawthorn. My love for them is infinite, and the suffering (hay fever) that their proximity causes me permits me each spring to give them proofs of this love that are not available to everyone. But even for them, non-literary as they are, unconnected with an aesthetic tradition, not being 'the very flower in such and such a painting by Tintoretto', as Ruskin would say, or 'in such and such a drawing by Leonardo', as our contemporary would say (he who has revealed to us, among so many other things about which everyone is talking and which nobody looked at before him – the drawings at the Academy of Fine Arts in Venice) I will always guard against an exclusive cult that would attach to them anything but the joy they give us, a cult in the name of which, by an egoistical self-reference, we would make them 'our' flowers, and would take care to honour them by adorning our room with works of art in which they appear. No, I will not find a painting more beautiful because the artist has painted a hawthorn in the foreground, although I know of nothing more beautiful than the hawthorn, for I wish to remain sincere and because I know that the beauty of a painting does not depend on the things represented in it. I will not collect images of hawthorn. I do not venerate hawthorn, I go to see it and breathe in its scent. I have permitted myself this short incursion – which has nothing of an offensive about it – into the terrain of contemporary literature, because it seems to me that the characteristics of idolatry seen in embryonic form in Ruskin would appear clearer to the reader here where they are magnified, and so much more so since here they are also differentiated. I beg our contemporary at any rate, if he has recognised himself in this clumsy sketch, to think that it was done without malice and that, as I have said, I had to reach the utmost limits of sincerity for myself to reproach Ruskin in this way and to find this weak spot in my otherwise absolute admiration for him. Now not only 'sharing with Ruskin has nothing at all dishonourable about it', but also I could find no higher praise for this contemporary than to reproach him in the same manner as I have reproached Ruskin. And if I have been discreet enough not to name him, I almost regret it. For when one is admitted near Ruskin, even in the attitude of the giver, and only to support his book and assist in a closer reading of it, it is not a burden but an honour.

I return to Ruskin. I am today so 'familiar' with Ruskin that I have to search my innermost self to understand the source and study the nature of this idolatry and the little artifice that it mingles at times with the more vivid literary pleasures that he gives us. But this idolatry must often have shocked me when I began to love his books, before little by little closing my eyes to their defects, as happens with every kind of love. Love for living creatures sometimes has a vile origin which is subsequently purified. A man becomes acquainted with a woman because she may help him reach a goal which has nothing to do with herself. Then once he knows her, he loves her for herself and sacrifices to her without hesitation this goal which she simply had to help him reach. Similarly, mixed in with my love of Ruskin's books at the start was something of a selfish interest, the joy of the intellectual benefit I was going to get from them. Certainly at the first pages that I read, feeling their power and their charm, I tried not to resist them, not to argue too much with myself, because I felt that if one day the charm of Ruskin's thought should for me permeate everything it had touched, in a word if I were entirely captivated with his thought, the universe would be enriched with everything that I had known until then, Gothic cathedrals, and however many paintings of England and Italy, which had not yet roused in me this desire without which there is never true knowledge. For Ruskin's thought is not like that of Emerson, for example, which is entirely contained within a book, that is to say an abstract thing, a pure sign of itself. The object to which a way of thinking such as Ruskin's is applied, and from which it is inseparable, is not immaterial, it is scattered here and there over the surface of the earth. One must go and look for it where it is, in Pisa, Florence, Venice, the National Gallery, Rouen, Amiens, the mountains of Switzerland. Such a way of thinking which has an object other than itself, which has materialised in space, which is no longer infinite and free, but limited and subdued, which is incarnated in bodies of sculpted marble, in snowy mountains, in painted faces, is perhaps less sublime than pure thought. But it makes the universe more beautiful to us, or at least certain individual parts, certain specifically named parts of the universe, because it has touched on them, and because it has introduced us to them, by obliging us, if we want to understand them, to love them.

And so it was, in effect; all at once the universe took on an infinite value again in my eyes. And my admiration for Ruskin gave such importance to the things he had made me love that they seemed to be charged with a value greater even than that of life. This was literally the case, and at a time when I believed my days to be numbered, as I left for Venice to be able before dying to approach, touch and see incarnated in decaying but still standing and rosy palaces, Ruskin's ideas on domestic architecture of the Middle Ages. What importance, what reality in the eyes of one who must soon leave the earth, can be possessed by a city so special, so fixed in time, so specific in space as Venice, and how could the theories of domestic architecture which I could study and verify there on living examples be those 'truths which are more powerful than death, which prevent us from fearing it, and which almost make us love it'?[46] It is the power of genius to make us love a beauty more real than ourselves in these things that in the eyes of others are as particular and perishable as ourselves.

The 'I will say they are beautiful when your eyes say it too' of the poet is not particularly true if it refers to the eyes of a beloved woman. In a certain sense, and whatever may be, even in the field of poetry, the wonderful compensations it has for us, love takes the poetry out of nature. For the lover, the earth is only 'the carpet of the beautiful childish feet' of his mistress, nature is only 'her temple'. Love, which makes us discover so many profound psychological truths, on the contrary shuts us off from the poetic feeling for nature,[47] because it puts us in an egoistic frame of mind (love is the highest form of egoism, but is egoism nonetheless) where it is difficult for the poetic feeling to flourish. Admiration for a thought on the other hand gives rise to beauty at every step because at each moment it arouses in us the desire for it. Mediocre people generally believe that to let oneself be guided by books one admires takes away a part of our ability to judge independently.

'What is it to you how Ruskin feels: feel for yourself.' Such an opinion rests on a psychological error that will get the treatment it deserves by all those who, having thus accepted an intellectual discipline, feel that their power to understand and to feel is infinitely increased and their critical sense never paralysed. We are then simply in a state of grace in which all our faculties, our critical sense as much as our other senses, are in play. Also, this voluntary servitude is the beginning of freedom. There is no better way of becoming aware of one's feelings than by trying to recreate in oneself what a master has felt. In this profound effort it is our thought, together with his, that we bring to light. We are free in life, but while having goals: the sophism of the freedom of indifference was revealed long ago. The writer who constantly empties his mind, thinking to free it from any external influence in order to be sure of staying personal, yields unwittingly to a sophism just as naïve. In reality the only occasions when we truly have all our mental powers are those when we do not believe ourselves to be acting with independence, when we do not arbitrarily choose the goal of our effort. The subject of the novelist, the vision of the poet, the truth of the philosopher are imposed on them in an almost inevitable way, external as it is to their way of thinking. And it is by submitting his mind to express this vision and to approach this truth that the artist really becomes himself.

But in speaking of this passion that I had for Ruskin's thought, a little artificial at first and then so deep, I speak with the help of memory and a frozen memory that recalls only facts, 'but from the distant past can recapture nothing'. It is only when certain periods of our lives are closed forever, when, even during the hours in which power and freedom seem to have been given to us, we are forbidden from reopening their doors furtively, it is when we are incapable of putting ourselves back again even for an instant in our former state, it is only then that we refuse to believe that such things have been abolished entirely. We can no longer sing of them, having ignored the wise warning of Goethe that there is poetry only in those things that one still feels. But unable to rekindle the flames of the past, we want at least to gather its ashes. Lacking a resurrection that is no longer possible, with the frozen memory we have kept of these things – the memory of facts telling us: 'you were thus' without permitting us to become that way again, affirming to us the reality of a lost paradise instead of giving it back to us through memory – we want at least to describe it and thereby give it structure. It is when Ruskin is far away from us that we translate his books and try to create a fair likeness of the characteristics of his way of thinking. Thus you will not know the sounds of our faith or of our love, and it is our piety alone that you will perceive here and there, cold and furtive, occupied, like the Theban Virgin, in restoring a tomb.

Marcel PROUST

# "Our Fathers Have Told Us"

SKETCHES ON THE HISTORY OF CHRISTIANITY
FOR BOYS AND GIRLS
WHO HAVE BEEN HELD AT ITS BAPTISMAL FONTS

by

JOHN RUSKIN, LL. DL., D. C. L.

HONORARY STUDENT OF CHRIST CHURCH, OXFORD
AND HONORARY MEMBER OF CORPUS CHRISTI COLLEGE, OXFORD

\*\*\*\*

# THE BIBLE OF AMIENS

# Preface

1

The long-abandoned project of which the following pages begin a first attempt at fulfilment has been resumed at the request of a young English governess, who asked me to write some history studies which her pupils could find useful, the fruit of historical documents placed by modern educational systems at their disposal being for them only pain and boredom.

What else may be said for this book, if it ever becomes one, it must say for itself: as preface, I do not wish to write more than this, especially as some recent events of English history, at this present moment, call for immediate, though brief, comment.

I am told that the Queen's Guards have left for Ireland, playing *God Save the Queen*. And being to the best of my knowledge, as I have declared in the course of some letters to which public attention has been lately more than enough directed, the staunchest conservative in England,[48] I am disposed seriously to discuss the question whether the service for which the Queen's Guards had been commanded could properly be called their mission.

My own conservative notion of the role of the Queen's Guards is that they should guard the Queen's throne and life if either one or the other is threatened by a domestic or foreign enemy, but not that they should become a substitute for her inefficient police force in the execution of her domiciliary laws.

2

And even less so, if the domiciliary laws which they are sent to execute while playing *God Save the Queen* happens by chance to be precisely opposite to the law of this God the Saviour, and consequently such that, in the long run, no quantity of Queens or Queen's men *could* execute. Which is a question I have, for ten years, attempted to get the English to consider – vainly enough until now; and I will add nothing at present to everything I have already said on the subject. But a book has just been published by an English officer who, if he had not been otherwise and more actively employed, could not only have written all my books on landscape and painting, but is very unusually also in agreement with me (God knows how few Englishmen I can say that of at present) on matters regarding the Queen's safety and the nation's honour. Of this book *Far Away: New Travel Writings* different passages will be given further on in my endnotes. Also I will content myself with quoting, for the end of my Preface, the memorable words which Colonel Butler himself quotes, as spoken to the English Parliament by its last Conservative leader, an English officer who had also served with honour and success.[49]

3

The Duke of Wellington said: 'Your Lordships already know that of the troops that our gracious sovereign did me the honour to entrust to my command at different periods of the war – a war undertaken for the express purpose of safeguarding the flourishing institutions and independence of the country – half at least were Roman Catholics. My lords, when I remind you of this fact, I am sure that all further eulogy is unnecessary. Your Lordships are well aware for what long period and under what difficult circumstances they maintained the Empire buoyant upon the flood which overwhelmed the thrones and destroyed the institutions of all the other peoples – how they kept alive the only spark of freedom which had not been extinguished in Europe.

'My lords, it is mainly to the Irish Catholics that we all owe our proud superiority in our military career, and that I am personally indebted for the laurels with which you have been pleased to crown my forehead.

'We should recognise, my lords, that without Catholic blood and Catholic valour, we could never have obtained victory, and the most exalted military talents might have been spent in vain.'

Let these noble words of tender justice be the first example for my young readers of what all history ought to be. It has been told to them in the Laws of Fiesole that all great Art is praise.[50] So is all faithful History, and all high Philosophy. For these three things, Art, History and Philosophy, are each but one part of the Heavenly Wisdom which does not see as man sees, but with an eternal charity; and because she does not rejoice in Iniquity, therefore rejoices in Truth.[51]

For true knowledge is of virtues only; of poisons and vices, it is Hecate who teaches, not Athena. And of all wisdom, that of politics principally must consist in this divine prudence; it is not in fact always necessary for men to know the virtues of their friends or their masters, since the friend will still manifest them, and the master still apply them. But woe betide the nation that is too cruel to cherish the virtue of its subjects and too cowardly to recognise that of its enemies!

# Chapter I
# By the Rivers of Waters[52]

The intelligent English traveller, in this fortunate century for him, is aware that, half-way between Boulogne and Paris, there is an important[53] railway station to which his train, while slowing down, carries him with many more than the average number of noises and shocks expected at the entry to every great French station, to startle the sleepy or distracted traveller into a sense of his situation. He probably also remembers that, at this halt in midjourney, there is a well-stocked buffet at which he has the privilege of a ten minute stop. He is not however always so clearly conscious that this ten minute stop is accorded to him within not so many minutes walk of the central square of a city which was once the Venice of France. Leaving aside the lagoon islands, the French 'Queen of the Waters' was nearly as large as Venice herself; and crossed, not by slow currents of ebbing and returning tide,[54] but by eleven beautiful trout streams (of which four or five are each as large as our Surrey Wandle or Isaac Walton's Dove[55]), which reunite again after they have eddied through its streets, are bordered as they flow down (not forded except where the two Edwards rode them, the day before Crécy) to the sands of St Valéry, by groves of aspen and glades of poplar[56] whose grace and gladness seem to spring in every magnificent avenue with the image of the just man's life: 'Erit tanquam lignum quod plantatum est secus decursus aquarum.'

But the Venice of Picardy did not only owe her name to the beauty of her streams, but to the burden that they carried. She was a worker, like the Adriatic princess, in gold and glass, in stone, in wood, in ivory; she was skilled like an Egyptian in the weaving of fine linens, and married the different colours in her needlework with the delicacy of the maids of Judah. And of those, the fruits of her hands which celebrated her in her own gates, she sent also portions to foreign nations and her fame spread into all lands.

'A local by-law of 12 April 1566 revealed that multicoloured velvets for furniture, *colombettes* with large and small tiles, and *burailles croisées* were made at this time for shipment to Germany, to Spain, to Turkey, and to Barbary!'[57]

Multicoloured velvets, pearl-iridescent colombettes (I wonder what they could be?) and sent to challenge the variegated carpets of the Turk and shine on the arabesque towers of Barbary![58] Was not that a phase of old provincial Picardy life to excite the interest of an intelligent English traveller?

Why should this fountain of rainbows leap up here near the Somme? Why was a little French maid able to call herself the sister of Venice and the servant of Carthage and of Tyre?

And if she, why could not others also of our northern villages do the same? Has the intelligent traveller on his way from the gate of Calais to the station at Amiens discerned anything by the sea or in the country that appears particularly favourable to an artistic project or a commercial enterprise? He has seen unfold league after league of sandy dunes. We also, we have our sands of the Severn, of the Lune, of Solway. He has seen extensive plains of useful and not unfragrant peat, an article sufficiently accessible also to our Scottish and Irish industries. He has seen jutting cliffs of the purest chalk, but on the opposite bank perfidious Albion gleams no whit less white beyond the blue. He has seen pure waters issuing out of the snowy rock, but are ours less bright at Croydon, at Guildford and at Winchester? And yet one never heard tell of treasures sent from the sands of Solway to the Africans; nor that the architects of Romsey could give lessons of colour to the builders at Granada. What can it be in the air or the earth of this country, in the light of her stars or her sun that could have put this flame into the eyes of the little white-capped Amiénoise to the point of rendering her capable of matching herself against Penelope?[59]

4

The intelligent English traveller has of course no time to waste on any of these questions. But if he has brought his ham sandwich and if he is ready for the 'All aboard, gents!' perhaps he may condescend for an instant to hear what a lounger about the place, neither wasteful of his time nor sparing of it, can suggest as worth looking at while his train slowly leaves the station. He will see first, and without any doubt with the respectful admiration which an Englishman is obliged to accord such spectacles, the coal-sheds and carriage-sheds of the station itself, extending in their ashy and oily splendours for about a quarter of a mile out of the town; and then, just as the train gets up to speed, under a chimney in the shape of a tower which he can hardly see to the top of, but will be enveloped by the thick shadow of its smoke, he may see, if he wants to risk his intelligent head out of the window and look back, fifty or fifty-one (I am not sure of my count to the nearest one) similar chimneys, all smoking in the same way, all provided with similar oblong works, made of brown brick walls with innumerable portholes of black square windows. But in the middle of these fifty tall things that smoke, he will see one, a little taller than all the others, and more delicate, that does not smoke;[60] and in the middle of these fifty masses of blank wall enclosing 'works' and without doubt producing works profitable and honourable to France and the world, he will see a mass of wall not blank but strangely wrought by the hands of foolish men of a good long time ago for the purpose of enclosing or producing no manner of profitable work whatsoever but one: 'There is the work of God; so that you will believe in him whom he has sent.'[61]

5

Leaving the intelligent traveller now to fulfil his vow of pilgrimage to Paris – or wherever else God may be sending him – I will suppose that one or two intelligent boys from Eton, or a thoughtful English girl, may wish to walk quietly with me to this place with a commanding view, and to reflect on what the workless – shall we say also worthless? – building, and its minaret without smoke may perhaps signify.

I have called it a minaret for want of a better English word. Flèche – arrow – is its proper name; vanishing into the air you know not when by its simple fineness. It does not throw a flame, it produces no movement, it does not do any harm, the beautiful arrow;[62] without plume, without poison and without barbs; aimless, shall we say also, readers old and young, travelling or abiding? It and the edifice from which it rises, what have they once meant? What meaning do they keep within them yet for you or for the people who live around them who do not lift up their eyes to them as they pass by?

Let us first set ourselves to learn how they came to be there.

6

At the birth of Christ, the whole hillside and the brightly watered plain below, with the corn-yellow fields that dominate it, were inhabited by a race taught by the Druids, wild enough in thoughts and customs, but placed under the government of Rome and gradually becoming accustomed to hear the names, and in a certain measure to confess the power, of Roman gods. For three hundred years after the birth of Christ they heard the name of no other God.

Three hundred years! And neither apostles nor inheritors of their apostolate had yet gone into all the world and preached the gospel to all the creatures. Here, on their peaty ground, the wild people still trusting in Pomona for apples, in Silvanus for acorns, in Ceres for bread, in Proserpina for rest, had no other hope than for the season's blessing from the gods of the harvest and feared no eternal anger from the Queen of Death.[63]

But at last, three hundred years having come and gone, in the year of Christ 301 there came to this hillside of Amiens, on the sixth day of the Ides of October, the messenger of a new life.

7

His name, Firminius (I suppose) in Latin, is Firmin in French – he is the one we must remember here in Picardy: Firmin, not Firminius; as Denis, not Dionysius; coming from afar – nobody tells us from how far. But received with a surprised welcome by the pagan Amiénois who see him – forty days – a great many days we may read – preaching agreeably and binding with baptismal vows even persons in good society; and that in such numbers, that at last he is brought before the Roman governor, by the priests of Jupiter and Mercury who accuse him of wanting to turn the world upside down. And on the last of the forty days – or of the indefinite number of days meant by forty – he is beheaded, as martyrs ought to be, and the role of his mortal being is terminated.

The old, old story, you say? So be it, you will the more easily remember it. The Amiénois remembered it so carefully, that twelve hundred years afterwards, in the sixteenth century, they judged well to sculpt and paint the four stone pictures, numbers 1, 2, 3 and 4 of our first choice photographs: 1st scene, *St Firmin arriving*; 2nd scene, *St Firmin preaching*; 3rd scene, *St Firmin baptising*; and 4th scene, *St Firmin beheaded*, by an executioner with very red legs, and a dog which accompanies him of the character of the dog in *Faust*, of whom we may have more to say presently.[64]

8

Following in the meantime the history of St Firmin, as of old time known, his body was received and buried by a Roman senator, his disciple (a kind of Joseph of Arimathea to St Firmin), in the

Roman senator's own garden; who also built a little oratory over his grave.

The Roman senator's son built a church to replace the oratory, dedicated to Our Lady of Martyrs, and established it as an episcopal seat – the first of the French nation's. A most memorable place for the French nation, surely? And deserving, perhaps, some little memory or monument – cross, inscription or something similar? Where therefore do you suppose this first cathedral of French Christianity stood, and with what monument has it been honoured? It stood where we now stand, my companion, whoever you may be, and the monument wherewith it has been honoured is this chimney, whose banner of smoke overshadows us, the most recent effort of modern art in Amiens, the chimney of St Acheul.

The first cathedral, you will note, of the *French* nation; more accurately, the first germ of cathedral *for* the French nation – who are not yet here; only this grave of a martyr is here, this church of Our Lady of Martyrs, abiding on the hillside until the power of the Romans disappears.

The city and the altar fall with it, trampled down by the feet of savage tribes; the tomb is forgotten – when, at last, the Franks of the north covering with their last wave these dunes of the Somme are stopped *here* and here the Frankish standard is planted, and the French kingdom founded.

9

Here their first capital, here the first footsteps[65] of the Franks in France! Think of it. All over the South there are Gauls, Burgundians, Bretons, nations with a sadder heart, with a more sullen mind. Past their frontier, their outermost border, here at last are the Franks, the source of all Franchise for our Europe. You have heard the word in England, before now, but for English word there is none to mean that. *Honesty* we have, and that comes from ourselves, but *Frankness* we must learn of these; further, all our western nations will in a few centuries be known by this name of

Frank. Franks, of Paris that is to be, in time to come, but French of Paris is in year of grace 500 a language as unknown in Paris as in Stratford-att-ye-Bowe. The French of Amiens is the kingly and courtly form of Christian speech, Paris lying yet in Lutetian mud to become one day a field of tiles perhaps, in due time. Here, by the softly glittering Somme, reign Clovis and his Clotilde.

And by the tomb of St Firmin speaks now another gentle evangelist, and the first Frank king's prayer to the king of kings is addressed to him only as to the 'God of Clotilde'.

10

I must appeal to the reader's patience for a date or two and for some dry facts – two – three – or more.

Clodion, the leader of the first Franks who reached definitively beyond the Rhine, fought his way through irregular Roman cohorts as far as Amiens, which he took in 445.[66]

Two years later, at his death, the scarcely asserted throne falls – perhaps inevitably into the hands of his children's tutor, Mérovée, whose dynasty is founded on the defeat of Attila at Châlons.

He died in 457. His son Childéric, giving himself up to the love of women, and scorned by the Frankish soldiery, is sent into exile, the Franks preferring to live under the law of Rome than under a disgraced leader of their own. He receives asylum at the court of the king of Thuringia and settles there. His chief officer at Amiens, at his departure, breaks a ring in two and, giving him half of it, tells him to come back when he receives the other half. And, after many days, the half of the broken ring is sent to him; he comes back and the Franks accept him as their king.

The queen of Thuringia follows him (I cannot find out if her husband died first – and still less, if dead, how he died), and offers herself to him as wife.

'I have known your usefulness, and that you are very powerful, and I have come to live with you. If I had known beyond the sea someone more useful than you I would have sought to live with *him*.'

He took her for his wife and their son is Clovis.

## 11

A surprising story; how far it is literally true has no interest for us; the myth and its effective scope uncover for us the nature of the French kingdom and prophesy its future destiny. Personal courage, personal beauty, loyalty to kings, love of women, disdain of loveless marriage, not that all these things were held essential, and that in their corruption will be the end of the Frank as in their force was his first glory.

Personal courage is valued. *Utilitas*, key to the vault of all. Birth nothing, unless it brings with it courage; the law of primogeniture unknown; and propriety of conduct apparently also (but remember that we are all still pagans).

## 12

Let us at least separate out our dates and our geography from the great 'nowhere' of confused memory, and organise them well before going any further.

457. Merovée dies. The useful Childéric, counting his exile and reign in Amiens, is king for a total of twenty-four years, from 457 to 481, and during his reign Odoacer puts an end to the Roman empire in Italy (476).

481. Clovis is only fifteen when he succeeds his father as king of the Franks in Amiens. At this time a fragment of Roman power persists in isolation in central France, while four strong and partly savage nations form a cross around this dying centre; the Franks to the north, the Bretons to the west, the Burgundians to the east, the Visigoths, strongest of all and gentlest, from the Loire to the sea.

Sketch for yourself first a map of France on any scale you like as in Plate $1^{67}$ (fig. 1), marking only the courses of the five rivers,

Somme, Seine, Loire, Saône and Rhône; then, roughly, you will find that it was divided at the time thus as indicated in fig.2: fleur de lys part figuring the Franks; other parts[68] indicating the Bretons,[69] the Burgundians,[70] the Visigoths. I do not know exactly how far these reached across the Rhône into Provence; but I think it best to indicate Provence as strewn with roses.

13

Now under Clovis the Franks fight three great battles. The first against the Romans, near Soissons, which they win, and become masters of France as far as the Loire. Copy the rough map (fig. 2) and put the fleur de lys over the whole of the middle of it, wiping out the Romans (fig. 3). This battle was won by Clovis, I believe, before he married Clotilde. He wins his princess as a result; however, he cannot get his pretty vase to give her as a present. Keep this story well in mind, as also the battle of Soissons, winning the centre of France for the French and putting an end to Roman domination here for ever. Secondly, after marrying Clotilde, the wild Germans attack *him* from the north, and he has to fight for his life and his throne at Tolbiac. This is the battle in which he prays to the God of Clotilde and is delivered from the Germans thanks to his support. Whereupon he is crowned at Rheims by St Rémy. And now in the new strength of his Christianity, and his double victory over Rome and Germany, and his love for his queen, and his ambition for his people, he looks often towards this vast kingdom of the Visigoths situated between the Loire and the snowy mountains. Shall not Christ and the Franks be stronger than the villainous Visigoths, 'who are even more Arian'? All the Franks share this opinion with him. So he marches against the Visigoths, meets them and their Alaric at Poitiers, finishes off their Alaric and their Arianism and leads his faithful Franks to the Pic du Midi.

14

And now you must draw the map of France once more and put the fleur de lys over the whole of the central mass from Calais to the Pyrenees. Only still remaining outside are Brittany to the west, Burgundy to the east and the white rose of Provence beyond the Rhône. And now poor little Amiens has become a simple border town like our Durham and the Somme a border watercourse like our Tyne. The Loire and the Seine are now the two great French rivers, and the men will have the idea of building towns on their courses, while the well-watered plains providing not peat, but rich pasture, will be able to repose under the protection of rebel castles on the rocks and fortified towers on the islands. But let us examine a little more closely what the change of symbols on our map may signify: five fleur de lys instead of horizontal bars.

They certainly do not mean that all the Goths have left, and that there is nobody in France but the Franks. The Franks have not massacred the Visigoth men, women and children, from the Loire to the Garonne. On the contrary, where the seat of their own throne is by the Somme, the people born on the peat whom they found there live there still, though subdued. Franks, Goths or Romans may fluctuate here and there in invading or fleeing troops; but unchanging across all the torments of war, the rural people whose huts they pillage, whose farms they ravage, and over whose arts they reign, must still be diligently and silently, without having any time to complain, working, sowing, feeding their cattle.

Otherwise, how could Franks or Huns, Visigoths or Romans live there for a month, or fight for a day?

15

Whatever the name or the customs of the masters, at bottom, the working population has to remain the same; and the goatherd of the Pyrenees, the vintner of the Garonne, the milkmaid of Picardy, whatever masters you give them, will always live on their land, blossoming as the trees of the field, enduring as the rocks of the desert. And these, the warp and first substance of the nation, are divided, not by dynasties, but by climates, and are strong here and powerless there, by privileges that no invading tyrant can abolish and through faults which no preaching hermit can correct. So please let us now leave our history for a minute or two, and read the lessons of immutable earth and sky.

### 16

In the old days when one travelled from Calais to Paris, there was about half an hour's trot on the level from the gate of Calais to the long chalk hill which had to be climbed before arriving at the village of Marquise, where the first overnight stop was.

This chalk hill is truly the front of France; the last bit of plain to the north is the last of Flanders; to the south stretches now a region of chalk and fine building limestone; if you keep your eyes open, you may see a large quarry to the west of the railway, half way between Calais and Boulogne, where formerly there was a blessed little rocky valley opening on to velvet lawns; this chalky region, raised up but never mountainous, sweeps around the chalk basin of Paris away to Caen on one side and Nancy on the other and south as far as Bourges and the Limousin. This limestone tract, with its keen fresh air, everywhere arable surface soil and everywhere quarries above well-watered meadows, is the real country of the French. Here only have their arts found their original development. Further south they are Gascons or Limousins or Auvergnats or the like. To the west are the Bretons of a granite pallor, to the east Burgundians, similar to Alpine bears, here only on the chalk and fine-grained marble between, say, Amiens and Chartres on one side, and between Caen and Rheims on the other, you have the true *France*.

### 17

Of which before we pursue the history of its true life, I must ask the reader to consider a little with me how history, or what one may call such, has been for the most part written and in what particulars it ordinarily consists.

Suppose that the history of King Lear were a true one; and that a modern historian were giving a summary of it in a school manual purporting to contain all the essential facts of the history of England which could prove useful to English youth from the point of view of examinations. The history would be recounted somewhat as follows:

'The reign of the last king of the seventy-ninth dynasty ended in a series of events of which it is painful to sully the pages of history. The weak old man wished to divide his kingdom into dowries for his three daughters; but on proposing this arrangement to them, seeing that the youngest received it with coldness and reserve, he drove her from his court and divided his kingdom between the two older children.

'The youngest found refuge at the court of France where in the end the prince royal married her. But the two elder daughters, having obtained absolute power, treated their father at first with disrespect, and soon with contempt. Seeing himself ultimately refused the support necessary to his declining years, the old king, in a transport of rage, left his palace with, it is said, the court fool as his sole attendant and, falling prey to a sort of madness, wandered half-naked through the storms of winter, in the woods of Britain.

18

'At the news of these events, his youngest daughter assembled an army in haste and invaded the territory of her ungrateful sisters, with the intention of restoring her father to his throne; but, encountering a well-disciplined force under the command of her eldest sister's lover, Edmond, bastard son of the Earl of Gloucester, she was herself defeated, thrown into prison and soon after strangled on the orders of her adulterous sister. The old king died on receiving the news of her death; and the participants in these crimes soon after received their reward; for the two wicked queens being rivals for the love of the bastard, the one who was regarded with less favour poisoned the other and afterwards killed herself. Edmond then met his death at the hand of his brother, the legitimate son of Gloucester, under whose authority, with that of the Earl of Kent, the kingdom remained for several years.'

Imagine this succinctly graceful exposition of what the historians consider to be facts, ornamented with starkly contrasting black and white woodcuts representing the moment when Gloucester's eyes were gouged out, the delirium of Lear, the strangling of Cordelia and the suicide of Goneril, and you have the typical nineteenth century popular history which, as you can appreciate after a little reflection, is as profitable a reading for young persons (so far as concerns the general colour and purity of their thoughts) as the *Newgate Reporter* would be, with this infinitely aggravating circumstance that, while the reports of prison crime would teach a thoughtful youth the dangers of low life and bad company, the picture of royal crimes destroys his respect for all manner of government and his faith in the decrees of Providence itself.

## 19

Books having loftier pretensions, written by bankers, members of Parliament or orthodox clergymen are of course not lacking; they show that the progress of civilisation consists in the victory of usury over ecclesiastical prejudice or in the extension of parliamentary privileges to some borough of Puddlecombe, or in the extinction of the dark superstitions of the Papacy in the glorious light of the Reformation. Finally you have a summary of philosophical history which proves to you that there is no evidence whatsoever that human affairs have been governed by Providence; that all virtuous actions have selfish motives; and that a scientific selfishness, with appropriate telegraphic communications and a perfect knowledge of all the species of bacteria, will entirely secure the future well-being of the upper classes of society and the respectful resignation of the lower classes.

Meanwhile, the two influences left aside, the Providence of heaven and the virtue of men have ruled and rule the world, and not in an invisible way – and they are the only powers of which history has ever to teach us some profitable truth. Hidden beneath all sorrow, there is the force of virtue; above all the ruins, the restorative charity of God. These alone we have to consider; in these alone we may understand the past and predict the future, the destiny of the centuries.

### 20

I return to the history of Clovis, king now of all central France. Fix the year 500 in your minds as the approximate date of his baptism at Rheims and of the sermon that St Rémy made to him, telling him of the sufferings and passion of Christ till Clovis sprang from his throne, grasping his spear and crying: 'If I had been there with my brave Franks, I would have avenged his injuries.'

'There is little doubt,' proceeds the cockney historian, 'that the conversion of Clovis was as much a matter of politics as of faith.' But the cockney historian would do better to limit his remarks on the characters and beliefs of men to those of the curates who have recently taken orders in his fashionable neighbourhood or of the bishops who have recently preached to the population of its manufacturing suburbs. The Frankish kings were made of other clay.

### 21

The Christianity of Clovis does not in fact produce any fruit of the kind that one notices in a modern convert. We do not hear that he repented of the least of his sins nor that he resolved to lead a new life in any way. He was not impressed with the doctrine of sin at the battle of Tolbiac; nor in asking for the help of the God of Clotilde had he felt or professed the remotest intention of changing his character or abandoning his projects. What he was before he believed in the God of his queen, he remained only with more intensity afterwards, in the renewed confidence in the supernatural support of his previously unknown God. His natural gratitude towards its liberating power and pride in its protection added only violence to his soldiership, and deepened his political hatred with all the force of religious indignation. The demons have never set a more dangerous trap for human frailty than the belief that our enemies are also the enemies of God; and it is perfectly conceivable to me that the conduct of Clovis might have been the more unscrupulous precisely in the measure that his faith was more sincere.

If Clovis or Clotilde had fully understood the precepts of their master, the future history of France and Europe would have been other than it was. What they were capable of understanding or at any rate what they were taught, you will see that they obeyed, and that they were blessed in obeying. But their history is complicated with several other persons relative to whom we must now note several too often forgotten details.

22

If from beneath the apse of the cathedral of Amiens we take the street leading due south, after having left the route of the railway on our left, it brings us to the foot of a gradually climbing hill – approximately half a mile long; it is a pleasant and quiet enough walk, which terminates on the level of the highest land near Amiens; from where, looking back, we see beneath us the entire cathedral, all but the spire, the height we have reached being on a level with the cathedral's rooftop; and, to the south, the plain of France.

It is near this location, or on the way from there to St Acheul, that stood the ancient Roman Gate of the Twins on which Romulus and Remus were seen being suckled by the wolf; and through which, one bitter winter's day, one hundred and seventy years before Clovis was baptised, rode on horseback a Roman soldier, wrapped in his cavalry coat,[71] on the causeway which was part of the great Roman road from Lyon to Boulogne.

23

And it is well worth your while also, some frosty autumn or winter day, when the east wind is high, to stay a few moments in this spot to feel its breath, while recalling what happened there, memorable for all men, and profitable, in this winter of the year 332, while men were dying of the cold in the streets of Amiens; namely, that the Roman horsemen, hardly through the city gate, met a naked beggar, shivering with cold; and that, seeing no other way of sheltering him, he drew his sword, divided his coat in two, and gave him half of it.

Not a ruinous gift, not even enthusiastically generous: Sydney's cup of cold water needed more self-denial; and I am quite certain that more than one Christian child of our day, himself well warmed and dressed, meeting a frozen naked man, would be ready to take the *whole* coat from his shoulders and give it to the needy one if his better-advised muse, or his mama, would let him. But the Roman soldier was not a Christian and accomplished his serene charity in total simplicity, and yet with prudence.

Nevertheless, this same night he beheld in a dream the Lord Jesus, who was before him in the midst of angels, having on his shoulders the half of the coat he had given to the beggar.

And Jesus said to the angels who were around him:

'Do you know who has dressed me thus? My servant Martin, although not yet baptised, has done that.' And Martin, after this vision, hastened to receive baptism, being then in his twenty-second year.[72] Whether these things were ever so, or to what extent they were so, credulous or incredulous reader, is no business of yours or mine. But of these things, what is and will be eternally *so* – namely, the infallible truth of the lesson here taught, and the actual effects of the life of St Martin on the spirit of Christianity –

is, very absolutely, the business of every rational being in any Christian kingdom.

24

You are to understand then first of all that the proper character of St Martin is a serene and sweet charity to all the creatures. He is not a preaching saint – still less a persecuting one, not even an anxious one. Of his prayers we hear little – of his wishes nothing. What he does always is merely the right thing at the right moment; rightness and bounty being in his soul one: an extremely exemplary saint, in my opinion.

Converted, baptised, and conscious of having seen Christ, he does not torment his officers for that, does not seek to make proselytes in his cohort. 'It is Christ's business, surely! – If he needs them, he can appear to them as he has to me' seems to be his feeling in the days following his baptism. He remains seventy years in the army, always this calm. At the end of this time, thinking that it might be well to take on other responsibilities, he asks the Emperor Julian to accept his resignation. On being accused of pusillanimity, Martin offers, unarmed and bearing only the sign of the cross, to lead his cohort into battle. Julian takes him at his word, holds him until the time of battle comes, but the day before he counts on putting him thus to the test, the enemy sends an ambassador with offers of submission and peace.

25

This story is not often insisted on; how far it is literally true, again observe, does not in the least matter; here the lesson *is* given for ever of the way in which a Christian soldier should meet his enemies. A lesson thanks to which, if John Bunyan's Mr Greatheart[73] had understood, the celestial gates would have opened by this time to more than one pilgrim who has failed to beat a path to them with the sword of violence.

But the story *is* true in some practical and effectual way; for, after a certain time, without any discussion, or anathema, or any kind of disturbance, we find the Roman knight made Bishop of Tours and becoming an influence for unquestionable good for the whole of humankind, then and afterwards. And in fact the story of his knight's cloak is repeated for his bishop's robe, and it should not be rejected because it is probably an invention for it is just as probably an act.

26

Going in his most beautiful robes to say prayers in church, with one of his deacons he encountered on the road an unfortunate man without clothes, and ordered his deacon to give him some sort of coat or tunic.

The deacon objecting that he had at hand no such profane apparel, St Martin, with his accustomed serenity, takes off his own episcopal stole or whatever other majestic and flowing finery it might be, throws it on the destitute shoulders of the beggar and, continuing on his way, goes on to perform the divine service, incorrectly, in his waistcoat or such mediaeval underclothes as remained to him.

But, as he stood at the altar, a globe of light appeared above his head, and when he raised his bare arms with the Host, angels were seen around him hanging golden chains and jewels not of the earth around his head.

27

This is not credible for you, or in the nature of things, wise reader, and too evidently no more than a gloss that monastic extravagance gives to a primitive story.

So be it. Yet this creation of monastic extravagance understood with the heart would have been the chastisement and the brake of every form of the church's pride and sensuality, which in our day have literally debased the service of God and his poor into the service of the clergyman and his rich; and changed what was once the garment of praise for the disheartened spirit into the spangling of pantaloons in an ecclesiastical masquerade.

28

But one more legend, and we will have enough to see the roots of the strange and universal influence of this saint on Christianity.

'What particularly distinguishes St Martin was his sweet, serious and unfailing serenity; no one had ever seen him angry, or sad, or gay; there was nothing in his heart but piety towards God and pity towards men. The Devil, who was particularly jealous of his virtues, detested above all his extreme charity, because it was the most injurious to his own power and, one day, he reproached him ironically for so quickly receiving into favour the sinners and the repentant. But St Martin answered him sadly: "Oh! How miserable you are! If you also could cease to persecute and seduce wretched creatures, if you also could repent, you would find grace and forgiveness through Jesus Christ." '[74]

29

In this gentleness was his strength; and its practical effect cannot be better appreciated than by comparing the scope of his work with that of St Firmin.

The impatient missionary rants and raves in the streets of Amiens, insults, exhorts, persuades, baptises, turns everything, as stated previously, upside down for forty days: after which he has his head cut off, and his name is never heard again *outside* Amiens.

St Martin upsets nobody, spends not one breath in unpleasant exhortation, understands by Christ's first lesson to himself that unbaptised people may be as good as baptised if their hearts are pure; he helps, forgives, consoles (sociable to the point of sharing the loving cup) paying as much attention to the clown as to the king; he is the patron of honest drinking,[75] the fragrance of the stuffing of your Martinmas goose is agreeable to his nostrils and sacred for him are the rays of departing summer. And somehow, near and far, the idols totter before him, the pagan gods disappear, *his* Christ becomes the Christ of all men, his name is invoked at the foot of innumerable altars in every country, on the tops of the Roman hills as well as down in the English fields. St Augustine baptised the first English converts in St Martin's church at Canterbury; and in London, Charing Cross station itself has not entirely effaced from the minds of Londoners his memory or his name.

30

The story of the episcopal robe is the last story relating to St Martin of which I will risk telling you that it is wiser to suppose it literally true than a simple myth; whilst remaining assuredly a myth of the greatest value and beauty; finally, I have yet another story to tell you. This is truly the last story and one which I admit you will be wiser in thinking a fable than the exact expression of truth, although some grain of truth is doubtless at its root. This grain of truth, of those which, cast on good ground, sprouting a hundred fold, it must be some tangible and unforgettable trait of the way St Martin behaved in high society; while as a myth, its value and meaning are for all times.

St Martin then, as the tale has it, was one day at dinner at the first table of the terrestrial globe – namely, with the Emperor and Empress of Germany! You do not need to enquire which Emperor, or which of the Emperor's wives! The Emperor of Germany is in all the ancient myths the expression of the highest sacred power in the State, as the Pope is the highest sacred power in the Church. So St Martin was at dinner, as we have said, with the Emperor sitting next to him on his left, the Empress on his right; everything went according to the rules; St Martin much enjoying his dinner, and making himself agreeable to the company, not in the least a John the Baptist sort of a saint. You also know that in Royal feasts of those days, persons of much inferior rank in society had access to the dining hall: they got behind the guests' chairs, saw and heard what was going on while they casually picked up crumbs and licked the plates.

When the dinner had got going, and it was time to serve the wines, the Emperor fills his cup, fills the Empress's, fills St Martin's, affectionately clinks glasses with St Martin. The Empress, equally amiable and even more sincerely believing, looks across the table, humbly, but also royally, expecting St Martin of course to approach her in turn to touch glasses with her. St Martin first looks around him with an air of reflection, notices that he has by his chair a poor ragged beggar, thirsty looking, who has managed to get *his* cup filled somehow, by a charitable lackey.

St Martin turns his back on the Empress and chinks glasses with *him*!

### 31

For which charity – mythic if you like, but ever more exemplary, he remains, as we have said, the patron of good Christian topers to this day.

As the years told upon him, he seems to have felt that he had carried the weight of the crosier long enough, that busy Tours now had need of a busier bishop, that for himself he might henceforth innocently take his pleasure and his rest where the vine grew and the lark sang. For episcopal palace he takes a little cave in the chalk cliffs of the upper river basin and organises everything for his bed and board, at little cost. Night by night, the stream murmurs for him, day by day, the vine leaves give him their shade; and the sun, his herald, going over the horizon earlier every day, goes down for him beyond the crimson water – there, where now, the peasant woman trots homewards between her baskets, where the saw stops in the half-cleft wood, and the village spire rises grey against the farthest light in Turner's *On the Banks of the Loire*.[76]

## 32

All these things that I have recounted, though not themselves without profit, my special reason for telling you now has been that you might understand the significance of a fact which marked the start of Clovis's march south against the Visigoths.

Having passed the Loire at Tours, he traversed the lands of the abbey of St Martin which he declared inviolate, and refused his soldiers permission to touch anything, except water and grass for their horses. His orders were so strict and the rigour with which he demanded they be obeyed so inflexible, that a Frankish soldier having taken without the consent of the owner some hay which belonged to a poor man, and saying jokingly that 'it was only grass', he had the aggressor put to death, exclaiming that 'victory could not be expected, if St Martin should be offended.'

## 33

Now mark well, this passage of the Loire at Tours represents the fulfilment of the proper bounds of the French kingdom, and the sign of its recognised and securely set power of 'Honour to the poor!' Even a little grass is not to be stolen from a poor man under pain of death. So wills the Christian knight of Roman armies, placed now on a high throne next to God. So wills the first Christian king of far victorious Franks, baptised by God, here, in the Jordan of his promised land, as he goes over to take possession of it.

For how long?

Until this same sign is read backwards by a degenerate throne; until, news arriving that the poor of the French people had no bread to eat, the reply was: 'Let them eat grass.'[77] Whereupon, near St Martin's faubourg and St Martin's gate, orders are given by the knight for the poor against the King which end his feasting.

And all these examples should remind you of the influence over French souls, present and to come, of St Martin of Tours.

## Notes to Chapter I

### 34

The reader will please observe that notes immediately necessary to the understanding of the text are given, in numerical order, at the foot of each page;* while the references to the writers with authority over the matter under discussion, or the texts that can be quoted in support, are indicated by a letter and thrown together at the end of each chapter. One good thing about this method[78] is that, after numbered notes are put in order, I will be able, if I see in rereading the proofs the need for a more complete explanation, to insert a letter referring to a *final* note without possibility of typographical confusion. The final notes will also be useful in summarising the chapters and making what is to be more carefully remembered stand out. Thus it is just now without importance to remember that the first taking of Amiens was in 445, because that is not the date of the founding of the Merovingian dynasty; or that Merovée seized the throne in 447 and died ten years later. The real date to be remembered is 481 which is when Clovis acceded to the throne at the age of fifteen; and the three battles of Clovis's reign to be remembered are Soissons, Tolbiac and Poitiers – remembering also that this was the first of the three great battles of Poitiers; how this Poitiers district came to have such importance as a field of battle, we will afterwards discover if we can. Of Queen Clotilde and her flight from Burgundy to find again her Frank lover, we will learn more in the following chapter; the story of the vase of Soissons is given in the *Illustrated History of France*, but we will also defer it with such commentary as it needs to the following chapter; for I would like the reader's mind, at the end of this first chapter, to be fixed on two descriptions of the modern Frank (taking this word in its Saracen sense) as distinguished from the modern Saracen. The first description is by Colonel Butler,

---

*In our edition, all the notes are regrouped at the end of the work.

entirely true and admirable without reserve, except in the (implied) extension of this contrast to ancient times, for the Saxon soul under Alfred, the Teutonic soul under Charlemagne, and the Frankish soul under St Louis were quite as religious as any Asiatic's, although more practical; it is only the modern mob of western miscreants without kings who have abased themselves by gambling, swindling, machine making, and gluttony into the most reprehensible louts who have ever fouled the earth with the carcases she lent them.

35

Of the English character traits brought to light by the spread of English domination in Asia, there is nothing more remarkable than the contrast between the religious bias of Eastern thought and the innate absence of religion in the Anglo-Saxon mind.

The Turk and the Greek, the Buddhist and the Armenian, the Copt and the Parsee, all manifest in a hundred acts of daily life the great fact of their belief in God. Above all their vices as well as their virtues reveal that they recognise a God.

For the westerner, on the contrary, all outward practice is an object of shame, something to hide. A procession of priests in some *Strade Reale* would probably be regarded by an ordinary Englishman with a less tolerant eye than a *Juggernaut*[19] festival in Orissa; but to each alike he would display the same iconoclastic zeal, both expressing the same idea, not the less fixed because it is seldom expressed in words. 'You pray, therefore I do not think much of you.'

But, in reality, this impatience of temper of the modern English to accept the religious habit of thought appears to hide a more profound difference between the East and the West. All Eastern peoples possess this habit of religious thought. It is the tie which links together their widely differing races. Here is an example to serve as an illustration of what I mean.

On an Austrian Lloyd's steamboat in the Levant, a traveller from Beirut will often see strange groups of men crowded together on the quarterdeck. In the morning the missal books of the Greek church will be placed on the bulwarks of the ship, and a couple of Russian priests coming from Jerusalem will be busy murmuring mass. A yard to the right or left a Turkish pilgrim returning from Mecca is seated respectfully watching the scene. It is in effect prayer and, consequently, something sacred to his eyes. So too when the evening hour is come, and the Turk spreads out his piece of carpet for the sunset prayers and the bowing towards Mecca, the Greek looks on in silence without any air of disdain, for it is again the worship of the Creator by the created. They are both fulfilling the *first* law of the East, prayer to God; and whether the altar is Jerusalem, Mecca or Lhasa,[80] the sanctity of worship communicates itself to the faithful and protects the pilgrim.

Into this society comes the Englishman generally lacking any feeling of sympathy for the prayers of any people or the faith in any religious idea; which is why our authority in the East has always rested and will always rest on the bayonet. We have never got beyond the stage of conquest; never assimilated a people to our customs, never even civilised a single tribe in the vast domain of our empire. It is curious to see how often it happens that a well-meaning Englishman will speak of a foreign church or temple as though it had presented itself to his mind in the same way as the City of London appeared to Blücher, as an object of pillage. The other idea, to know that a priest is a good man for hanging, is an idea that is often observable in the English brain. One day when we were trying to shed a little light into our minds on the Greek question, in questioning a naval officer whose vessel had been stationed in Greek and Adriatic waters during our occupation of Corfu and the other Ionian isles, we could only elicit from our informant the fact that one morning, before breakfast, he had hanged seventeen priests.

## 36

The second passage which I put in reserve in these notes for future use is the following, absolutely marvellous, taken from a book full of marvels – if one can put a true idea on the same rank as deeds and attribute to it the same strength: *Grains of Good Sense* by Alphonse Karr. I cannot praise this book or his more recent *Buzzings* highly enough, simply because they are by a man who is entirely after my own heart, who has been saying in France this many a year what I also, this many a year, have been saying in England, neither of us knowing the other, and both of us in vain (see paragraphs 11 and 12 of *Buzzings*).

The passage given here is from chapter 63 of *Grains of Good Sense*.

'And all that, sir, comes from the fact that there are no longer beliefs – that people no longer believe in anything.

'Ah! Fiddlesticks, sir, you're pulling my leg! You say nobody believes in anything any more! But never, in any age, have people believed in so much nonsense, such trivia, so many lies, stupidities, absurdities as today.

'First, people *believe* in incredulity – incredulity is a belief, a very demanding religion, which has its dogmas, its liturgy, its practices, its rites! ... its intolerance, its superstitions. We have our incredulous and impious Jesuits, and our impious Jansenists; our impious molinists, and our impious quietists; our impious practising, and non-practising; our impious indifferents, and our impious fanatics; our incredulous despised minorities and our impious hypocrites and impostors. The religion of incredulity does not even deny itself the luxury of heresies.

'Nobody believes any more in the bible, which I like, but people *believe* in the "articles" in the newspapers, people believe in the "priesthood" of the magazines and broadsheets, and in their daily "oracles".

'People *believe* in the "baptism" by the correctional service and the criminal court – people call the "missing" of Nouméa "martyrs" and the "brothers" from Switzerland, England and Belgium "confessors" – and, when people talk about "martyrs of the Commune", they don't mean the assassinated, but the assassins.

'People have "civil" burials, they don't want church prayers said over their caskets, they don't want candles, or religious chanting – but people want a procession carrying everlasting red flowers behind the coffin; – people want an "oration", a "sermon" by Victor Hugo who has added this speciality to his other specialities, to the degree that one day recently, as he was following a funeral rehearsal, an undertaker approached him, nudged him, and said to him smiling: "Won't we be having anything from you today?" – And this sermon he will read or recite – or, if he doesn't feel he should "officiate" himself, if it's just another death, he will send Mr Meurice to chant it, or another "priest" or "child of the heart" of "God". – In the absence of Mr Hugo, if it's an obscure citizen, people are happy with a homily improvised for the tenth time by whatever intransigent deputy – and the *Miserere* is replaced by cries of "Long live the Republic!" ringing out in the cemetery.

'People don't go to churches any more, but they frequent restaurants and night clubs; people officiate there, they celebrate the mysteries there, they sing the praises there of a claimed, *sacrosanct* republic, one, indivisible, democratic, social, athenian, intransigent, despotic, invisible but everywhere existing. People take communion in different ways; in the morning (matins) they "kill the worm" with white wine – later on there are the vespers of absinthe, in which it's considered a crime to lack assiduity.

'People no longer believe in God, but they *believe* piously in Mr Gambetta, in Messrs Marcou, Naquet, Barodet, Tartempion, etc., and in a whole long litany of saints and of *dii minores* such as Gouttenoire, Polosse, Bariasse and Silibat, the hero of Lyon.

'People *believe* in the immutability of Mr Thiers, who has said with self-assurance "I never change", and who today is at the same time the protector of and protected by those with whom he has spent part of his life as a gunner, and whom he shot again yesterday.

'People *believe* in the immaculate republicanism of the lawyer of Cahors who has thrown overboard all the republican principles – who is at the same time for his part the protector of and protected by Mr Thiers, who was yesterday calling him "mad dog", deporting and shooting his friends.

'Both of them, it is true, at the same time hypothetical protectors, and duped protected.

'Nobody believes any more in the miracles of the past, but people *do believe* in new miracles.

'People *believe* in a republic without the religious and almost fanatical respect of the laws.

People *believe* that they can enrich themselves while remaining uncircumspect, careless and lazy, and otherwise than by work and thrift.

'People *believe* themselves free while blindly and stupidly obeying two or three cliques.

'People *believe* themselves independent because they have killed or hunted a lion and replaced it with two dozen yellow-coloured poodles.

'People *believe* they have conquered "universal suffrage" in voting for words arranged so as to mean the opposite of universal suffrage – led to the vote as a flock is led to pasture, with the difference that there is no nourishment. Besides, by this universal suffrage that people think they have when they haven't, people would have to *believe* that soldiers have a duty to give orders to their general, that horses lead the coachman; *believe* that two radishes are worth more than a truffle, two pebbles more than a diamond, two pieces of dung more than a rose.

'People *believe* they are in a Republic, because some half-baked jokers occupy the same places, sign the same attendance sheets, practise the same abuses as those who have been kicked out for their benefit.

'We *believe* ourselves to be a heroic oppressed people, who break out of our chains, but are nothing more than a flighty domestic servant who loves changing masters.

'People *believe* in the genius of top drawer barristers, who have only thrown themselves into politics and aspire to the despotic government of France for want of having been able to achieve honestly, without a great deal of work, in the exercise of a correct profession, a quiet life with the occasional pint.

'People *believe* that delinquents and outcasts, hollowed out men and dried fruit, etc., who have only studied "four man dominoes" and "ten penny pinochle" wake up one morning, after a sleep made heavy with tobacco and beer, possessing the science of politics, and the art of war, and suited to being dictators, generals, ministers, prefects, sub-prefects, etc.

'And the so-called conservatives themselves *believe* that France can pick itself up and live so long as we do not do justice to this pretend universal suffrage which is the opposite of universal suffrage.

'The beliefs have suffered the lot of the snake of fable, cut, hacked into pieces, each section of which became a snake.

'The beliefs have been exchanged for money, into billions of credulities.

'And to finish the list, albeit incomplete, of beliefs and credulities, you *believe*, you, that people don't believe in anything!'

# Chapter II
# Under the Drachenfels

1

Not wanting to trust ignobly in the stratagems of artificial memory and far less slight what gives real strength to a firm and thoughtful memory, my young readers will perceive that it is extremely useful to note any instances of coincidence between the numbers, which help to recall what could be called dates of anchorage: around which others, less important, can oscillate at the end of cables of various lengths.

Thus we will first make use of one of the most simple and convenient arrangements for counting the years since the birth of Christ, by dividing them up into periods of five centuries, that is to say by the marked periods of the fifth, tenth, fifteenth, and now fast approaching us, the twentieth centuries.

And this division, which at first appears formal and arithmetical, will be found, as we use it, to give a singular meaning to events which mark a notable change in the knowledge, disciplines and morals of the human race.

2

Every date, it should further be remembered, belonging to the fifth century, will start with the number 4 (401, 402, etc.). Every date in the tenth century, with the number 9 (901, 902, etc.) and every date in the fifteenth century, with the number 14 (1401, 1402, etc.).

In the immediate subject of study, we have to occupy ourselves with the first of these centuries, the fifth, of which I will therefore ask you to observe two very interesting divisions.

All the dates in the century, we have said, must begin with the number 4.

If you halve this number for the second figure you have 42.

And if you double it for the second figure, you have 48; add one for the third figure for each of these numbers and you have 421 and 481, two dates which you will please fix in your heads without permitting the least wavering in their regard.

For the first is the date of the birth of Venice itself and her dukedom (See *St Mark's Rest*, part I, page 30); and the second is the date of the birth of the French Venice and of her kingdom, Clovis being crowned in that year at Amiens.

3

These are the two great anniversaries of birth, 'birthdays', of nations, in the fifth century; we will give the dates of their death-days at another time.

And it is not only because of dark Rialto's dukedom, nor because of the beautiful kingdom of France, that these two dates must dominate all the others in the wild fifth century, but because they are also the birthdays of a great lady and an even greater lord, of all future Christendom, St Genevieve and St Benedict.[81]

Genevieve, 'the white wave' (laughing water), the purest of all the virgins who have taken their name from the sea-foam or the rivulet's ripples, without blemish, not the troubled or troubling Aphrodite, but the Leucothea of Ulysses, the wave that leads to deliverance.

White wave on the blue of the lake or of the sunny sea which have since been the colours of France, silver lilies on a field of azure; she is forever the type of purity, in active splendour of the whole soul and life (thus distinguished from the quieter and more reserved innocence of St Agnes), and all the legends of sorrow in the trial or fall of the noble soul of woman are connected with her name, in Italian Ginevra becoming the Imogen of Shakespeare; and Guinevere,[82] the torrential wave of the mountain of waters of

Great Britain, of whose pollution your modern sentimental minstrels lament in the useless lugubrious songs; but nobody tells you, so far as I know, of the victory and power of this white wave of France.

4

She was a shepherdess, a tiny creature, barefoot, bareheaded, such as you may see running wild and innocent, less well looked after than her flock, over many a hillside of France and Italy.

Tiny enough, seven years old, that is all we are told when we first hear of her: 'Seven times one are seven (I am old, you can believe me, linnet, linnet)[83] and all around her, fierce as the Furies, wild as the minds of heaven, the Gothic armies, the thunder of which reverberates over the ruins of the universe.

5

Two leagues from Paris (Roman Paris soon to pass away with Rome herself) the little creature keeps her flock, not even her own, nor her father's flock, like David; she is the hired servant of a rich farmer from Nanterre. Who can tell me anything about Nanterre? Which pilgrim of our all-speculating, all-ignorant age has thought of visiting what relics may still be there? I don't even know on which side of Paris this place is located,[84] nor under what heap of railway cinders and iron ore one must conceive the pastures and fields of flowers of this fairy St Phillis.[85] There were such fields, even in my time, between Paris and St Denis (see the prettiest of all the chapters in the 'Mysteries of Paris', where Fleur-de-Marie runs free in them for the first time); but, at present, I suppose the native earth of St Phillis is all thrown up into bastions and strategic slopes (profitable and blessed by all the saints and by her as they have since proved themselves), or else are covered with factories and nightclubs.

She was seven years old when, on his way from Auxerre to England, St Germain stopped for a night in her village and, among the children who next morning set him on his way in a more kindly way than Elisha's escort, noticed this one looking at him wider-eyed in reverence than the rest; he had her come to him, questioned her, and was sweetly answered that she would be happy to be Christ's servant. And he hung round her neck a small copper coin marked with the cross. From this moment on Genevieve held herself 'separated from the world'.

6

It did not turn out so, however. Quite the opposite, you must think of her instead as the first of the Parisiennes. Queen of Vanity Fair, she was to become quiet, poor St Phillis with her copper farthing marked with a cross around her neck! More than Nicotris was to Egypt, more than Semiramis to Nineveh, more than Zenobia to the city of palm trees, this seven year old shepherdess became for Paris and her France. You have not heard her spoken of this way? No, how could you have? For she did not lead armies, but stopped them, and all her power was in peace.

7

There are however some twenty-seven or twenty-eight lives of her, I believe, into the literature of which I cannot and do not need to enter, all having shown themselves equally ineffective in producing a clear picture of her in the minds of the French or English of today, and I leave one's own poor sagacities and imagination to touch her sanctity, shape it and give it an intelligible, I do not say credible, form, for there is no question here of belief: the creature is as real as Joan of Arc and has a great deal more power. She is distinguished by her quietness of force (exactly as St Martin by his patience distinguishes himself from the provocative prelates) from the pitiable crowd of female martyr saints.

There are thousands of pious girls who have never figured in any calendar, but who have passed and wasted away their lives in sadness, God knows why, for we cannot, but here is one, at any rate, who does not sigh after martyrdom nor does she consume herself in torments, but became a tower of the flock[86] and all her life builds a fold for them.

8

The first thing then you have to note of her is that she is absolutely a Gaul by birth. She does not come as a missionary from Hungary or Illyria, or from Egypt, or from some mysterious nameless region, but she grows up at Nanterre, like a marguerite in the dew, the first 'White Queen' of Gaul.

I have not previously used this ugly word 'Gaul', and we must be quite sure of its meaning, at once, even though it will cost us a long parenthesis.

9

At the time of the growing power of Rome, the people called Gaul all those who lived north of the sources of the Tiber. If this general definition fails to satisfy you, you can read the article *Gallia* in Smith's *Dictionary* which consists of seventy-one columns of close print, each the length of three of my pages, and he tells you at the end: 'Though long, it is not complete.' You may however, after an attentive reading, gather as much from it as I have told you above.

But from the second century after Christ and, much more distinctly, in the time with which we ourselves are concerned – the fifth century – the wild nations opposed to Rome, and partly subdued or held in check by her, had formed themselves into two distinct masses, belonging to two distinct *latitudes*. One having settled in the pleasant temperate zone of Europe: England with her western mountains, the healthy limestone plateaus and granite mountains of France, the German labyrinths of wooded hills and winding valleys from the Tirol to the Harz, and all the vast enclosed basin of the Carpathians with its network of valleys branching out. Think of these four countries and call them, briefly and clearly, 'Britain', 'Gaul', 'Germany' and 'Dacia'.

### 10

North of these sedentary populations, rude but enduring, possessing fields and orchards, peaceful flocks, homes of a sort, customs and traditions not without grandeur, lived, or rather drifted and shook a chain, here or there broken, of sadder tribes, above all piratical and predatory, essentially nomadic; homeless of necessity, finding no rest, no comfort in earth or sad sky; desperately wandering along the arid sands and boggy waters of the flat country stretching from the mouths of the Rhine to those of the Vistula and, beyond the Vistula, nobody knows where, or needs to know. Desert sand and rootless bogs, such was their lot; a prison of ice and shallow pools, oozings or windings of sluggish watercourses, black decay of neglected woods, barely habitable, impossible to love. Since this epoch the inner mainlands have scarcely improved.[87] And their inhabitants have now fallen on even sadder times.

### 11

For in the fifth century they had herds of cattle[88] to drive and eat, lands which were true unmanaged hunting grounds, full of game and wild deer and also tameable reindeer, even in the south, spirited hogs good for fighting, as in Meleager's time, and afterwards for bacon; innumerable furry beasts useful for their flesh and skin. Fish of the infinite sea breaking their nets, innumerable birds, migrating in the skies, easy targets for their sharp-pointed arrows, horses bred for riding, ships of no mean size and of all sorts, flat-bottomed for the muddy puddles, keeled and decked for the impetuous current of the Elbe and the furious Baltic on the one side, to the south for the mountain-cleaving Danube and the black lake of Colchos.

## 12

And they were in all outward aspect and also in their proven strength the living powers of the world, in this long hour of its transfiguration. All the rest once regarded as redoubtable had become formalism, folly or shame. The Roman armies nothing but a mechanism armed with a sword, collapsing in disorder sword against friendly sword – the Roman civil order a multitude of mixed slaves, slave masters, and prostitutes. The East, separated from Europe by the weakness of the Greeks. These starving troops of the Black forests and the White seas, themselves half wolf, half driftwood (as we called ourselves Lion-hearts, Hearts of Oak, so did they) merciless as the herded hound, enduring as the wild birch and pine. You will hear of few besides them for five centuries yet to come; Visigoths, to the west of the Vistula; Ostrogoths, to the east of the Vistula and, radiating around little Holy Island (Heligoland), our own Saxons and Hamlet the Dane, and in a sleigh on the ice, his enemy the Pole, all these to the south of the Baltic; and throwing her force non-stop across the Baltic, Scandinavia issues forth from the mountains – until at last *she* for a time rules all, and the Norman name sees its authority uncontested from the North Cape to Jerusalem.

## 13

*This* is the apparent history, this is the only known world history, as I have said, for the five centuries to come. And yet it is only the surface, beneath which the real history plays itself out.

The wandering armies are only, in reality, living hail and thunder and fire over the land. But the suffering life, the deep heart of primitive humanity, growing up in an eternal gentleness, however ravaged, forgotten, spoiled, itself staying where it is and never devastating, nor murdering, but unconqerable by grief or death – became the seed of all love that was to be born in due time, gave then to mortal humanity what hope, joy or genius it could receive and – if there is an immortality – led, beyond the grave, to the Church her protector Saints and to Heaven her helpful Angels.

14

Of this order of creatures of humble condition, silent, inoffensive, infinitely submissive, infinitely devoted, no historian ever takes the slightest notice, except when they are robbed or killed. I can give you no picture of it, bring to your ear no murmur of it, no cry. I can only show you the absolute 'must have been' of its unrewarded past, and the idea that all of us are made of them, and the things which we have been told are founded on the deeper facts in its history, which have never been conceived of, or recounted.

15

The great mass of this innocent and invincible peasant life is, as I have told you above, grouped in the fruitful and temperate districts of (relatively) mountainous Europe, going from west to east from Cornwall's Land's End to the mouth of the Danube.

Already, in the times we are now dealing with, it was full of a naturally generous ardour and an intelligence open to all. Dacia gives to Rome her four last great emperors;[89] Britain gives to Christianity the first exploits and the last legends of her chivalry; Germany to all men the sincerity and the fire of the Frank; Gaul, to all women the patience and strength of St Genevieve.

16

The *sincerity* and the fire of the Frank, I must repeat with insistence, for my youngest readers have probably been in the habit of thinking that the French were more polite than sincere. They will find, if they look deeper into the matter, that sincerity alone can be polished, and that all we recognise of beauty, delicacy and proportion in the manners, the language or the architecture of the French, comes of a pure sincerity in their nature, which you will soon find in the living creatures themselves if you love them; and if you have a sane understanding of even their worst faults, you will see that their Revolution itself was a revolt against lies, and against the betrayal of love. Never was a people so loyal in vain.

17

That they were originally German, they themselves I suppose would now be happy to forget; but how they shook the dust of Germany off their feet and gave themselves a new name is the first of the phenomena that we now have to observe attentively concerning them. 'The most sagacious critics,' says Mr Gibbon in his tenth chapter, '*suppose* that *around* the year 240' (we will therefore *suppose*, for greater comfort, that it was *around* the year 250, half way to the end of the fifth century, where we are – ten years more or less in cases of 'supposing that around' matter little, but we will have at least some floating buoy of a date ready to hand).

'About AD 250 then, "a new confederacy" was formed under the name of Franks by the old inhabitants of the Lower Rhine and the Weser.'

18

My own impression concerning the old inhabitants of the Lower Rhine and the Weser would have been that they consisted mostly of fish, with frogs and ducks on the surface, but a note added by Gibbon on this passage informs us that the new confederation composed itself of human creatures, listed as follows:

1. The Chauci who lived we are not told where;
2. The Sicambri, in the Principality of Waldeck;
3. The Attuarii, in the Duchy of Berg;
4. The Bructeri, on the banks of the Lippe;
5. The Chamavii, in the country of the Bructeri;
6. The Catti, in Hessia.

All that will be, I believe, clearer in your heads if you forget it than if you remember it; but, if it pleases you to read or reread (or, best of all, find some real Miss Isabelle Wardour[90] to read to you) the story of Martin Waldeck in *The Antiquary*, you will gain from it a sufficient notion of the principal character 'the Principality of Waldeck', clearly linked to this important German word 'woody' (that is to say 'woodish', I suppose?) – descriptive of rocks and half-grown forests; together with a healthy respect for the deep foundations that Scott gives instinctively to the proper names in his work.

19

But let us not lose sight of our goal. The most pressing is seriously to come back now to our maps, and locate things in a space determined by linear limits.

All the maps of Germany which I myself have the privilege of possessing become very confused just to the north of Frankfurt, and happen to resemble a painted window broken into a thousand pieces by Puritan malice, and restored by ingenious churchwardens who put every piece of it back upside down, this curious glassware purporting to represent the sixty, seventy, eighty or ninety hereditary dukedoms, marquisates, counties, baronies, electorates, etc., into which Germany cracked and pieced itself in this latitude.

But under the mottled colours and through the jotted and jumbled alphabets of truncated dignities to which the three networks of railways are spread over all, networks not united, but bristling with legs like centipedes, a hard day's work with a good magnifying glass enables one approximately to discover the course of the Weser, and the names of certain neighbouring towns near its sources worth remembering.

20

In case you don't have an afternoon to spare, nor eyesight to waste, you will have to content yourself with this, which is necessarily a simple summary: knowing that from the Drachenfels[91] and from its six brother Felsen, bearing from the east to the north, there runs and extends a scattered group of little gnarled crags, mysterious crests which jut superciliously over valleys bordered by small woods, where a torrent will be now furious and now melodious; the crests, mostly crowned with castles by Christian piety form long ago for distant or fanciful ends; the valleys resounding with the sounds of woodmen, and burrowed into by miners, inhabited below ground by gnomes and above ground by forest and other spirits. The entire country grasping rock by rock, connecting from valley to valley for some 150 miles (with intervals) the Dragon mountain above the Rhine to the Rosin mountain, the 'Harz', still shadowy today, towards the south of the territory trampled underfoot by the black Brunswickers of indisputable bodily presence; long ago obscured by the 'Hercynian' forest (hedge or fence) from which by corruption Harz, where today we have the Harz or Rosin forest, haunted by dark foresters, of at least resinous, not to say sulphurous, extraction.

21

One hundred and fifty miles from east to west, say half as much from north to south, about ten thousand square miles in total of metalliferous, coniferous and phantomiferous mountains, fluent and diffluent for us, in the middle ages and in modern times, with the most essential oil of turpentine, and this myrrh, or this incense, of imagination and character which Germany produces naturally and of which oil of turpentine is the symbol. I am thinking particularly of how the more delicate uses of resin, as indispensable to the bow of the violin, have developed themselves, from the days of St Elizabeth of Marbury to those of St Mephistopheles of Weimar.

## 22

As far as I know, this cluster of capricious rocks and valleys has no general name as a group of hills; and it is altogether impossible to discover its different branchings on any of the maps I can lay my hands on, but we can easily, and usefully, recall that it is *all* north of the Main, that it rests on the Drachenfels at one extremity, and suddenly throws itself vaulting towards the morning light, up to the Harz (summit of the Brocken, 3,700 feet above sea level, nothing higher), with a broad space reserved for the course of the Weser, of which we will speak presently.

## 23

We will call this in future the chain or group of enchanted mountains; and then we shall all the more easily link them to the Giant mountains, Riesen Gebirge, when we need them; but these are altogether higher, more severe, and we have not yet to approach them; these nearer ones through which our road lies, we might perhaps more aptly call the demon mountains; but that would be scarcely respectful for St Elizabeth, or for the innumerable pretty ladies of the manor of towers, or for the princesses of park and valley, who have made German domestic manners sweet and exemplary and have let their life flow freely transparent and light down the valleys of ages until enchantment takes a form perhaps a little too canonical in the Almanach de Gotha.

We will call them therefore the enchanted mountains, not the demons; noting also gratefully that the spirits of their rocks have really much more of the character of healing fairies than of gnomes, each (as it were with magic hazel wand instead of smiting rod), surging from underground ferruginous caves of effervescent springs, healthily salt and warm.

24

At the very heart of this enchanted chain (and the most beneficent, if one use it and direct it well, of all the fountains in the region) sprang the source of the most ancient Frank race; 'in the principality of Waldeck', you can go back to no further source; there it rises out of the earth.

'Frankenburg' (Burg) on the right bank of the Eder and nineteen miles to the north of Marburg, clearly indicated in map number 13 of Black's General Atlas, in which the cluster of enchanted mountains which surrounds the valley of the Eder, otherwise 'Engel-Bach', 'Angel Brook' (as the village situated higher up the valley still calls itself) which rejoins the Fulda, just above Cassel, is also delineated in a way intelligible to attentive mortal eyes. I would be plagued by the names if I tried a drawing; but a few careful pen strokes or a few sketches that you made yourself by hand, would give you all the actual sources of the Weser with sufficient clarity, with the memorable towns on its course or just to the south of it on the other slope of the watershed towards Maine: Frankenberg and Waldeck on the Eder, Fulda and Cassel on the Fulda, Eisenach on the Werra, which forms the Weser after taking the Fulda for bride (as Tees the Greta),[92] beyond Eisenach, under the Wartzburg (which you have heard spoken of as a castle handling Christian missions, and for Bible Society purposes). The streets of the town are paved in hard basalt (its name – iron water – recalling the Thuringian armouries of old), and it is still active with mills serving every purpose.

25

The rocks all the way from the Rhine are up to here jets and spurts of basalt across ferruginous sandstone, with one or two strips of coal towards the north, thanks be to God, not worth extracting; at Frankenberg even a gold mine; also by heaven's mercy poor in iron ore; but the country produces a sufficient quantity of wood and of iron if the right amount of effort is expended; and there are softer riches on the surface of the ground: game, corn, fruit, flax, wine, wool and hemp. Finally crowning all, monastic zeal in the houses of Fulda and Walter which I find marked by a cross as built by some pious Walter, knight of Meiningen on the Bodenwasser 'bottom water', that is to say water having finally found its way well down (in the sense in which 'Boden See' is said of the Rhine to be descended from the Via Mala).

### 26

And thus, having got your springs of the Weser well clear of the rocks, and as it were having gathered up the reins of your river, you can draw easily enough for your personal use the further course of its stream going to the north in a straight line, to the North Sea. And trace it with an energetic line on your sketch of the map of Europe, after the border of the Vistula, leaving aside the Elbe for a time. For the moment, you can take the whole space between the Weser and the Vistula (north of the mountains) as wild and barbarous (Saxon and Goth); but allow for the source of the Franks at Waldeck and you will find them gradually but swiftly filling all the space between the Weser and the mouths of the Rhine and, foaming in the mountains, spreading into a calmer blanket over the Netherlands, where their straying forest and pastoral life has at last to embank itself into muddy farm fields and in frozen sea mist forgets the sunshine on its basalt crags.

### 27

Whereupon we must also stop to embank ourselves somewhat; and before doing anything else, see what we can understand in this name of Frank relative to which Gibbon tells us in his sweetest tone of satisfied moral serenity: 'The love of freedom was the ruling passion of these Germans. They deserved, they took, they kept the honourable epithet of Franks, or free men.' He does not tell us though in what language of the time (Chaucian, Sicambrian, Chamavian, or Cattian) 'Frank' ever meant Free; and I cannot myself find out what language, of whatever time, this word first belongs to; but I do not doubt that Miss Yonge (*History of Christian Names*, articles on Frey and Frank) gives the time root when she speaks of what she calls the High German 'Frang', Free *Lord*. Not by any means a free man of the people, nothing of the sort; but a person whose nature and name implied the existence around him and beneath him of a considerable number of other persons who were by no means 'Frang' nor Frangs. His title was one of the proudest of those that existed at that time; consecrated at last by the dignity of age added to that of valour in the name of Seigneur, or Monseigneur, not even yet in the last cockney form of it 'Mossoo' wholly understood as a republican term!

28

So that, reflecting on it well, the quality of Frankness gives only its flat side in the learning of 'Libre', but with all its cutting edge and pointedness, without any doubt and for all time meaning brave, strong and honest, above other men.[93]

The old people of the woodlands were never in any bad sense 'free'; but in a truly human sense Frank, meaning exactly what they said, and sticking to it until it was accomplished. Quick and clear in words and action, absolutely fearless and always restless; but lawless, undisciplined or weakly lavish they were not, either in word or deed. Their frankness, if you read the word as a scholar and a Christian, and not as a modern half-breed infidel with half a brain, knowing none of the languages of the world but its slang form, is really opposed not to servitude, but to timidity.[94]

It is today the mark of the sweetest and most French of the French character that it produces quite the most perfect servants. Indefatigably attached to their protectors, addressing every action with sweetness, under a latent tutorship; the most amiably useful of valets, the kindliest of housekeepers (with mentality and personality altogether good). But in no sense are they intimidated by you. Though you be the Duke or Duchess of Montalissimo, you will not see them troubled by your elevated rank. They will answer back at you if they have a mind to.

### 29

Best of servants; best of subjects too when they have an equally frank king, or count, or chief, to lead them; of which we will see ample proof in due time; but, at the moment, note this further, whatever accessory gleam of the thing subsequently called by them Liberty may be meant by the name Frank, you must from now on and always in the future guard yourself from confusing their Liberties with their Power to act. What the attitude of the army may be towards their chief is one question: whether chief or army can keep quiet for six months, another and totally different one. They must always be fighting someone or going somewhere, their life otherwise does not seem worth living to them; and this activity, this flashing and flickering of mercury which shines here and everywhere at once, which in its essence is love neither of war nor of rape, but simply the need to change place and mood, so to say, modus and tempus – and intensity) among men who never want to let their spurs rest but have them always shining on their feet, and prefer to be fasting on horseback than feasting at rest, this infantile fear of being put in the corner, and continual need to have something to do, all that has to be considered by us with an astonished sympathy in all its sometimes splendid, but too often unlucky or disastrous consequences for the nation itself as well as for its neighbours.

### 30

And this activity which we, heavy beef eaters that we are, before we had been taught by modern science that we were no better than baboons ourselves, were wont to compare discourteously to that of the livelier tribes of monkey, made in fact such a great impression on the Hollanders (when for the first time Frank irrigation gave motion and current to their marshes) that the most ancient heraldry in which we find the Frank power blazoned seems to have been the work of a Dutch man who wanted to give a disdainfully satirical representation of it.

'For,' says a very ingenious historian, Mr André Favine, Parisian and advocate in the high court of the French parliament in the year 1626, 'these people who bordered on the river Sala, called "Salts" by the Germans, were on their descent into Dutch lands called by the Romans "Franci Salici" (whence note the future "Salique" law) and by abbreviation "Salii", apparently from the verb *salire*, that is to say "saulter", "to jump" (and in future consequently duly also to dance – in an incomparable manner), to be quick and nimble of foot, to jump and climb, qualities most particularly requisite for such as dwell in wet and marshy places. So that while such of the French as dwelt on the main arm of the river (Rhine) were called "Nageurs" (Swimmers), they of the marshes were called "Saulteurs" (Jumpers); it was a nickname given to the French by reason of their natural disposition and of their residence; and even today, their enemies call them French Toads (or Frogs more exactly) whence came the fable that their ancient kings carried such creatures in their arms.'

## 31

Without at present addressing the question of whether it is a fable or not, you will easily remember the epithet 'Salian', characterising the people who jump the ditches, swim across the rivers, so well that, as we have said previously, all the length of the Rhine must be refortified against them, epithet however, in which it appears in its origin to be delicately Saline, so that we can justly, as we call our hardened mariners 'Old Salts', think of these more brilliant, more sparkling Franks as 'Young Salts'; but the Romans were to play with the word to a certain extent, and in their natural respect for the martial fire and 'élan' of the Franks, they were to make of them 'Salii exsultantes'[95] which name they gave even to their own armed priests who followed them to war.

Going to a little further, but subtle, derivation, we can consider this first 'Salient' as a promontory shaped like the beak of an eagle, over the France we know, towards what we call today France; and ever more in its brilliant elasticity of temperament, a nation of jumps and sallies, furnishing to us English, for we can risk just this once this little heraldic erudition, their 'Leopard' (not as a spotted and dotted creature, but as a naturally springing and bounding one) for our kingly and princely shields.

That should be enough for their 'Salian' epithet, but from the interpretation of the Frankish one we are still as far as ever, and we must be content in the meantime to stay so, noting however two ideas afterwards entangled with this name, which are for us of a very definitional importance.

### 32

'The French poet in the first books of his Franciade,' (says Mr Favine, but what poet I know not, nor can find out)[96] 'recounts'[97] (in the sense of en-quarters, or paints as a herald does) 'certain fables on the name of the French by the adoption and reunion of two Gaulish words joined together, Phere-Encos which means "Bear-Lance" (Brandish-Lance, we may perhaps venture to translate), a lighter weapon than the spear beginning here to quiver in the hands of their chivalry and Fere-Encos becoming quite quickly in the spoken language "Francos" – a derivation certainly not to be accepted, but because of the idea that it gives to the weapon it is worth paying attention to the following: among the weapons of the ancient French, above and beyond the lance, there was the battle axe which they called anchon, and which still exists today in many of the provinces of France where it is called an achon; they served themselves in war by throwing it from a distance at the enemy with the sole purpose of discovering the man and cleaving his shield. This achon was darted with such violence that it would cleave the shield, forcing its holder to lower his arm and thus leave him discovered and disarmed allowing him to be more easily and quickly surprised. It seems that this weapon was properly and specially the weapon of the French soldier, as well on foot as on horseback. For this reason, it was called *Franciscus*. Francisca, *securis oblonga, quam Franci librabant in hostes*. For the horseman, besides his shield and Francisca (a weapon common, as we have said, to the footman and the horseman), had also the lance; when it was broken and could no longer serve, he laid his hand on the Francisca, the use of which we learn from the Archbishop of Tours, in his second book, chapter 27.'

33

It is agreeable to see how respectfully the lessons of the Archbishop of Tours were received by the French knights, and curious to note the preference for using the Francisca by all the best of them, not only to the time of the Coeur de Lion, but even to the days of Poitiers. In the last engagement of this battle at the gates of Poitiers: 'There the King Jehan made wonderful weapons with his own hands, and used a battle axe so well in defence and attack – if a quarter of his men had done the same, they would have held the day.' Still more remarkable from this point of view is the episode of combat which Froissart stops to tell us about before beginning his story, and which pits the Sire de Verclef (on the Severn) against the Picard squire Jean de Helennes; the Englishman losing his sword dismounts to pick it up; whereupon Helennes *casts* his own at him with such aim and force 'that he sunders the Englishman's thigh protection such that the sword enters the thigh and severs it right through, all the way to the haunch.'

On this the knight rendering himself, the squire binds his wound, and nurses him, staying fifteen days 'for the love of him', at Châtellerault, while his life was in danger, and afterwards carrying him in his litter all the way to Picardy. His ransom is 6,000 nobles. I think that is worth about 25,000 pounds in today's money and you can take as a particularly fatal sign of how near we are to the decline of the times of chivalry that 'this squire was made a knight by reason of the huge profit that he made from the Seigneur de Verclef.'

I return gladly to the dawn of chivalry when, hour by hour, men were becoming more gentle and more wise, while even through their worst cruelties and errors, native qualities of the most noble cast may be seen asserting themselves at first, by virtue of an innate principle, and then submitting themselves to the test of future tasks.

34

The two principal weapons, that is all we yet know of the Salian Frank; but his silhouette begins to take shape in the mist of the Brocken, carrying the light lance which will become the javelin; but the axe, his woodman's weapon, is heavy – for economical reasons, in scarcity of iron, it is the weapon preferable to all others, giving the greatest force of thrust and most powerful blow with the least quantity of metal, and the roughest forging. Gibbon gives them also a 'weighty' sword, suspended from a 'broad' belt; but Gibbon's epithets are always given gratis,[98] and the belted sword, whatever its measure, was probably destined for the leaders only; the belt, itself of gold, the destination of the Roman courts and doubtless adopted, from their example, by the allied Frank leaders; afterwards taking the symbolic meaning given to it by St Paul[99] of the girdle of truth; and so finally the principal emblem of the chivalric order.

35

The shield for all was round, wielded like a highlander's shield, armour which probably was nothing but hard-tanned leather, or patiently solidly knitted hemp: 'Their close apparel,' says Mr Gibbon, 'exactly figured the shape of their limbs', but 'apparel' is only a Miltonic-Gibbonian expression for 'nobody knows what'. He is more intelligible when referring to their persons. 'The lofty stature of the Franks and their blue eyes, denoted a Germanic origin; the warlike barbarians were trained from their first youth to run, to jump, to swim, to throw the javelin and battle axe without hesitation against an enemy superior in numbers, and to maintain in life or in death the invincible reputation of their ancestors' (VI, 93). For the first time, in 358, appalled by the victory of Emperor Julian at Strasbourg, and besieged by him on the Meuse, a body of six hundred Franks 'dispensed with the ancient law which ordered them to conquer or die'. 'Although the lust for rape was strong in them, they professed a disinterested love of war which they considered as the supreme honour and supreme happiness of human nature, and their minds and bodies were so hardened by perpetual activity, that according to the lively expression of an orator, the snows of winter were as agreeable to them as the flowers of spring' (III, 220).

### 36

These moral and bodily virtues or this hardening were probably universal in the military ranks of the nation; but we will soon learn with surprise of so remarkably 'free' a people, that nobody but the King and the royal family could wear their hair as they liked. The kings wore theirs in floating ringlets on their backs and shoulders, the queens in undulating tresses down to their feet, but all the rest of the nation were obliged either by law or custom to shave the back part of their head, to comb their short hair over their forehead, and to content themselves with the ornament of two small whiskers.[100]

### 37

Moustaches, Mr Gibbon means I imagine, and I permit myself also to suppose that the nobles and their wives could wear their tresses and ringlets as they wished. But again, as unexpectedly and embarrassingly, light is shed on the democratic institutions of the Franks when we learn 'that the various trades, the labours of agriculture and the arts of hunting and fishing were *exercised* by *servile* hands for a *salary* from the Sovereign.'

'Servile and salary' however, though at first they sound terrible and unjust, are only Miltonic-Gibbonian expressions of the general fact that the Frankish kings had workers in their fields, employed weavers and blacksmiths to make their clothes and swords, hunted with huntsmen, hawked with falconers, and were in other respects tyrannical in the same way that an English master of hounds may be. 'The castle of the long-haired kings was surrounded by convenient yards and stables for poultry and cattle, the garden was planted with useful vegetables, the stores filled with corn and wine either for sale or consumption, and the whole administration conducted with the strictest rules of private economy.'

### 38

I have assembled these often incomplete and not very consistent remarks, about the aspect and character of the Franks, out of Mr Gibbon's references to them, during a period of more than two centuries, and the last passage quoted – which he accompanies with the statement that 'one hundred and sixty of these rural palaces were scattered across the provinces of their kingdom,' without telling us which kingdom, or at what period – must be held descriptive of the customs and general system of their monarchy after the victories of Clovis. But from the first hour you hear tell of him, the Frank, properly considered, is always an extremely ingenious, well-intentioned and industrious personage; if he is impatiently acquisitive, he is also intelligently conservative and constructive; there is an element of order and clarity of architecture which will one day find its supreme expression in the aisles of Amiens; and things generally unrivalled and indestructible, if those who lived among them had been as stout-hearted as those who built them so many years before.[101]

### 39

But for the moment we must retrace our steps, for lately, in rereading some of my books for new and revised editions, I have observed, and not without remorse, that every time in one paragraph or chapter I promise for the next chapter a careful examination of some particular point, the next paragraph never does touch upon the promised point at all, but is sure to attach itself passionately to some antithetic, antipathic or antipodic point in the opposite hemisphere; I find this manner of putting a book together extremely conducive to impartiality and largeness of view; but I can conceive it to be for the general reader not only disappointing (if I can truly flatter myself that I ever interest enough to disappoint), but even capable of confirming in his mind some of the fallacious and absolutely absurd insinuations of hostile critics respecting my inconsistency, my vacillations, and my facility for being influenced by changes of temperature in my principles or opinions. So I propose in these historical sketches, at least to watch myself, and I hope partly to correct myself in this fault of failing in my promises and, at whatever cost to the various flux and reflux of my humour, to tell in some measure in each chapter what the reader has the right to be told.

### 40

I abandoned in my first chapter, after having simply glanced at it, the story of the vase of Soissons. It can be found (and it is very nearly the only thing that can be found concerning the life or personal character of the first Louis) in every cheap popular history of France with cheap popular morality imprinted on it. If I had the time to trace it to its first sources, perhaps it would take another aspect. But I give it to you as you can find it everywhere asking you only to consider – even as so read – whether it may not properly bear a somewhat different meaning.

41

The story is then that after the battle of Soissons, in the division of Roman or Gallic spoils, the king wished to have a superbly worked silver vase for – 'himself', I was on the point of writing – and in my last chapter I *did* mistakenly imply that he wanted it for his better self, his queen. But he wanted it for neither one nor the other, it was to restore it to St Rémy, that it might remain among the consecrated treasures of Rheims. This is the first point on which the popular histories do not insist, and which one of his warriors claiming an equal share of the treasure also preferred to ignore. The vase was demanded by the king in addition to his own portion and the Frank knights, while they rendered true obedience to their king as leader, did not have the least intention of according him what more modern kings call 'royalties', taxes levied in advance on everything they touch. And one of these Frank knights or counts, a little franker than the others and as incredulous of St Rémy's sainthood as a Protestant bishop or a positivist philosopher, took it upon himself to dispute the claim of the king and the church, in the manner, I suppose, of a Liberal opposition in the House of Commons; and disputed it with such confidence in being supported by the public opinion of the fifth century that, the king persisting in his request, the fearless soldier dashed the vase to pieces with his battle axe exclaiming: 'You will have no more than your share by lot.'

42

It is the first clear affirmation of French 'Liberty, Fraternity and Equality', supported then as now by the destruction of art, which is the only possible active manifestation of 'free' personages, who are incapable of creating anything themselves.

The king did not continue the quarrel. Cowards will think that he paused in cowardice, and evil people that he paused in evil. It is certain, at least it is well accepted, that he did pause; but he bided his time; which the anger of a strong man always can, and burn hotter for the waiting, and it is one of the principal reasons why Christians are taught not to let the sun go down on it.[102] Precept which Christians are nowadays perfectly ready to obey if it is somebody else who has been offended, and in fact the difficulty in such cases is usually to get them to think of the injury, even when the sun has not yet gone down on their indignation.[103]

43

The sequel is truly shocking for the modern sensibility. I give it in the, if not polished, at least delicately varnished, language of the illustrated history.

'About a year afterwards, on reviewing his troops, he went to the man who had broken the vase and, *examining his arms, complained* that *they* were in a bad state!' (the italics are mine) and 'threw them' (what? shield and sword?) 'on the ground.' The soldier bent down to recover them and at that moment the king hit him on the head with his battle axe, crying: 'Thus did you to the vase of Soissons.' The moral modern historian adds this remark, that: 'This as evidence of the state of the Franks and of the ties by which they were united gives but the idea of a band of robbers and of their chief.' Which is in effect, so far as I can penetrate and decipher the nature of things, the primary idea to be entertained respecting most of the kingly and military organisations in the world right down to our own day (unless perchance it be the Afghans and the Zulus who are stealing our own land in England instead of we theirs in their respective countries). But concerning the manner in which this type of military execution was accomplished, I must for the moment ask the reader's permission to consider with him, if it be less kingly, or more cruel, to hit an insolent soldier over the head with one's own battle axe, than to strike a person like Sir Thomas More[104] on the neck with an executioner's, using for the mechanism – as if it were cleaver, guillotine or rope, to give the final blow – manageable forms of national law and the graciously intermingled intervention of an elegant group of noblemen and bishops.

### 44

There are things quite a bit blacker to say about Clovis than this, as his proud life draws towards its end, things which you should be told in all their truth, if any of us could see clear through the darkness. But we can never know the truth of sin; for its nature is to deceive equally on the one hand the sinner, and on the other hand the judge. Diabolic, betraying us whether we yield to it or condemn it; here on this subject are Gibbon's facetious comments, if you care for them; but I gather first, from the confused paragraphs that lead to them, sentences of praise no less generous than the Sage of Lausanne ordinarily accords to those of his heroes who have confessed the power of Christianity.

### 45

'Clovis was no more than fifteen years of age when, by his father's death, he succeeded as chief of the Salian tribe. The narrow limits of his kingdom stopped at the island of the Batavians, with the ancient dioceses of Tournay and Arras; and at the baptism of Clovis, the number of his warriors could not exceed 5,000. The tribes of the same race as the Franks who had installed themselves along the Scheldt, the Meuse, the Moselle and the Rhine, were governed by their autonomous kings of the Merovingian race, the equals and the allies, and sometimes the enemies of the Salic prince. When he started the campaign, he had neither gold nor silver in his coffers, nor wine and corn in his stores; but he imitated the example of Caesar who, in the same country, had enriched himself at the point of a sword, and bought mercenaries with the fruits of conquest.

'The untamed spirit of the Barbarians learned to recognise the advantages of regular discipline. At the annual review of the month of March, their arms were diligently inspected; and, when they crossed a peaceful territory, they were forbidden from touching a blade of grass. The justice of Clovis was inexorable; and those of his soldiers who proved to be careless or disobedient were punished with instant death. It would be superfluous to praise the valour of a Frank, but the valour of Clovis was governed by a cold and consummate prudence. In all his relations with men he took the balance between the weight of interest, of passion and of opinion; and his measures were sometimes in harmony with the sanguinary manners of the Germans, and sometimes moderated by the milder genius of Rome and of Christianity.'

46

'But the savage conqueror of Gaul was incapable of discussing the value of proofs of a religion which depend on the laborious investigation of historic evidence and on speculative theology. He was still more incapable of feeling the mild influence of the Gospel which persuades and purifies the heart of a true convert. His ambitious reign was a perpetual violation of moral and Christian duties: his hands were stained with blood in peace as in war; and, as soon as Clovis had dismissed a synod of the Gallican church, he calmly assassinated *all* the princes of the Merovingian race.'

47

It is too true;[105] but at first it is rhetorical – for we ought to be told how many *all* the princes were – in second place we should note that supposing Clovis had in any degree 'studied the scriptures' as presented to the western world by St Jerome, he was likely, as a soldier-king, to have thought more of the mission of Joshua[106] and Jehu than of the patience of Christ, whom he thought more of avenging than of irritating his passion; and the fear that the other Frank kings would succeed him or, in envy of the vast kingdom that he had enlarged, would attack and dethrone him, could easily appear to him as inspired not by a personal danger, but by the possible return of the whole nation to idolatry. And, in the last place, his faith in the divine protection given to his cause had been shaken by the defeat that the Ostrogoths had inflicted on him before Arles, and the Frank leopard had not so wholly changed his spots[107] as to surrender to an enemy the opportunity of the first bound.

48

Finally, and placing ourselves above these personal questions, the diverse forms of cruelty and ruse – the first, observe, arising much out of a scorn of suffering which was a condition of honour for the women as well as for the men – are in these savage races always founded on their love of glory in war; which can only be understood by comparing what remains of the same temper in the highest castes of the North American Indians; and before finally exposing clearly the actual events of the reign of Clovis to their end, the reader will do well to learn this list of the personages of the great Drama, taking to heart the meaning of the *name* of each, both in its probable influence on the mind of its bearer, and as a fatal expression of the sum total of their acts and their consequences for the future generations.

1. Clovis. Frank form, Hluodoveh.[108] 'Glorious sanctity' or sacred. Latin Chlodovisus, when baptised by St Rémy, softening across the centuries into Lhodovisus, Ludovicus, Louis.

2. Albofleda. 'White household fairy?' His youngest sister married Theodoric ('Theudreich, ruler of the people'), the great king of the Ostrogoths.

3. Clotilde. Hlod-hilda, 'Glorious battle maiden'. His wife. 'Hilda' first meaning battle, pure; and then becoming queen or battle maiden. Christianised to St Clotilde in France, and St Hilda of Whitby rock.

4. Clotilde. His only daughter, died for the catholic faith, under Arian persecution.

5. Childebert. His eldest son by Clotilde, the first Frank king in Paris. 'Battle Splendour' softening into Hildebert, and then Hildebrandt as in the Nibelung.

6. Chlodomir. 'Glorious Fame.' His second son from the bed of Clotilde.

7. Clotaire. His youngest son by Clotilde; virtually the destroyer of his father's house. 'Glorious Warrior.'

8. Chlodowald. Youngest son of Chlodomir. 'Glorious Power', afterwards St Cloud.

### 49

I will now follow without further ado, through their light and shadow, the course of Clovis's reign and deeds.

A.D. 481 – Crowned when he was only fifteen. Five years afterwards he provokes 'in the spirit and almost in the language of chivalry' the Roman governor Syagrius, holding the district of Rheims and Soissons: '*Campum sibi praeparari jussit*, he commanded his antagonist to prepare him a battlefield' (See Gibbon's note and reference, chapter xxxviii). The Benedictine abbey of Nogent was afterwards built on the battlefield, marked by a circle of Pagan sepulchres. 'Clovis gives the adjacent lands of Leuilly and Coucy to the church of Rheims.'[109]

A.D. 485 – The Battle of Soissons. Gibbon does not give its date: the subsequent death of Syagrius at the court of Alaric (the younger) was in 486, take 485 for the battle.

### 50

A.D. 493 – I cannot find any account of the relations between Clovis and the King of Burgundy, the uncle of Clotilde, which preceded his betrothal to the orphan princess. Her uncle, according to all historians, had killed her father and mother and forced her sister to take the veil. No motive is given, and no source quoted. Clotilde herself was pursued on her way to France[110] and the litter in which she travelled was captured with part of her dowry. But the princess herself climbed on horseback and rode with part of her escort towards France, 'ordering her servants to set fire to everything that pertained to her uncle and his subjects which they might meet on the way'.

### 51

The fact is not usually recounted among the sayings or doings of the saints; but punishing kings by destroying the property of their subjects is too well accepted a method of modern warfare to allow our indignation to burn too strongly against Clotilde who was acting under the impulse of grief and anger. The years of her youth are not recounted to us: Clovis was already twenty-seven and had for three years maintained the faith of his ancestors against all the influence of his queen.

### 52

A.D. 496 – I did not in the opening chapter attach nearly enough importance to the battle of Tolbiac, thinking of it as merely compelling the Allemanni to recross the Rhine, and establishing the power of the Franks on its western bank. But infinitely broader results are indicated in the short sentence with which Gibbon closes his account of the battle. 'After the conquest of the western provinces, the Franks alone kept their ancient possessions beyond the Rhine. They gradually submitted and civilised the peoples whose resistance they had broken as far as the Elbe and the mountains of Bohemia; and the *peace of Europe* was assured by the submission of Germany.'

### 53

For, in the south, Theodoric had already 'sheathed the sword in the pride of his victory and the vigour of his age, and his reign which continued for thirty-three years was consecrated to the duties of civil government.' Even when his son in law Alaric fell by Clovis's hand at the battle of Poitiers, Theodoric was content to stop the power of the Franks at Arles, without pursuing his success, and protect his infant grandchild, correcting at the same time certain abuses in the civil government of Spain. So the beneficent sovereignty of the great Goth was established from Sicily to the Danube and form Sirmium to the Atlantic Ocean.

### 54

Thus then, at the end of the fifth century, you have a Europe divided simply by her watershed; and two Christian kings[111] reigning, with an entirely beneficent and healthy power – one in the north, the other in the south – the most powerful and noble of the two married to the younger sister of the other: a saint of a queen in the north, a catholic queen mother, pious and sincere, in the south. It is a conjunction of circumstances memorable enough in the earth's history and worth thinking about, if ever in the whirlwind of your travels, O reader, you can separate yourself for an hour from the pent up cattle driven across the Rhine or the Adige, to walk peacefully out of the south gate of Cologne, or over Fra Gioconda's bridge at Verona. Then, stop and look through the clear air across the battlefield of Tolbiac, towards the blue Drachenfels, or across the plain of St Ambrogio towards the mountains of Garda. For there were fought and won if you think about it seriously the two great battles of the Christian world. That of Constantine alone gave another form and a new colour to the falling walls of Rome; but the Frank and Gothic races, by their conquests and under their governments, founded the arts and established the laws which gave to all future Europe her joy and her virtue. And it is charming to see how, and also how early, feudal chivalry depended for its life on the nobility of its womankind.

There was no vision seen at Tolbiac and no tradition has been claimed since. The king prayed simply to the God of Clotilde. On the morning of the battle of Verona, Theodoric visited the tent of his mother and sister 'and asked that for the most illustrious festival of his life, they would adorn him with the rich vestments which they had worked with their own hands.'

### 55

But over Clovis there was extended yet another influence, greater than that of his queen. When his kingdom reached to the Loire, the shepherdess of Nanterre was already old – she was no torch-bearing maiden of battle, like Clotilde, no knightly guide to deliverance like Jeanne; she had grown white in the sweetness of wisdom and was now 'more and more full of crystal light'. Clovis's father had known her; he himself made her his friend and, when he left Paris for the plain of Poitiers, he made a vow that, if he was victorious, he would build a church on the hills of the Seine. He returned victorious and, with St Genevieve at his side, stopped at the site of the ruined Roman thermae, just above the 'Isle' of Paris, to fulfil his vow: and to determine the limits of the foundation of the first Metropolitan Church of Frankish Christendom.[112]

The king swung his battle axe and tossed it with all his force – measuring thus in its flight the place of his own tomb, and that of Clotilde, and of St Genevieve.

'There they rested and rest, in soul, together. The whole hill still carries the name of the patron saint of Paris; a small and poorly lit road has kept that of the conquering king.'

# Chapter III
# The Lion Tamer

1

It has been announced often of late as an entirely new discovery that man is a creature of circumstances, and our attention is insistently called to this fact, in the hope, so seductive to the eyes of certain people, of being able to resolve into a succession of splashes in mud or whirlwinds in air, the circumstances responsible for his creation. But the more important fact that his nature does not depend like that of a mosquito on the mists of a marsh, nor like a mole's on the crumblings of a burrow, but has been endowed with the sense to discern, and with the instinct to adopt the conditions that will make him draw from his life the best that can be, is very necessarily ignored by the philosophers who propose to humanity, as a beautiful accomplishment of its destinies, a life entertained by scientific gossip in a cellar lit by electric sparks, heated by steam pipes, drained by buried rivers, and that the ministry of less learned and better provisioned races feeds with extract of beef and potted crocodile.[113]

2

From these chemically analytic conceptions of a Paradise in catacombs, which is not troubled in its alkaline or acid virtues by the fear of the Divinity, or by the hope of a future life, I do not know at what point the modern reader will be able to consent to withdraw himself for some time to hear speak of men who in their darkest and most foolish days sought by their labour to make from the desert itself the garden of the Lord and by their love become worthy of permission to live with him forever.

And yet hitherto, it has only been by such labour and in such hope that man has been able to find happiness, skill and virtue; and even at the dawn of the new law and on the threshold of the promised Canaan, rich in beatitudes of iron, steam and fire, there are here and there some among us who in a feeling of filial piety will stop to look back towards this solitude of Sinai where their fathers worshipped and died.

3

Even admitting for the moment that the main streets of Manchester, the district immediately surrounding the Bank of London, the Bourse and the avenues of Paris, are already part of the future Kingdom of Heaven when the Earth will be all Bourse and avenues, the universe of which our fathers tell us was divided among them, as you already know, partly into climatic zones, partly into races, partly into historical periods, and the circumstances in which a human creature has been called to his life had to be considered under these three heads: Under what climate was he born? Of what race? In what era?

He would not know how to be other than these conditions permit him to be. It is with reference to these that he must be heard – understood, if it is possible; – judged, by our love first, by our pity, if he need it, by our humility at the end of the day and for always.

4

To this end it is evidently necessary that we should have reliable maps of the world to begin with and reliable maps of our own hearts to end with; and neither one nor the other of these maps is easy to draw at any time, and perhaps least of all now when the purpose of a map is principally to indicate hotels and railways, and when humility is held to be the most unpleasant and despicable of the seven deadly sins.

5

Thus at the beginning of Sir Edward Creasy's *History of England* you find a map purporting to exhibit the possessions of the British nation, and which illustrates the extremely wise and courteous behaviour of Mr Fox to a Frenchman of Napoleon's inner circle, when 'advancing towards a terrestrial globe of uncommon size and definition and spreading his arms around it over the oceans and the Indies', he made the observation while in this impressive attitude that 'while Englishmen live, they extend themselves over the whole world and clasp it in the circle of their power.'

6

Inflamed by Mr Fox's enthusiasm, Sir Edward who, with this exception, was seldom noted for his fieriness, proceeds to tell us that 'our island home is the favourite domicile of freedom, domination and glory.'

He does not give himself or his readers the trouble of wondering how long the nations, subjected by the free people that we are and of whose shame our glory is made, may find their satisfaction in this arrangement of the globe and its affairs; or even if from the present the method that he uses in drawing his maps may not suffice to convince them of the degraded position that they occupy.

For the map, being drawn after the system of Mercator's projection, happens to represent the British possessions in America as twice the size of the United States and considerably larger than the whole of South America put together, while the brilliant crimson with which all our landed property is coloured can only deeply engrave in the mind of the innocent reader the impression of a universal flush of freedom and glory throughout all these fields and all these spaces.

So that he is scarcely likely to carp at results so marvellous, by inquiring into the nature and degree of perfection of the government that we operate at such and such a place, for example in Ireland, in the Hebrides or at the Cape.

7

In the chapter that ends the first volume of the *Laws of Fiesole*, I have laid down the mathematical principles of how to draw maps properly – principles which for many reasons it is well that my young readers should learn and of which the most important is that you cannot flatten the skin of an orange without opening it and that you should not, if you draw countries on the unsplit skin, stretch them afterwards to fill the empty spaces.

The British pride, which does not deny itself the luxury of penny Walter Scotts and penny Shakespeares, will assuredly be able in its future grandeur to possess itself of penny universes pirouetting conveniently on their axes. I can therefore assume that my readers can look at a round globe while I am talking about the world; and of a properly reduced drawing of its surfaces while I am talking about a country.

8

If the reader can consider them now or at least refer to a fairly drawn double circle map of the globe with converging meridians, I will beg him first to observe that, although the old division of the world into four quarters is today almost effaced by emigration and the transatlantic cable, still the great question that dominates the history of the globe is not to know how it is divided here and there by the ins and outs of land and sea, but how it is divided into zones of latitude by irresistible laws of light and air. It is often a matter of very secondary interest to know if a man is an American or an African, a European or an Asiatic; but it is a matter of extreme and decisive interest to know if he is Brazilian or Patagonian, Japanese or Samoyed.

9

In the course of the last chapter I asked the reader to hold firmly the conception of the great climatic division which separated the wandering races of Norway and Siberia from the calmly settled nations of Britain, Gaul, Germany and Dacia.

Now fix this division definitively in your mind by drawing however grossly the course of the two rivers, little thought of usually by geographers, but of quite unspeakable importance in the history of humanity, the Vistula and the Dniester.

10

Their sources are thirty miles from each other[114] and each runs its three hundred miles (not counting detours) – the Vistula to the north west, the Dniester to the south east; the two of them together cut Europe at the neck so to speak and separate, examining the thing more deeply, Europe properly so called (Europe's own and Jupiter's), the small educable, civilisable and more or less mentally rational fragment of the globe, from the great muscovite desert, as Cis-Ural as Trans-Ural; the chaotic space that we cannot conceive of, occupied from time immemorial by Scythians, Tartars, Huns, Cossacks, Bears, Ermines and Mammoths, with variable thicknesses of skin, shapes of skulls, and varying levels of suffering and discomfort according to whether they were settled or wandering. No history worth the trouble of retracing has anything to do with them; for the force of Scandinavia never looked to come out by the isthmus of Finland, but always navigated by means of large contingents of sailing or roving vessels across the Baltic, or down the rocky west coast; and the Siberian and Russian ice pressure simply drives the really memorable races into a higher degree of concentration, and kneads them into exploring masses made fiercer by necessity.

But by these exploring masses, of true European birth, our own history was fashioned for ever; and consequently these two frontier and barrier rivers must be marked on your map with extreme clarity: the Vistula, with Warsaw astride of it half way down, flowing out into the Baltic, the Dniester, in Euxine, the course of each of them measuring in a straight line a distance equal to that from Edinburgh to London. And if one takes account of the meanders,[115] the Vistula six hundred miles, the Dniester five hundred;[116] put end to end they form a moat of a thousand miles between Europe and the desert, going from Danzig to Odessa.

11

Your Europe thus enclosed by this moat in a clear and distinct space, you will then have to fix the frontiers which separate the four Gothic countries, Britain, Gaul, Germany and Dacia, from the four Classical countries, Spain, Italy, Greece and Lydia. There is generally no other term opposed to Gothic except Classical; I use it voluntarily for love of practical divisions and clarity, although its precise meaning must for some time remain indeterminate. Only get the geography clear in your head and the nomenclature will sort itself out in good time.

12

Broadly, you have the sea between Britain and Spain, the Pyrenees between Gaul and Spain, the Alps between Germany and Italy, the Danube between Dacia and Greece. You must consider everything south of the Danube as Greek, variously influenced by Athens on one side and Byzantium on the other; then from the other side of the Aegean sea, you have the vast country absurdly called Asia Minor (for we might just as well call Greece, Europe Minor, or Cornwall, England Minor), but which is to be remembered as 'Lydia', the country which awakes the passion and tempts with wealth, which taught the Lydians measure in music and softened the Greek language on its borders with Ionia, which gave to ancient history everything pertaining to Troy, and to Christian history, the grandeur and the decline of the seven churches.[117]

### 13

Opposite and to the south of these four countries, but separated from them either by sea or desert, are four more, as easily remembered – Morocco, Libya, Egypt and Arabia.

Morocco consists essentially in the chain of the Atlas and in the coasts which depend on it; the easiest way is to think of it as including the modern Morocco and Algeria, with the Canaries as a dependent group of islands.

Libya, in the same way, will include modern Tunisia and Tripoli: it will begin on the west with St Augustine's town of Hippo; its coast, colonised by Tyre and Greece, divides it into two districts, that of Carthage and that of Cyrene. Egypt, the country of the river, and Arabia, the country without a river, will remain in your mind as the two great southern homes of non-christian religions.

### 14

You have thus, easy to remember clearly, twelve countries forever distinct by natural laws, and forming three zones from north to south, all healthy and inhabited, but the races of the extreme north acclimatised to the cold, those of the central zone made more perfect by the enjoyment of the sun alike in summer and winter, those of the southern zone trained to bear the heat. Now showing their names in tabular form:

| Britain | Gaul  | Germany | Dacia   |
| Spain   | Italy | Greece  | Lydia   |
| Morocco | Libya | Egypt   | Arabia, |

you have mapped out in the simplest of terms everything of profane history that is worth knowing.

Then finally you have to conceive perfectly for all these countries as the source of inspiration that all the souls that have been endowed with it have held for a sacred and supernatural power, the small mountainous region of the Holy Land, with Philistia and

Syria on its flanks, both of them chastising forces, but Syria herself at the beginning the origin of the chosen race: 'My father was a Syrian ready to perish'[118] and the Syrian Rachel coming to be regarded for always as the true mother of Israel.

### 15

And remember, in all future study of the relations of these countries among themselves, that you must never permit your mind to become preoccupied with accidental variations of a political demarcation. No matter who governs a country, no matter what it is officially called or what conventional borders it has, eternal barriers and gates are placed against it by the mountains and seas, and the clouds and stars bend beneath the yoke of eternal laws. The people who are born on it are its people, be they conquered thousands and thousands of times, exiled or captive. The foreigner cannot be its king, the invader cannot be its master and, although just laws, whether maintained by the people or their conquerors, have always the virtue and power which are the privilege of justice, nothing can assure any race or any class of men of durable benefits but the flame that burns in their own hearts, lit by the love of their native land.

### 16

Naturally, in saying that the invader of a country can never possess it, I speak only of invasions such as those by the Vandals of Libya, or by ourselves of India; where the conquering race cannot become its permanent inhabitant. You could not call Libya Vandalia, or India England, because these countries are temporarily under the law of the Vandals or the English, any more than we could call Italy Gothland under the Ostrogoths, or England Denmark under Canute. National character modifies itself when invasion or corruption weakens it, but if ever it glows again into a new life, this life must be tempered by the earth and the sky of the country itself. Of the twelve names of the countries now given in their order, we will only see one changed as we advance in our history; Gaul will properly become France when the Franks come to inhabit it for all time. The eleven other primitive names will serve us to the end.

17

One moment's more patience to glance towards the Far East, and we will have established the bases of all the geography necessary to us. As the northern kingdoms are separated from the Scythian desert by the Vistula, so those of the south are separated from the dynasties properly called 'Oriental' by the Euphrates which, 'plunging for part of its course into the Persian Gulf, goes from the shores of Beluchistan and Oman to the mountains of Armenia, and forms an immense hot air funnel the base' (or mouth) 'of which is on the tropics while its extremity reaches 37 degrees of northern latitude.

'That is why the Simoon itself (the specific and gaseous Simoon) pays occasional visits to Mosul and Djezerat Omer, while the barometer at Baghdad attains in summer a level capable of beggaring belief of even an old Indian.'[119]

18

This valley in ancient days formed the kingdom of Assyria as the valley of the Nile formed that of Egypt. We have in this study nothing to do with its people who were nothing but an enemy as far as the Jews were concerned, the nation of captivity itself, inexorable as the clay of its walls, or the stone of its statues; and after the birth of Christ, the marshy valley is no more than a field of battle between west and east. Beyond the great river, Persia, India and China form the 'Southern Orient'. Persia is properly to be conceived as extending from the Persian Gulf to the mountain chains which dominate and feed the Indus, and is the true vital power of the Orient in the days of Marathon, but has no influence on Christian history except through the intermediary of Arabia;

while of the northern Asiatic tribes, Mede, Bactrian, Parthian and Scythian, becoming later the Turks and the Tartars, we do not have to preoccupy ourselves until they come to invade us, in our own historic territory.

### 19

Using the terms 'Gothic' and 'Classic' simply to separate the northern and central zones of our own territory, we may conveniently also use the word 'Arab'[120] for the whole southern zone. The influence of Egypt disappears soon after the fourth century, while that of Arabia, powerful from the beginning, grows in the sixth century to form an empire of which we have not yet seen the end.[121] And you may most judiciously conceive the religious principle on which this empire is built by remembering that, while the Jews themselves forfeited their prophetic power by exercising the profession of usury over the whole earth, the Arabs returned to the simplicity of prophecy beginning near the well of Agar[122] and are not opponents of Christianity, but only of the faults or follies of the Christians. They keep still their faith in a single God who spoke to Abraham[123] their father and are simply his children far more truly than the nominal Christians who lived, and live, only to discuss in vociferous councils or in a furious schism the relations of the Father, the Son and the Holy Spirit.

### 20

Counting on my reader in future to retain in his mind, and without any confusion, the idea of the three zones, Gothic, Classic and Arab, each divided into four countries clearly recognisable across all the ages of ancient or modern history, I must simplify for him yet another idea, that of the Roman *Empire* (see the note to the last paragraph), from the point of view that it will be relevant to him. Its nominal extent, its temporary conquests or its internal vices have scarcely any historical importance at all; the real empire only corresponds to something true, is an example of just law, of military discipline, of the skills of the hand, given to undisciplined races, and as a translation of Greek thought into a system more concentrated and more assimilable for them. The Classic zone, from the beginning to the end of its effective reign, rests on these two elements: Greek imagination with Roman order; and the divisions or dislocations of the third and fourth centuries simply allow their differences to appear in an entirely natural way, when the political system which concealed them was tested by Christianity.

The historians also seem ordinarily to have almost entirely lost from view that, in the wars of the last Romans with the Goths, the great Gothic captains were all Christians; and that the vigorous and naïve form which the birth of faith took in their minds is a more important subject of investigation by far than the inevitable wars which followed the retreat of Diocletian, or the confused schisms and crimes of the lascivious court of Constantine.

I am however forced to note the conditions in which the last arbitrary dissolutions of the empire took place, so that they can clarify instead of confusing the arrangement of the nations that I would like to fix in your memory.

21

In the middle of the fourth century you have politically what Gibbon calls 'the final division of the eastern and western empires'. This means above all that the Emperor Valentinian, yielding, not without hesitation, to this feeling which dominated then in the legions, that the empire was too vast to stay in the hands of a single person, takes his brother as his colleague, and divides not properly speaking their authority, but their attention, between the east and the west.

To his brother Valens he assigns the extremely vague 'Prefecture of the East, from the lower Danube to the confines of Persia', while he reserves for his own immediate government 'the prefectures still at war of Illyria, Italy and Gaul, from the extremity of Greece to the Caledonian rampart to the foot of Mount Atlas'.

This means, in less poetically rhythmic prose (Gibbon would have done better to put his history into hexameters at once), that Valentinian keeps under his own surveillance the whole of Roman Europe and Africa and leaves Lydia and the Caucasus to his brother. Lydia and the Caucasus never did, and never could, form an Eastern empire, they were simply kinds of colonies, useful for taxation in times of peace, dangerous because of their numbers in times of war. There never was from the seventh century before to the seventh century after Christ but one Roman Empire,[124] expression of the power over humanity of men like Cincinnatus[125] or Agricola; it expires when their race and character expire; its nominal extension, or brilliancy at any moment, is no more than the reflection farther or nearer upon the clouds of the flames rising on an altar whose fuel was of noble souls. There is no true date for its division, there is none for its destruction. Whether the Dacian Probus or the Noric Odoacer be on the throne, the force of its living principle alone is to be considered, residing in the arts, in the laws, in the habits of thought, reigning still in Europe up to the twelfth century; reigning still today in language and example over all educated men.

22

But, for the nominal division made by Valentinian, let us note the definition that Gibbon gives (I suppose it is his and not the Emperor's) of European Roman Empire in 'Illyria, Italy and Gaul'. I have already told you that you have to hold everything south of the Danube for Greek. The two principal regions situated immediately to the south of the river are Lower and Upper Moesia formed from the slope of the Thracian mountains northward to the river, with the plains which separate them from the river. You must pay attention to this region because of its importance in forming the Moeso-Gothic alphabet in which 'the Greek is by far the principal element';[126] providing sixteen of the twenty-four letters. The Gothic invasion under the reign of Valens is the first to establish a Teutonic nation within the frontier of the empire; but it only thereby brings itself more immediately under its spiritual power. Its bishop, Ulphilas, adopts this Moesian alphabet, two-thirds Greek, for his translation of the bible, and this translation disseminates it everywhere and assures its perpetuation until the extinction or absorption of the Gothic race.

23

South of the Thracian mountains you have Thrace herself and the countries confusingly called Dalmatia and Illyria, bordering the Adriatic, and going inland in an eastern direction, up to the mountain watershed. I have never been able to form a clear notion myself of what the people of these regions were like, in any given period; but they can all be considered in mass as northern Greek, having more or less of Greek blood and dialect following their degree of proximity to Greece proper; although neither sharing in her philosophy nor submitting to her discipline. But it is of course far more accurate to speak in broad terms of these Illyrian, Moesian and Macedonian regions as being all Greek, than to talk with Gibbon or Valentinian of Greece and Macedonia as being all Illyrian.[127]

24

In the same imperial or poetic generalisation, we find England reunited with France under the term Gaul, and bounded by 'the Caledonian rampart'. Whereas, in our own divisions, Caledonia, Hibernia and Wales are from the beginning considered as essential parts of Britain,[128] and their link with the continent conceived as formed by the establishment of Britons in Brittany, and not at all by Roman influence beyond the Humber.

25

So then, going over once again the order of our countries and remarking only that the British Isles while situated for the most part, if one looks at the degrees, much to the north of the rest of the northern zone, are placed by the influence of the Gulf Stream under the same climate, you have, at the time when our history of Christianity begins, the Gothic zone not yet converted, and having not yet even heard of the new faith. You have the Classic zone variously and increasingly conscious of it, disputing it and striving to extinguish it, and your Arab zone, which is the home and sustenance of it, enveloping the Holy Land with the heat of its own wings and cherishing (cinders of the phoenix[129] consumed over all the earth) the hope of resurrection.[130]

26

What would have been the course, or even the fate, of Christianity, if it had only been preached orally, instead of being sustained by its poetic literature, might be the object of deeply instructive speculation – if a historian's duty were to reflect instead of recount. The power of the Christian faith was in fact however always founded on the written prophecies and histories of the Bible; and on the interpretations that the great monastic orders gave of their meaning, far more by their example than by their precepts. The poetry and the history of the Syrian testaments were given to the Roman church by St Jerome, while the virtue and efficiency of monastic life are expressed in the rule of St Benedict. To understand the relation of the work accomplished by these two men, with the general organisation of the church, is the first requirement for its subsequent intelligible history.

In his thirty-seventh chapter, Gibbon professes to give us an account of the 'institution of the monastic life' in the third century. But the monastic life had been instituted somewhat earlier and by many prophets and kings. By Jacob when he took the stone for his pillow;[131] by Moses when he turned aside to contemplate the burning bush;[132] by David before he had left 'this little flock of sheep in the desert'[133] and by the prophet who 'was in the deserts up to the moment of appearing before Israel'.[134] We see the first 'institution' for Europe under Numa, in his vestal virgins and his college of augurs, founded on the originally Etrurian and eventually Roman conception of pure life dedicated to the service of God and of practical wisdom guided by him.[135]

The form which the monastic spirit took later depended far more on the corruption of the world from which it was forced to recoil, either in indignation or in terror, than on any change brought about by Christianity in the ideal of human virtue and happiness.

27

'Egypt,' Mr Gibbon thus begins to account for the new institution, 'the fertile mother of superstition, provided the first example of monastic life.' Egypt had her superstitions like other countries; but she was so little the mother of superstition that one can say that the faith of no people – among the imaginative races of the world – perhaps knew so little missionary zeal as hers. She never prevailed on even the nearest of her neighbours to worship cats or cobras with her; and I am alone, as far as I know, among recent writers in maintaining Herodotus' opinion[136] on the influence she exerted on the archaic theology of Greece. But this influence, if influence it be, consisted only in delineating its form and not in giving it rites; so that in no case and in no country was Egypt the mother of superstition: while, beyond all possible dispute, she was, for all peoples and for all times, the mother of geometry, of astronomy, of architecture and of chivalry. She was for the material and technical elements the mistress of literature, teaching authors, who before could only scratch on wax and wood, how to make paper and engrave porphyry. She was the first to expose the law of judgement for sin after death. She was the educator of Moses; and the hostess of Christ.

28

It is both probable and natural that in such a country the disciples of every new spiritual doctrine led it to a perfection that it would not have attained among the illiterate warriors or in the solitudes tormented by the storms of the North. It would however be an absurd error to attribute to the isolated ardour of Egyptian monarchism the future power of cloistered fraternity. The anchorites of the first three centuries vanish like spectres of fever when the rational, merciful and laborious laws of Christian societies are established; and the clearly recognisable laws of heavenly solitude are accorded only to those who seek the desert for its redemption.[137]

### 29

'The clearly recognisable reward,' I repeat and with energetic intent. No man has the means of appreciating, far less a certain way of judging, until he has the courage to try it himself, the results of a life of sincere renunciation; but I believe no reasonable person will wish or dare deny the advantages he has occasionally felt both in body and mind during periods of accidental privation from luxury, or exposure to danger. The extreme vanity of the modern Englishman who makes of himself a momentary Stylite on the summit of a Horn[138] or a Needle and his occasional confession of the charm of solitude in the rocks, of which he modifies nevertheless the poignancy by having his newspaper in his pocket and from the prolongation of which he gratefully escapes to the nearest restaurant meal, ought to make us less disdainful of the pride, and more understanding of the state of mind in which the mountain anchorites of Arabia and Palestine condemned themselves to lives of retreat and suffering, without any comfort but visions of the supernatural or celestial hope. That pathological forms of the mental state are the necessary consequence of excessive and totally subjective emotions of any kind must be remembered when reading the legends of the desert; but neither physicians nor moralists have yet tried to distinguish the morbid states of the intelligence[139] leading to a noble enthusiasm from those which are the punishments of ambition, of avarice or of debauchery.

### 30

Leaving aside for the moment all questions of this nature, my young readers need only retain the broad fact that during the whole of the fourth century, multitudes of devoted men led lives of extreme poverty and misery in an effort to arrive at a more intimate knowledge of the Being and Will of God. We have no light which would allow us to reach any useful knowledge of what they suffered or what they learned. We cannot appreciate the edifying or disapproving power of their examples on the less zealous Christian world; and God alone knows how far their prayers were heard or their persons accepted. We can only observe with respect that in their great number not one seems to have repented having chosen this sort of existence, not one perished as a result of melancholy or suicide; the sufferings to which they condemned themselves were never inflicted in the hope of shortening the lives which they embitter or purify; and the hours of dream or meditation on the mountain or in the cave appear rarely to have dragged so heavily for them as those which, without vision or reflection, we pass ourselves on the embankment or in the tunnel.

### 31

But whatever judgement one should give, after a final and conscientious examination on the follies or virtues of the anchorite life, we would be unjust to Jerome if we were to look upon him as its introducer into the West of Europe. He passed through it himself as a phase of spiritual discipline; but he represents, in his entire nature and in his final work, not the sad inactivity of the hermit but the ardent labour of a benevolent master and pastor. His heart is in a continual fervour of admiration or of hope – remaining up to the end not only as impetuous as a child's but just as affectionate; and the contradictions of the Protestant point of view which have confused or concealed his character are clarified in an obscure portrait of his real personality when we come to understand the simplicity of his faith, and sympathise a little with the ardent charity which can so easily be wounded to the point of indignation and is never bounded by calculation.

### 32

The little confidence that modern readings must inspire in us is demonstrated by comparing the two passages in which Milman has exposed in an entirely different way the leading principles of his political conduct. 'Jerome begins (!) and ends his career as a monk of Palestine; he arrived at, *he aspired to*, no dignity in the Church. Though ordained a priest against his will, he escaped the episcopal dignity which was imposed on the most distinguished priests of his time.' (*History of Christianity*, Book III.)

'Jerome cherished in secret the hope, if it was not the avowed object of his ambition, to succeed Damascus as Bishop of Rome. Must the refusal of an aspirant so singularly unfit for this situation by reason of his violent passions, his insolent treatment of his adversaries, his absolute lack of self-control, his almost unrivalled faculty of awakening hatred, be attributed to the instinctive and informed wisdom of Rome?' (*History of Latin Christianity*, Book I, Chapter II.)

### 33

You can observe as a very frequent characteristic of 'informed wisdom' of the Protestant clerical mind, that it instinctively assumes that the desire for power and position is not only universal in the clergy, but is always purely egotistical in its motives. The idea that it be possible to seek influence for the sake of its benevolent use does not once occur in the pages of a single ecclesiastical historian of recent date. In our studies of times past, we will calmly put out of court, with the reader's permission, all the stories of 'hopes cherished in secret' and we will give very little attention to the reasons for the conduct of the men of the Middle Ages which appear logical to the rationalists, and probable to the politicians.[140] We concern ourselves only with what these singular and fantastic Christians of the past really said and did for certain.

### 34

Jerome's life by no means begins as that of a monk of Palestine; Dean Milman has not explained to us how any man's could; but the childhood of Jerome in any case was entirely other than as a recluse, or precociously religious. He was born of rich parents living on their own estate; it is perhaps the name of his native town to the north of Illyria (Stridon) which has been softened today into Strigi, near Aquileia.[141] In any case it was under the Venetian climate and in sight of the Alps and the sea. He had a brother and sister, a good grandfather, a disagreeable tutor, and was still a young man studying grammar when Julian died in 363.

### 35

A young eighteen year old man who had begun well in all the establishments of classical studies, but far from being a monk, not yet a Christian nor at all disposed to fill the for him too severe offices of Roman life itself! And contemplating without aversion the splendours, either worldly or sacred, which shone in his eyes during the year of college that he spent in the capital.

For 'the prestige and the majesty of paganism were still concentrated at Rome, the divinities of the ancient faith found their last refuge in the capital of the Empire. For a stranger Rome still offered the appearance of a pagan city. It contained 132 temples and 180 smaller chapels or altars still sacred to their tutelary God and serving for the exercise of public worship. Christianity had never ventured to usurp these few moments which might be transformed for her use, still less had she the power to destroy them. The religious edifices were under the protection of the prefect of the city and the prefect was usually a pagan: at all events he would not permit any breach of the public peace, or any violation of public property.

'Dominating the whole city with its towers, the Capitol, in its unassailed and solemn majesty, with its 30 temples or altars, which bore the most sacred names in the religious and civil annals of Rome, those of Jupiter, of Mars, of Romulus, or Caesar, of Victory. Some years after the accession of Theodosius to the Eastern Empire the sacrifices were still performed as national rites at public expense, *the pontiffs made their offerings in the name of the entire human race*. The pagan orator ventures to declare that the Emperor had feared endangering the security of the Empire by their abolition. The Emperor still bore the title and insignia of the Supreme Pontiff; the consuls before entering on their functions ascended to the Capitol, the religious processions passed along the crowded streets and the people thronged to the festivals and performances which still formed part of the pagan worship.'[142]

### 36

At this point Jerome must have heard of what all the Christian sects held to be the judgement of God between them and their main enemy – the death of the Emperor Julian. But we possess nothing that would permit us to trace, and I do not want to conjecture, the course of his own thoughts until the moment when the direction of his entire life was changed by baptism. We owe to the candour which lies at the base of his character one sentence of his respecting this change which is worth volumes of an ordinary confession. 'I left not only my parents and my family, but the luxurious habits of a refined life.'

These words shed plenty of light on what to our less courageous nature seems the exaggerated interpretation by the early converts of Christ's words to them: 'He who loves his father and his mother more than me is not worthy of me.'[143] We are happy to leave for much lesser interests our father or our mother, and do not see the necessity of any greater sacrifice; we would know more about ourselves and about Christianity if we had more often to uphold the test that St Jerome found the most difficult. I have seen that his biographers here and there gave indications of their contempt because of an indulgence that he found himself incapable of renouncing, that of scholarship; and the usual sneers at the ignorance and laziness of monks are in his case transferred to the weakness of a pilgrim luxurious enough to carry his library in his haversack. And it would be curious to know (putting, as it is the modern fashion to do, the idea of Providence wholly aside) if, but for this literary enthusiasm which was to a certain degree a weakness of this old man's character, the Bible would ever have become the library of Europe.

37

For observe, that is the real meaning in its first sense of the word *Bible*:[144] not simply book; but 'Bibliotheca', treasury of books; and it was, I repeat, curious to know how far – if Jerome, at the very moment when Rome, which had instructed him, was dispossessed of her material power, had not made her language the oracle of Hebrew prophecy, had not constituted an original literature and a religion disengaged from the terrors of the Mosaic law – the spirit of the Bible might have penetrated the hearts of the Goths, the Franks and the Saxons, under Theodoric, Clovis and Alfred.

38

Destiny had determined otherwise and Jerome was such a passive instrument in her hands that he began the study of Hebrew as a discipline only and without any conception of the task he was to fulfil,[145] still less of the scope of its fulfilment. I would have joy in believing that the words of Christ: 'If they do not hear Moses and the Prophets, they will not be persuaded even if one dead were to rise again,'[146] haunted the spirit of the recluse until he resolved that the voice of Moses and the Prophets would be made audible to the churches of all the earth. But as far as we have proof of it, no such will or hope exalted the quiet instincts of his natural industry. It was partly as a writer's exercise, partly as an old man's recreation, that he pleased himself by softening the severity of the Latin language, just as Venetian crystal, at the variable fire of Hebrew thought; and the 'Book of Books' took the abiding form of which all future art of the Western nations was to be a day by day expanding interpretation.

39

And on this subject you have to note that the main point of it lies, not in the translation of the Greek and Hebrew Scriptures into an easier and more common language, but in their *presentation to the Church as a universal authority*. The first Gentiles among the Christians had naturally a tendency towards an oral tradition of exaggerating or altering the teaching of the Apostle of the Gentiles, until their freedom from the servitude of the Jewish law was replaced by doubt of its inspiration; and even after the fall of Jerusalem, into terrible interdiction of its observance. So that, only a few years after the remaining exiled Jews in Pella had elected the Gentile Marcus as bishop, and had obtained authorisation to return to Aelia Capitolina built by Hadrian on Mount Zion, 'it became a matter of doubt and controversy whether a man who sincerely recognised Jesus as the Messiah, but who continued to observe the law of Moses, could hope for salvation.'[147] While on the other hand the most learned and the wealthiest of those called Christians, designated generally by the title of 'knowing' (Gnostic), had more insidiously effaced the authority of the Evangelists by separating themselves during the course of the third century 'into more than fifty distinct sects that could be counted, and gave birth to a multitude of works in which the actions and discourses of Christ and his apostles were adapted to their respective doctrines.'[148]

40

It would be a task of very great and unprofitable difficulty to determine in what measure the consent of the general Church and in what measure the life and influence of Jerome contributed to fix, in their ever since untouched harmony and majesty, the canons of Mosaic and Apostolic Scripture. All that the young reader need know is that, when Jerome died at Bethlehem, this great fact was virtually accomplished; and the series of historic and didactic books which form our present Bible (including the Apocrypha) reigned from then over the nascent thought of the noblest races of men living on the globe, as a message addressed directly to them by its creator and which – containing whatever it was necessary for them to learn of his designs in their regard – commanded or advised them, with divine authority and infallible wisdom, what was best for them to do and happiest to desire.

41

And it is only for those who have sincerely obeyed the law to say how far the hope that has been given to them by the dispenser of the law has been fulfilled. The worst 'children of disobedience'[149] are those who accept of the word what they like and reject what they hate; this perversity is not always conscious in them, for most of the sins of the Church have been engendered in it by enthusiasm, which in the contemplation and passionate defence of parts of the Scripture easily grasped, have neglected the study and finally destroyed the balance of the rest. What forms and ways does the opinionated mind follow to result in forcing the sense of the Scriptures to man's perdition? This is for those who have charge of our consciences to examine, not for us. The history we have to learn must be held absolutely outside such debate, and the influence of the Bible observed exclusively on those who receive the word with joy and obey it in truth.

## 42

There has however always been a greater difficulty in appreciating the influence of the Bible than in distinguishing honest from dishonest readers. The hold of Christianity on the souls of men must be considered, when we come to a close study of it, under three headings: there is first the power of the cross itself, and of the theory of salvation, upon the heart; then the action of the Jewish and Greek scriptures on the mind; then the influence on morals of the teaching and example of the existing hierarchy. And when one wants to compare men as they are and as they might have been, these three questions must be kept separately in mind: first, what would have been the character of Europe without the charity and work meant by 'carrying the cross'; then, secondly, what would the intellect of Europe have become without biblical literature; and finally what would the social order of Europe have become without the hierarchy of the Church.

## 43

You see that I have reunited the words 'charity' and 'work' under the general term of 'carrying the cross'. 'If anyone wants to follow me let him deny himself (through charity) and carry his cross (through work) and follow me.'[150]

The idea has been exactly reversed by modern protestantism which sees in the cross not a gallows to which it must be nailed but a raft on which it and all its valuable properties[151] are to be carried over the waves to paradise.

## 44

It is also only in days when the Cross was received with courage, the Scripture considered in conscience, and the Pastor heard in faith, that the pure word of God and the bright sword of the Spirit[152] can be recognised in the heart and hand of Christianity. The effect of biblical poetry and legend on its thinking can be followed further across decadent ages and in unbounded fields;

giving birth for us to *Paradise Lost*, no less than the *Divine Comedy*; – to Goethe's *Faust* and Byron's *Cain* no less than the *Imitation of Jesus Christ*.

45

Furthermore, the writer who wants to understand as completely as possible the influence of the Bible on humanity must be capable of reading the interpretations of it given by the great arts of Europe at their culmination. In every province of Christendom, proportionately according to the degree of artistic power that it possessed, series of illustrations of the Bible appeared progressively, beginning with the vignettes that illustrated the manuscripts and, passing through life-sized sculpture, concluded by reaching its full power in realistic painting. These teachings and preachings of the church by means of art are not only one of the most important parts of the general apostolic acts of Christianity, but their study is a necessary part of biblical scholarship, so that no man can understand the deep thought of the Bible itself until he has learned to read these national commentaries and become aware of their collective value. The Protestant reader who believes he has an independent view of the Bible and studies it by himself is nevertheless at the mercy of the first preacher gifted with a pleasant voice and ingenious imagination;[153] receiving from him gratefully and often with respect whatever interpretation of texts the agreeable voice or lively wit may recommend; but, at the same time, he is entirely ignorant and, if left to his own devices, invariably destroys as injurious the deeply considered interpretations of Scripture which, in their essence, have been sanctioned by the consent of the whole Christian church for a thousand years and in their form have been carried to the highest perfection by the traditional art and inspired imagination of the noblest souls ever enclosed in mortal clay.

## 46

There are few of the fathers of the Christian church whose commentaries on the Bible or personal theories of its Gospel have not been, to the constant exaltation of the enemies of the church, altered and disgraced by furious controversies, or weakened and perverted by an irreconcilable heresy. On the contrary, the biblical teaching given through their art by men such as Orcagna, Giotto, Angelico, Luca della Robbia and Luini is literally free of all earthly trace of temporary passions. Its patience, its meekness and its calm are incapable of error coming from fear or anger; they can, without offence, say anything they like, they are bound by tradition and in a sort of brotherly solidarity which represents always identical scenes and unaltered doctrines; and they are forced by the nature of their work to a deliberation and method of composition which result in the purest state and frankest use of all intellectual power.

## 47

I can at once and without needing to return to this question illustrate the difference in dignity and safety between the influence on the mind of literature and art[154] by referring you to a page, otherwise beautifully illustrative of St Jerome's sweetness and simplicity of character, although quoted in the place where we find it without any favourable intention – namely, in the pretty letter of Queen Sophie Charlotte (paternal grandmother of Frederick the Great) to the Jesuit Vota, given in part by Carlyle in his first volume, chapter IV.

'How can St Jerome, for example, be a key to Scripture?', she insinuates, citing from Jerome this remarkable avowal of his method of composing books, particularly this book, *Commentaries on the Galatians*, where he accuses both St Peter and St Paul of falsity and even of hypocrisy. The great St Augustine has charged him with this unpleasant accusation (says Her Majesty, who gives chapter and verse), and Jerome answers: 'I have followed the commentaries of Origen, of ...' – five or six different persons who turned out mostly to be heretics before Jerome had quite done with them. 'And to confess the honest truth to you,' continues Jerome, 'I have read all that and, after having crammed my head with a great many things, I sent for my secretary and dictated to him, now my own thoughts, now those of others, without much recollecting the order, nor sometimes the words, nor even the sense.' In another place (further on in the same book),[155] he says, 'I do not myself write: I have a secretary and I dictate to him what comes to my lips. If I wish to reflect a little, or express the thing better, or a better thing, he frowns and his whole look tells me sufficiently that he cannot bear to wait.' Here is a sacred old gentleman whom it is not good to trust to interpret the Scriptures, thinks her Majesty; but she does not say so – leaving Father Vota to his reflections. Alas no, Queen Sophie, we must not depend for this sort of thing either on old St Jerome or on any other human lips or mind; but only the eternal Sophia,[156] the power of God and the wisdom of God. At least you can see in your old interpreter that he is absolutely frank, innocent, sincere and that through such a man, whether forgetful of his author, or pressed by his scribe, it is more than probable that you can hear what God knows to be the best for you; and extremely improbable that you would be perverted, in the least, while by a prudent master skilled in the literary arts, reticent in his doubts, and dexterous in his sayings, any number of prejudices and errors can be presented to you in an acceptable way, or even fixed in you irremediably, even though at no time were you in the least required to confide in his inspiration.

48

For to tell the truth, the only confidence and the only safety, which in such matters we can either hold or hope, reside in our own desire to be rightly guided and in our willingness to follow in simplicity the guidance granted. But all our ideas and reasonings on the subject of inspiration have been falsified by our habit – first of distinguishing erroneously or at least needlessly between the inspiration of words and of acts, and secondly by our attribution of inspired strength or wisdom to certain persons or certain writers only, instead of to the whole body of believers, insofar as they participate in the grace of Christ, the love of God, and the fellowship of the Holy Spirit.[157] To the extent that each Christian receives or refuses the multiple gifts expressed by this general benediction, he enters into the inheritance of the Saints or is cast out from it. To the exact extent that he denies Christ, angers the Father and grieves the Holy Spirit, he loses the inspiration of Sainthood; and to the extent that he believes in Christ, obeys the Father, and submits to the Spirit, he becomes inspired in the feeling, act, word and reception of the word, according to the capacities of his nature. He will not be endowed with higher aptitudes, nor called to a new function, but made capable of using the natural faculties accorded to him, in their appointed place, to the best purpose. A child is inspired as a child, and a girl as a girl; the weak even in their weakness, and the wise only in their hour. This is, to a degree determinable with certainty, the theory of inspiration among all true members of the church; its truth can only be recognised by putting it to the test, but I believe there is no record of any man who has proved it and declared it vain.[158]

### 49

Beyond this theory of general inspiration there is that of special call and command with immediate dictation of the actions that must be accomplished and the words which have to be said. I do not wish to enter at present into an examination of the testimonials of such an effective election; it is not claimed by the fathers of the Church, either for themselves, or even for the entire body of sacred writers.

It is only attributed to certain passages dictated at certain moments in view of special necessities; and it is not possible to attach the idea of infallible truth to any form of this human language in which even these exceptional passages have been given to us. But of the entire volume of them as we possess it and read it, for each of us as it may be rendered in his native tongue, one can affirm and demonstrate that, however mingled with a mystery which we are not required to unravel or difficulties which we would be insolent in desiring to resolve, it contains true teaching for men of every rank and station in life, teaching thanks to which, so far as they honestly and implicitly obey, they will be happy and innocent to the utmost power of their nature, and capable of triumphing over all adversities, whether residing in temptation or pain.

50

In effect the Psalter alone, which practically was the book of services for the church for many centuries, contains simply in its first half the sum of individual and social wisdom. The first, eighth, twelfth, fifteenth, nineteenth, twenty-third, and twenty-fourth psalms well learned and believed are enough for all personal guidance; the forty-eighth, seventy-second and seventy-fifth have in them the law and the prophecy of all just government, and every discovery of natural science is anticipated in the one hundred and fourth.

51

As for the contents of the entire volume, consider if another cycle of historic and didactic literature has a range comparable to it. It contains:

I. The story of the Fall and of the Flood, the two greatest human traditions founded on the horror of sin.

II. The story of the Patriarchs, of which the permanent truth is still visible today in the history of the Jewish and Arab races.

III. The story of Moses with its results for the moral law of the whole civilised world.

IV. The story of the Kings – virtually that of all royalty, in David, and of all philosophy, in Solomon, culminating in the Psalms and the Proverbs, with the still more serried and practical wisdom of Ecclesiasticus and the son of Sirach.

V. The story of the Prophets – virtually that of the deepest mystery, tragedy and perpetually immanent fatality of national existence.

VI. The story of Christ.

VII. The moral law of St John who finds eventually its fulfilment in the apocalypse.

Ask yourselves if you can compare its table of contents with, I do not say any other 'book', but with any other 'literature'. Try, so far as it is possible for any of us to extricate your intelligence from the association that habit has formed between it and moral sentiment based upon the Bible, and ask what literature could have taken its place or fulfilled its function even if all the libraries of the universe had remained intact and if all the words of the teachers richest in truth had been written down.

52

I am not contemptuous of profane literature, so far from it that I believe no interpretation of Greek religion has ever been so affectionate, none of Roman religion so reverent, as that which will be found at the base of my teaching of art and which runs through the entire body of my works. But it was from the Bible that I learned the symbols of Homer and the faith of Horace.[159]

The duty that was imposed upon me in my early youth[160] of reading every word of the gospels and prophecies, as if written by the hand of God, gave me the habit of respectful attention which later made many of the passages of the profane authors, frivolous to an irreligious reader, deeply serious for me. How far my mind has been paralysed by the faults and sorrows of life,[161] how far short my knowledge of life may be compared to what I might have learned if I had more faithfully walked in the light available to me, is beyond my conjecture or confession. But as I never wrote for my own pleasure or renown, I have been preserved, as men who write thus always will be, from errors dangerous to others,[162] and the fragmentary expressions of feelings or statements of doctrine that, from time to time, I have been capable of giving, will appear now to an attentive reader to bind themselves together in a general system of interpretation of sacred literature, simultaneously classic and Christian, which will enable him, without injustice, to sympathise with the faith of candid souls of all times and all countries.

53

That there is a sacred classic literature, following a parallel course with that of the Hebrews and harmonising with the symbolic legends of mediaeval Christianity,[163] is a fact which appears in the most tender and expressive way by the independent yet similar influence of Virgil on Dante and on Bishop Gawaine Douglas. At earlier dates, the teaching of every master formed in the schools of the East was necessarily grafted on the wisdom of Greek mythology, and thus the story of the Nemean Lion,[164] conquered with the aid of Athena, is the true root of the legend of St Jerome's companion, conquered by the healing sweetness of the spirit of life.

54

I call it a legend only. Whether Heracles ever killed, or St Jerome ever cherished the wild or wounded creature, is without importance for us in learning what the Greeks meant to tell us by representing the great content on their vases,[165] or the Christian painters with their predilection for their theme of the constancy of the friend of the lion. An earlier tradition, that of the struggle of Samson,[166] the disobedient prophet, of David's first inspired victory,[167] and finally of the miracle wrought for the defence of the most favoured and most faithful of the great prophets,[168] follows its symbolic course in parallel with the Dorian fable. But the legend of St Jerome takes up the prophecy of the millennium and predicts, with the Cumaean Sibyl,[169] and with Isaiah, a day when the fear of man will no longer be among the inferior beings of hatred but will be extended over them as a benediction, when it will not hurt or destroy throughout the extent of the holy mountain,[170] and the peace of the earth will be as far removed from its present sorrow as the present gloriously animated universe is from the nascent desert, whose deeps were the resting places of dragons, and its mountains domes of fire. Of that day knows no man,[171] but the kingdom of God has already come[172] to those who have tamed in their own hearts the runaway fire of the lower nature,[173] and have learned to cherish what is charming and human in the wandering children of the clouds and fields.

Avallon, 28 August 1882.

# Chapter IV
# Interpretations

1

It is a well-known privilege for every sacristan who loves his cathedral to depreciate by comparison all the cathedrals of his country that resemble, and all the edifices of the globe that differ from it. But I love too many cathedrals, although I have never had the happiness of becoming sacristan of any, to permit myself the easy and traditional exercise of the privilege in question, and I prefer to prove to you my sincerity and make my opinion known to you, from the start, by confessing that the cathedral of Amiens has nothing to boast of in the way of towers, that its central spire[174] is simply the pretty caprice of a village carpenter, that its architectural structure is in dignity inferior to Chartres,[175] in sublimity to Beauvais, in decorative splendour to Rheims, and for the grace of sculpted figures to Bourges. It has nothing resembling the artful painting and moulding of Salisbury; nothing of the power of Durham; it possesses none of the Daedalian encrustations of Florence, none of the glow of symbolic fantasy of Verona. And yet in all and more than these ways, outshone and overpowered by these, the cathedral of Amiens deserves the name given to it by Mr Viollet-le-Duc, 'the Parthenon of Gothic architecture'.[176]

Gothic, you hear; Gothic clear of all Roman tradition[177] and all Arabian influence; Gothic pure, exemplary, unsurpassable and beyond criticism, its proper principles of construction being once understood and admitted.

2

There is today no well-educated traveller who does not have some notion of what is commonly and rightly called 'purity of style' in the forms of art that have been practised by civilised nations, and few are ignorant of the distinctive intentions and proper character of the Gothic. The purpose of a good Gothic architect was to raise, with the stone extracted from the place where he had to build, an edifice as high and as spacious as possible, giving the impression of solidity guaranteed by reason and calculation, without it taking too long or being too wearisome, and without spending too much and needing overwhelming human labour.

He did not wish to exhaust for a city the energies of a generation or the resources of a kingdom; he built for Amiens with the strengths and the finances of Amiens, with chalk from the rocks of the Somme[178] and under the directions of two successive bishops; one presiding over the foundations of the edifice, and the other giving thanks in it for its completion. His goal as an artist, in common with all the sacred architects of his time in the north, was to admit as much light into the building as was compatible with its solidity; to make its structure intelligible and magnificent, but not curious or effete, and to add to the power of this structure with the aid of ornament sufficient to embellish it, yet without yielding to wanton enthusiasm by exaggerating its richness, or by showing his cleverness in a moment of insolent intoxication or egotism. And finally he wanted to make the sculpture of its walls and gates an alphabet and an epitome of the religion by the knowledge and inspiration of which worship might be rendered within those gates, acceptable to the Lord whose fear was in his holy temple and whose seat was in heaven.[179]

3

It is not easy for the citizen of the modern aggregate of bad building, and bad lives held in check by constables, which *we* call a town – in which it is convenient to consecrate the widest streets to encourage vice and the narrowest ones to conceal misery – it is not easy, I say, for the inhabitant of any such despicable city to understand the feeling of a burgher of the Christian ages for his cathedral. For him, the quite simply and frankly believed text: 'Where two or three are assembled in my name, I am in the middle of them,'[180] was extended into a wider promise, applying to a great number of honest and industrious persons asssembled in his name. 'They will be my people and I will be their God,'[181] and these words received for them a deeper meaning of some lovely local and simply affectionate belief that Christ, as he was a Jew among Jews, a Galilean among Galileans, was also wherever there were disciples, even the poorest, as one of their nation, and that their own *Beau Christ d'Amiens* was as real a compatriot of them as if he had been born of a Picard virgin.

4

It must be remembered however – and this is a theological point on which depends much of the architectural development of the basilicas of the north – that the part of the building in which the divine presence was believed to be constant, as in the Jewish Holy of Holies, was only the enclosed choir, in front of which the aisles and transepts could become the King's Hall of Justice, as in the throne-room of Christ; and whose high altar was protected always from the surrounding eastern aisles by a screen of the most finished workmanship, while from these surrounding aisles branched off a series of radiating chapels or cells, each dedicated to a particular saint. This conception of Christ in the company of his saints (the easternmost chapel being consecrated to the Virgin) was at the base of the entire disposition of the apse with its supporting and dividing buttresses and piers; and the architectural forms will never be able to delight us truly, unless in sympathy with the spiritual conception out of which it arose.[182] We talk foolishly and miserably of symbols and allegories: in the old Christian architecture all the parts of the building must be read literally; the cathedral is for its builders the House of God,[183] it is surrounded, like an earthly king's, with lesser lodgings for his servants; and the glorious sculptures of the choir, those of its exterior walls,[184] and on the interior, those of wood which, almost instinctively, an English rector would think destined for the glorification of the canons, was in reality the Amiénois carpenter's way of making his master-carpenter's [185] house comfortable;[186] and no less of showing his own native and unrivalled talent as a carpenter, before God and man.

5

Whatever you would like to see at Amiens, or are forced to leave aside without having seen, if the overwhelming responsibilities of your existence and the precipitate locomotion that they inevitably necessitate leave you only a quarter of an hour without being out of breath for the contemplation of the capital of Picardy, give it wholly to the cathedral choir.

The aisles and porches, lancet and rose windows, you can see elsewhere as well as here, but such carpenter's work, you cannot.[187] It is of the flamboyant in its full development just at the moment when the fifteenth century comes to an end. That has something of Flemish stolidity mixed with pleasing French fire; but sculpting wood is the Picard's joy from his youth and, as far as I know, nothing so beautiful has ever been cut out of the good trees of any country of the entire world. It is in sweet and young-grained wood, of oak, trained and chosen for such work, as resonant now as four hundred years ago. Under the sculptor's hand it seems to model itself like clay, fold itself like silk, to grow like living branches, to leap like a living flame. Canopies crowning canopies, pinnacles piercing pinnacles, that shoot and weave themselves into an enchanted clearing, inextricable, imperishable, fuller of foliage than any forest and fuller of story than any book.

6

I have never been capable of deciding what was the best way of approaching the cathedral for the first time. If you have plenty of leisure, if it is a beautiful day and if you are not afraid of an hour's walk, the best thing to do is to walk down the main street of the old town, cross the river and head out towards the chalk hill,[188] where the citadel's foundations are dug and from which it borrows its walls; climb to the top and look down into the citadel's dry 'ditch' or more truly dry valley of death; it is about as deep as a Derbyshire dale (or, more precisely, the upper part of the 'Happy Valley' at Oxford, above Lower Hinksey); and from there, raise your eyes to the cathedral while climbing the slopes of the city. By doing that you will understand the true height of the towers in relation to the houses, then returning find your way to its Mount Zion,[189] by any narrow cross streets and bridges that you find; the more winding and dirty the streets, the better, and whether you arrive first at the west front or the apse, you will find them worth all the trouble you have had to reach them.

7

But, if the day is dreary as can sometimes happen, even in France in recent years, or if you cannot or do not want to walk, which is also possible for all our athletics and lawn tennis, etc. – or if you must really go to Paris this afternoon and if you only want to see all you can in an hour or two – then supposing that, despite these weaknesses, you are still a nice sort of person, for whom it is of some importance to know which way to arrive at a pretty thing and first start to look at it, my estimation is that the best way is to walk from the Hôtel de France or the Place du Périgord, up the *rue des Trois-Cailloux* towards the railway station. Stop for a moment on the way so as to get in a good mood, and buy some tarts or bon-bons for the children in one of the charming pastry shops on the left. Just after passing them, ask for the theatre; and immediately after that you will find also on the left three open arches under which you can pass, you will leave behind the Palais de Justice, and go straight up to the south transept which has really something about it to please everybody.

It is simple and severe at the base, delicately traceried and pinnacled at the top, and appears all of a piece, even though it isn't. Everyone must like the tapering and transparent fretwork of the spire above, which seems to bend towards the west wind – even though it doesn't. At least its bending is a long habit gradually acceded to, with growing grace and submission, during these last three hundred years. And, coming right up to the porch, everybody must like the pretty little French Madonna which occupies the middle with her head a little to one side, and her nimbus a little to one side also, like a becoming hat. She is a madonna of decadence despite of or rather by reason of all her prettiness[190] and her gay soubrette's smile; and she has no business here either, for this is St Honoré's porch, not hers; rough and grey, St Honoré used to stand there to receive you; he is now banished to the north porch, where nobody ever enters.

That took place a long time ago, in the fourteenth century, when the people began to find Christianity too serious, imagined a more joyous faith for France and wanted to have soubrette Madonnas everywhere glancing brightly, letting their own dark-eyed Joan of Arc be burned as a witch; and since then things went their merry way, straight on, 'ça allait, ça ira,' up to the merriest days of the guillotine. But they still knew how to sculpt in the fourteenth century, and the Madonna and her hawthorn-blossom lintel[191] are worth looking at, and much more the sculptures as delicate and calmer[192] that are above and which tell St Honoré's own story, little talked of now in the Parisian *faubourg* that bears his name.

## 8

I do not want to keep you now to tell St Honoré's story (only too happy to leave you somewhat curious about it, if that were possible),[193] for certainly you are impatient to go into the church, and you cannot enter it in a better way than by this door. For all cathedrals of some importance have almost the same effect when you enter by the west door; but I do not know of any other which shows so much of its nobility from the south interior transept; the rose opposite is of an exquisite fineness of tracery and of a charming lustre; and the shafts of the transept aisles form marvellous groups with those of the choir and nave. You will also better appreciate the height of the apse, if it is revealed to you as you go from the transept to the central nave than if you see it at once from the west end of the nave; there it would be just possible for an irreverent person to find the nave narrow rather than the apse high. Therefore, if you would like me to lead you, enter at the south transept door and put some money into every beggar's box who asks it there; it is none of your business to know if they should be there or not – nor if they deserve to have your money – you should know only if you yourself deserve to have it to give, and give it kindly and not as if it burned your fingers. Then being once inside, give yourself the pleasure of the general sense of space – promising the sacristan to come back to see it properly (only mind you keep your promise), and in the first quarter of an hour see only what your fantasy will bid you to see, but at least, as I said, look at the apse from the nave and all the transverse parts of the building leading off from its centre. Then you will know, when you go outside again, to what end the architect was working and what his buttresses and traceries mean, for the outside of a French cathedral, except its sculpture, must always be thought of as the wrong side of a fabric which helps you to understand how the threads go that produce the inside or right-side pattern.[194]

And if you do not feel yourself gripped with admiration for this choir and its surrounding circle of light, when you look up into it from the middle of the cross centre, you have no need to travel farther in search of cathedrals, for the waiting room of any station is a better place for you; but if it confounds and delights you at first, then the more you know it, the more your amazement will grow. For it is not possible for the imagination and mathematics together to make with glass and stone anything nobler and more powerful than this procession of windows, nor anything which looks higher, with such a considered and prudent measure of actual height.

9

From the pavement to the keystone of the vault is but 132 French feet – about 130 English. Think only, you who have been in Switzerland – that the Staubbach falls are 900 feet![195] Even better, Dover cliff below the castle, just at the end of the promenade, is twice as high, and the little cockneys who parade on the asphalt to the military polka, think themselves just as tall I suppose; but with the little lodgings, huts and shacks that they have put up around it, they have succeeded in making it look no bigger than a medium sized lime kiln. Yet it is twice the height of the apse of Amiens! And it requires a solid construction with only such bits of chalk as one can extract in the neighbourhood of the Somme to make a work stand half that height for 600 years.

10

It requires good construction, I say, and you can even affirm the best that ever was, or is likely for many a day to be on the immovable and fruitful earth where one could count on a pillar's standing fast when it had been well built, and where aisles of aspen, orchards of apple, and clusters of vine provided the model of what might be most magnificently made sacred in the permanence of sculpted stone. From the unhewn block placed on end of the Druid's Bethel to *this* House of the Lord and this blue windowed gate of Heaven,[196] you have the entire course and accomplishment of all the love and art of the religious architects of the north.

11

But note further and attentively that this apse of Amiens is not only the best, but the *first* thing executed *perfectly* in its manner by northern Christianity. On pages 323 and 327[197] of the sixth volume of Mr Viollet-le-Duc you will find the exact history of the development of these rib vaults across which the eastern light shines on you at this moment, since the less perfect first hints of Rheims; and the culmination of the perfect rightness was so momentary that here, from the nave to the transept, built only ten years later, there is already a little change in the manner not towards decadence but to a precision greater than is absolutely necessary.[198] The point where decadence begins one cannot, among the charming fantasies that will follow, fix exactly; but exactly and indisputably we know that this apse of Amiens is the first work of a perfect virgin purity – the Parthenon, in this sense again – of Gothic architecture.

12

Who built it, shall we ask? God and man is the first and truest answer. The stars in their courses built it and the nations. Greek Athena has worked here, and the father of the Roman gods, Jupiter, and guardian Mars. The Gaul has worked here, and the Frank, the knightly Norman, the powerful Ostrogoth, and the scrawny anchorite of Idumea.

The man who built it scarcely concerned himself whether you would ever know, and the historians do not glorify him; all the possible heraldries of knaves and idlers you find in what they call their 'history'; but this is probably the first time you have read the name of Robert de Luzarches. I say he 'scarcely concerned himself,' we are not sure that he concerned himself at all. He signed his name nowhere, as far as I know. You will perhaps find here and there in the building some recently engraved initials by remarkable English visitors desirous of immortality. But Robert the builder or at least the master of building, engraved *his* on no stone of it. Only when, after his death, the headstone of the cathedral had been brought forth with shouting, to celebrate this event the following legend was written, recalling the names of all those who had been part or parcel of the work – in the middle of the labyrinth which then existed in the paving stones of the nave. You have to read it in a soft voice; it was rhymed gaily for you by pure French gaiety which does not in the least resemble that of the *Théatre des Folies*.

> In the year of Grace one thousand two hundred
> And twenty, was the work in ruins
> First begun again.
> Then was of this Bishopric
> Evrart, blessed bishop;
> And, King of France, Louis
> Who was the son of Philip the Wise.
> He who was master of the work
> Master Robert was his name
> And de Luzarches was his surname.
> Master Thomas was after him
> De Cormont. And after, his son
> Master Reginald, which master
> Made at this point this reading
> That the incarnatino was verified as
> Thirteen hundred, less twelve, it must have been.

13

I have written the numerals in letters, otherwise the metre would not have been clear – in reality, they were represented thus 'IIC and XX' 'XIIIC less XII'. I quote the inscription from the Abbé Rozé's admirable little book: *Visite à la Cathédrale d'Amiens* – (Sup. Lib. de Mgr l'Evêque d'Amiens, 1877) – which every grateful traveller should buy, for I am only going to steal a little of it here and there. I only wish there had been a translation of the legend to steal too; for there are one or two points both of doctrine and chronology on which I would have liked to have the Abbé's opinion. Anyway, the principal meaning of the poem, line by line, appears to us to be as follows:

> In the year of grace twelve hundred
> Twenty, the work then falling into ruin
> Was first started again.
> Then was of this bishopric
> Everard the blessed Bishop
> And king of France Louis
> Who was son of Philip the Wise.
> He who was master of the work
> Was called Master Robert
> And named further de Luzarche.
> Master Thomas was after him
> De Cormont. And after him his son
> Master Reginald who commissioned
> This inscription to be put here
> Indicating that it was
> the year of the Lord 1288.

Of this inscription, while you stand where it was formerly (it was put somewhere else when the old pavement was polished, in the year, I sadly observe, of my first visit to the continent, in 1825, when I had not yet turned my attention to religious architecture), some points are worth noting – if you still have a little patience.

### 14

'The work' that is to say the work of Amiens proper, her cathedral, was *déchéant*, falling into ruins for, I cannot at once say if it was, the fourth, fifth, or what time – in the year 1220. For it was an extraordinarily difficult matter for little Amiens that such work be well executed, so hard did the devil work against her. She built her first episcopal church (scarcely more than St Firmin's tomb chapel) about the year 350, just beside the railway station on the road to Paris.[199] But after having been nearly destroyed, chapel and all, by the Frank invasion, having recovered and converted her Franks, she built another, and properly called a cathedral, where this one stands now, under Bishop St Save (St Sauve or Salve). But even this true cathedral was only made of wood, and the Normans burnt it in 881. Rebuilt, it stood for two hundred years; but was in great part destroyed by lightning in 1019. Rebuilt again, it and the town were more or less burnt together by lightning in 1107. My authority says calmly: 'A fire provoked by the same cause destroyed the *town*, and a part of the cathedral.' The 'part' having been rebuilt once more, the whole was again reduced to ashes, 'reduced to ashes by the lightning storm in 1218, just as were all the volumes, catalogues of martyrs, the calendars, and the archives of the bishopric and the chapter.'

15

It was then the fifth cathedral, by my count, that was in 'ashes' according to Mr Gilbert – in ruins certainly – *déchéante* – and a ruin that would have meant absolute discouragement for the inhabitants of a less lively town – in 1218. But it was rather a great stimulant for Bishop Evrard and his people to see that the ground was cleared for them as it was; and the lightning (fire of hell, not of heaven, recognised for a diabolical plague, as in Egypt) had to be braved to the end. They only took two years, you see, to pull themselves together and they set to work in 1220, they, and their bishop, and their king, and their Robert de Luzarches. And this cathedral which receives you at this moment under its vaults was what their hands found to do, with all their might.

16

Their king was 'à donc', at this time, Louis VIII who is further designated by the name of son of Philip August or Philip the Wise, because his father was not dead in 1220; but he must have abandoned the governing of the kingdom to his son, as his own father had done to him; the old and wise king retiring to his palace and from there silently guiding his son's hands, very gloriously for three more years.

But then – and this is the point on which I would have particularly liked the Abbé's opinion – Louis VIII died of fever at Montpensier in 1226. And the entire direction of the essential works of the cathedral, and the main honour of its consecration, as we shall see presently, emanated from St Louis, for a time of forty-four years. And the inscription was placed 'à ce point-ci' by the last architect, six years after the death of St Louis. How is it that the great and holy king is not named?

17

I must not, in this traveller's summary, lose time in giving conjectural replies to the questions which every step here will raise from the ravaged temple. But this is a very serious one; and must be kept in our hearts until we can perhaps get an explanation for it. One thing only we are sure of, that at least the honour due alike by the sons of kings as the sons of craftsmen is given always to their fathers; and that apparently the greatest honour of all is given here to Philip the Wise. From his palace, not of parliament but of peace, came in the years when this temple was first being built, an edict of true pacification: 'That it would be criminal for any man to take vengeance for an insult or injury until forty days from receipt of the offence – and then only with the approval of the Bishop of the Diocese.' Which was perhaps a wiser effort to put an end to the feudal system taken in its Saxon sense[200] than any of our recent projects designed to put an end to the feudal system in its Norman sense.

18

'À ce point-ci.' The point particularly of the labyrinth encrusted in the paving stones of the cathedral: emblem of a great number of things consecrated to the people, who knew that the ground on which they stood was holy, as was the vault over their heads.

Above all, it was for them an emblem of noble human life – strait gates, narrow walls, with an infinite darkness and the *inextricabilis error* on all sides and, in its depths, the brutal nature to be tamed.

19

It is this meaning, since the most proudly heroic and most purely legislative days of Greece, that this symbol has always borne for men versed in her traditions: for the schools of craftsmen it meant further the nobility of their art and its direct descent with the divinely terrestrial art of Daedalus, the builder of labyrinths, and the first sculptor whose imagery of human life and death must be considered *pathetic*.[201]

20

Quite the most beautiful sign of the power of true Christian-Catholic faith is this continual recognition of it by its brothers – or rather the fathers, the older people who had not seen Christ; but had been filled with the Spirit of God; and had obeyed, as far as their knowledge permitted, his unwritten law. The pure charity and humility of this character are seen in all Christian art, according to its strength and purity of race, but it is nowhere as well and as fully realised and interpreted as by the three great Christian-heathen poets, Dante, Douglas of Dunkeld,[202] and George Chapman. The prayer by which the last ends his life's work is, as far as I know, the most perfect and deepest expression of natural religion given to us in literature; and if you can, pray it here, placing yourself on the spot where the architect one day wrote the history of the Parthenon of Christianity.

21

'I pray to you, Lord, father and guide of our reason, that we may remember the nobility with which you have adorned us and that you are always on our right hand and on our left,[203] while our wills are in motion; so that we may be purged of the contagion of the body and the affections of the savage and dominate and govern them; and use them, as it becomes men, as instruments. And then that you would be in communion with us for the vigilant correction of our mind and for its conjunction, by the light of truth, with the things that truly are.

'And in the third place, I pray to you the Saviour, to dissipate entirely the darkness and gloom which imprison the eyes of our souls, so that we can know well who should be held for God, and who for mortal. Amen.'[204]

## 22

And after having prayed this prayer or at least having read it with the desire for improvement (if you cannot, there is no hope that you will at present take pleasure in any human work of high inspiration, whether it be poetry, painting or sculpture), we can walk a little farther westward along the nave, in the middle of which, but only a few yards from its end, two flat stones (the sacristan will show you them), one a little further back than the other, are laid over the tombs of the two great bishops, all the strength of whose lives was given, with that of the architect, to raise this temple. Their true tombs have stayed in the same place; but the tombs raised over them, having been moved several times, are now to your right and to your left when you look back towards the apse, under the third arch between the nave and the aisles.

## 23

Both are in bronze, cast in a single flow and with an unsurpassable, and in certain respects inimitable, mastery in the caster's art.

'Masterpieces of casting, the whole cast in a single flow, and admirably.'[205] 'There are only two similar tombs still remaining in France, those of the children of St Louis. All others of their kind, and there were a large number in every great French cathedral, were first torn from the graves they covered in order to destroy the memory of France's dead; and then melted down into sous and centimes, to buy gunpowder and absynthe for her living – in the spirit of progress and civilisation in her first flame of enthusiasm and new light, from 1789 to 1800.

The children's tombs, placed one on either side of the altar of St Denis, are much smaller than these, although more beautifully wrought. These near where you are now are *the only two bronze tombs of her men of the great ages* that are left in France!

24

And they are the tombs of the pastors of her people, who built for her the first perfect temple of her God; that of Bishop Évrard is to your right and has this inscription engraved around its border:[206]

'He who fed the people, who laid the foundations
Monument, to whose care the city was of this given
Here in an eternal balm of glory rests Evrard.
A man compassionate to the afflicted, protector of the widow,
                                                                of the orphan
The guardian. Those whom he could, he comforted with gifts
To the words of men,
If gentle, a lamb; if violent, a lion; if proud, biting steel.'

English in its best days, those of Elizabeth, is a more noble language than Latin ever was; but its merit is in the colour and accent, not in what could be called metallic or crystalline condensation. And it is impossible to translate the last line of this inscription in as few English words. Note first that the friends and enemies of the bishop are mentioned as such in words, not in acts, because the proud, or mocking, or flattering words of men are what in effect the meek of this earth must know how to bear and even welcome; their deeds, it is for kings and knights to deal with; not that the bishops did not often take deeds in hand also; and in battle, they were permitted to strike with the mace, but not with the sword, nor with lance – that is to say, not to 'shed blood'. For it was assumed that a man can always recover from a blow with the mace (which however depended on the intuition of the bishop who gave it). The battle of Bouvines, which is in reality one of the most important of the Middle Ages, was won against the English (and further against auxiliary German troops marching under Otho) by two French bishops (Senlis and Bayeux) – who were both generals of the king of France's armies, and led their charges. Our Earl of Salisbury surrendered to the Bishop of Bayeux in person.

25

Note further that one of the deadliest and most diabolical powers of evil words, or to put it better, of blasphemy, has been developed in modern times in the effects of 'slang', sometimes quite innocently and joyously meant. Slang, in its essence, is of two types. 'Thieves' Latin', the special language of rascals used in order not to be understood; the other, the better word to give it would perhaps be Louts' Latin! – the abasing or insulting words invented by vile people to bring things that in themselves are held as good to their own level or beneath it.

Certainly the worst power of this kind of blasphemy is in its often making it impossible to use common words without attaching to them a degrading or ludicrous sense. Thus I have been unable to end my translation of this epitaph, as the old Latinist could, with the absolutely *exact* image: 'To the proud, a file', because of the abuse of the word in lower English which retains, but nastily, the thirteenth century idea. But the exact force of the symbol here is in its allusion to jewellers' work, filing facets. A proud man is often also a precious one and can be made brighter on the surface, and the purity of his inner being better revealed, by a good filing.

26

Such as they are, these six Latin lines – express – au mieux mieux[207] – the entire duty of a bishop[208] – beginning with his pastoral office – *Feed* my flock – Qui pavit populum. And be assured, good reader, that those times never could have told you what was the duty of a bishop, or of any other man, if they had not, each man in his place, done it well and had seen it well done. The tomb of Bishop Geoffroy is on your left and its inscription is:

'Look, Godfrey's limbs rest on their humble bed.
Perhaps a smaller one or one of the same size is prepared
for us
Whom the twin laurels of medicine adorned
And of divine law, the two ornaments became him.
Resplendent man of Eu, by whom the throne of Amiens
Rose into immensity, may you be increased in heaven.'
Amen

And now at last, this homage paid and this debt of gratitude acquitted, we will turn from these tombs and go out of one of the western doors, and in this way we will see gradually rising above us the immensity of the three porches and of the thoughts sculpted on them.

27

What degradations and changes they have had to endure, I will not tell you today, except the 'inestimable' loss of the great old steps dating from the foundation, open, extending broadly from one end to the other for all who came, without walls, without divisions, kept sunny for their whole length by the light from the west, lighted only by the moon and stars at night, falling steep and many down the side of the hill – finishing one by one, wide and few as they reached the ground, and worn by the feet of pilgrims for six hundred years. Thus I have seen them once and a second time – now such things can never be seen again.

In the west front itself, above, there is not much left of the old construction; but in the porches, nearly all – except the actual outside facing with its rose moulding, of which only a few flowers have been spared here and there. But the sculpture has been carefully and honourably conserved and restored in place, the pedestals and niches restored here and there with clay, and some which you see white and crude, entirely resculpted; nevertheless, the impression you may receive from the whole is still what the builder intended and I will tell you the order of its theology without further remarks on the decay of its work.

28

You will always do well, when looking at any cathedral, to fix in your mind the four points of the compass from the start; and to remember that, when you enter, you are looking and advancing towards the east, and that, if there are three entrance porches, the one on your left as you enter is the northern, that on your right, the southern porch. I will force myself in everything I write in future about architecture to observe the simple rule of always calling the door of the north transept the north door; and that on the same side of the west front, the northern door, and so for the doors on the other sides.

That will save, in the end, much printing and confusion, for a Gothic cathedral has almost always these five great entrances which are easily recognised, if one takes care at the start, under the names of the central door (or porch), the northern door, the southern door, the north door, and the south door.

But, if we use the terms right and left, we should always in using them consider ourselves to be going out of the cathedral and walking down the nave – the entire north side and aisles of the building being consequently its right side, and the south, its left side. For we have the right to use these terms right and left only relatively to the image of Christ in the apse or on the cross, or else to the central statue of the west front, whether of Christ, the Virgin, or a saint. At Amiens this central statue, or the 'trumean' or supporting and dividing pillar of the central porch, is that of Christ Emmanuel[209] – God *with* us. On his right and on his left, occupying the entire walls of the central porch, are the apostles and the four great prophets.

The twelve minor prophets stand side by side on the front, three on each of its great piers. The northern porch is dedicated to St Firmin, the first Christian missionary to Amiens.

The southern porch to the Virgin.

But these are both treated as retreating behind the great foundation of Christ and the prophets; and the narrow recesses where they are taking refuge[210] partly conceal their sculpture, up to the moment when you enter. What you first have to think of and to read is the scripture of the great central porch and the façade itself.

29

You have then in the centre of the front the image of Christ himself receiving you:

'I am the way, the truth and the life.'[211]

And the best way of understanding the order of the attendant powers will be to consider them as placed on Christ's right and left hand; this was also the order which the architect adopts in the scripture history on the façade – so that it has to be read from left to right, that is to say from the left of Christ to the right of Christ, as he sees it. Thus then, taking the great statues in order:

First, in the central porch, there are six apostles on the right of Christ, six on his left.

On his left, next to him, Peter; then in receding order, Andrew, James, John, Matthew, Simon; on his right, next to him, Paul; and successively, James the Bishop, Philip, Bartholomew, Thomas and Jude. These two symmetrical ranks of the apostles occupy what may be called the apse or curved bay of the porch, and form an almost semicircular group, clearly visible when one approaches. But on the sides of the porch, not in the same line as the apostles, and not seen clearly until one has entered the porch, are the four great prophets. On the left of Christ, Isaiah and Jeremiah; on his right, Ezekiel and Daniel.

### 30

Then in front, taking the entire length of the façade – read in order from Christ's left to his right – come the series of the twelve minor prophets, three to each of the four piers of the temple, starting at the south angle with Hosea, and ending with Malachi.

When you look at the entire front when positioning yourself in front of it, the statues which fill the secondary porches are either obscured in their narrower niches or concealed one behind the other so as to be unseen.

And the entire mass of the front is seen, literally as built on the foundation of the apostles and prophets, Jesus Christ himself being the cornerstone. And this to the letter; for the porch in opening itself forms a deep 'angulus' and the central pillar is the head of the angle.

Built on the foundation of the apostles and prophets, that is to say of the prophets who predicted the coming of *Christ* and the apostles who proclaimed him. Although Moses had been an apostle of *God*, he is not here. Although Elijah had been a prophet of *God*, he is not here. The voice of the entire moment is that of Heaven at the Transfiguration: 'This is my beloved son, hear him.'[212]

### 31

There is another and greater prophet still who, as it seems at first, is not here. Will the people enter the gates of the temple singing 'Hosanna to the son of David,'[213] and see no image of his father?

Christ himself declares: 'I am the root and offspring of David,' and yet has the root near it no memory of the earth that nourished it?

Not so, David and his son are together. David is the pedestal of the Christ.

## 32

So we will begin our examination of the temple front with this beautiful pedestal.

The statue of David, which is only two-thirds life size, occupies the niche in front of the pedestal. He holds his sceptre in his right hand, his scroll in the left. King and prophet, symbol for ever of all royalty which acts with a divine justice, claims it and proclaims it.

The pedestal which has this statue for sculpture on its west face is square and, on the two other sides, there are flowers in vases; on the north side the lily and on the south side the rose. And the entire monolith is one of the noblest pieces of Christian sculpture in the entire world.

Above this pedestal comes a less important one, carrying in front of it a tendril of vine which completes the floral symbolism of the whole.

The plant which I have called a lily is not the fleur de lys nor the Madonna's,[214] but an ideal flower with bells like the imperial crown (the type of 'lilies of all kinds' of Shakespeare),[215] representing the mode of growth of the lily of the valley which could not be sculpted so large in its literal form without appearing monstrous, and is thus represented on this piece of sculpture where it fulfils, together with its companions the rose and the vine, the triple saying of Christ: 'I am the Rose of Sharon and the Lily of the Valley.'[216] 'I am the true Vine.'[217]

### 33

On the sides of this plinth are supports of a different character. Supports, not captives, or victims; the Cockatrice and the Adder representing the most active of the evil principles on the earth in their extreme malignity; nevertheless pedestals of Christ, and even in their deleterious life, accomplishing his final will.

The two creatures are represented exactly in the mediaeval traditional form, the cockatrice, half dragon, half cock; the adder, deaf, putting one ear against the ground and stopping the other with its tail.[218]

The first represents the infidelity of pride. The cockatrice – king-serpent or the first among serpents – saying that he *is* God and that he *will be* God.

The second, the infidelity of death. The adder (the lowest serpent) saying that he *is* mud and *will be* mud.

### 34

Lastly, above all, placed under the feet of the statue of Christ himself, are the lion and the dragon; the images of carnal or human sin, as distinguished from the spiritual and intellectual sin of pride by which the angels fell as well.

To desire to reign rather than to serve – sin of the cockatrice – or deaf death rather than listening life – sin of the adder – these two sins are possible to all the intelligences of the universe. But the sins that are especially human, anger and covetousness, seen in our life of perpetual sadness, Christ in his own humanity has conquered and conquers them still in his disciples. This is why his foot is on their head, and the prophecy: 'Inculcabis super leonem et aspidem'[219] is always recognised as fulfilled in him, and in all his true servants, according to the height of their authority and the reality of their influence.

### 35

It is in this mystical sense that Alexander III used these words in re-establishing peace in Italy and pardoning the deadliest enemy of this country under the porch of St Mark's.[220] But the meaning of each action, as of every art of the Christian ages, lost now for three hundred years, can only be read backwards in our time,[221] if it can be read at all, through the contrary spirit which is now our own. We glorify pride and avarice as the virtues by which all things exist and move, we follow our desires as our only guides to salvation, and we exhale the bubbling of our own shame, which is all that our hands and lips can produce on this earth.

### 36

Of the statue of Christ itself I will not speak here at length, as no sculpture satisfies or should satisfy the hope of a loving soul that has learned to believe in him; but at this time it surpassed what had then been attained in sculpted tenderness; and it was known far and near under the name of 'Le Beau Dieu d'Amiens'.[222] Yet it was understood, observe, just as clearly to be no more than a symbol of the divine presence, as the poor coiling reptiles below were no more than symbols of the demoniacal presences. Not an idol, in our sense of the word – only a letter, a sign of the living spirit, which however every one of the faithful conceived as coming to meet him at the gate of the temple: 'the Word of Life, the King of Glory[223] and the Lord of Armies.'

*Dominus Virtutum*, the Lord of Virtues'[224] is the best translation given to a well-educated disciple of the thirteenth century by the words of the twenty-fourth psalm.

### 37

Also under the feet of his apostles in the quatrefoils of the apostolic foundation are represented the virtues which each apostle taught or manifested in his life – it may have been a virtue which sorely put him to the test and he may even have lacked the strength of character which subsequently led to his perfection. Thus St Peter denying through fear is afterwards the apostle of courage; and St John, who with his brother would have burnt the inhospitable village, is afterwards the apostle of love. Having understood this, you see that in the sides of the porches the apostles with their special virtues are placed in two opposing ranks.

| St Paul, Faith | Courage, St Peter |
| St James the Bishop, Hope | Patience, St Andrew |
| St Philip, Charity | Sweetness, St James |
| St Bartholomew, Chastity | Love, St John |
| St Thomas, Wisdom | Obedience, St Matthew |
| St Jude, Humility | Perseverance, St Simon |

38

Now you see how these virtues answer to each other in their symmetrical ranks. Remember that the left-hand side is always the first and see how the virtues on the left lead to those on the right.

| Courage | to | Faith |
| Patience | to | Hope |
| Sweetness | to | Charity |
| Love | to | Chastity |
| Obedience | to | Wisdom |
| Perseverance | to | Humility |

Note further that the apostles are all calm, nearly all with books, some with crosses, but all with the same message: 'That peace be on this house. And if the Son of Peace is here,'[225] etc.[226]

But the prophets, all searching, or pensive, or tormented, or praying, with the sole exception of Daniel. The most tormented of all is Isaiah, morally sawn in two.[227] The bas-relief which is above represents no scene of his martyrdom, but shows the prophet at the moment when he sees the Lord in his temple, and yet he has the feeling that he has impure lips. Jeremiah also carries his cross but with more serenity.

39

And now I give, in clear succession, the order of the statues of the entire front with the subjects of the quatrefoils placed under each of them, designating the quatrefoils placed highest with an A, the lower quatrefoils with a B.

The six prophets who are standing at an angle to the porches, Amos, Obadiah, Micah, Nahum, Zephaniah and Haggai each have four quatrefoils, designated, the upper quatrefoils with A and C, the lower with B and D.

Beginning then, on the left-hand side of the central porch and reading from the interior of the porch towards the outside, you have:

| | |
|---|---|
| 1. St Peter | A. Courage<br>B. Cowardice |
| 2. St Andrew | A. Patience<br>B. Anger |
| 3. St James | A. Sweetness<br>B. Vulgarity |
| 4. St John | A. Love<br>B. Discord |
| 5. St Matthew | A. Obedience<br>B. Rebellion |
| 6. St Simon | A. Perseverance<br>B. Atheism |

Now, to the right of the porch reading towards the outside:

| | |
|---|---|
| 1. St Paul | A. Faith<br>B. Idolatry |

|  |  |
|---|---|
| 2. St James the Bishop | A. Hope<br>B. Despair |
| 3. St Philip | A. Charity<br>B. Avarice |
| 4. St Bartholomew | A. Chastity<br>B. Lust |
| 5. St Thomas | A. Prudence<br>B. Folly |
| 6. St Jude | A. Humility<br>B. Pride |

Now, again on the left, the two statues farthest from the Christ.

13. Isaiah:

A. 'I see the Lord seated on a throne.' (VI. 1.)

B. 'See, this has touched your lips.' (VI. 7.)

14. Jeremiah:

A. The burial of the belt. (XIII. 4, 5.)

B. The breaking of the yoke. (XVIII. 10.)

And on the right:

15. Ezekiel:

A. The wheel within a wheel. (I. 16.)

B. 'Son of man, turn your face towards Jerusalem.' (XXI. 2.)

16. Daniel:

A. 'He has closed the lions' mouths.' (VI. 22.)

B. 'At the same moment the fingers of the hand of man went out.' (V. 5.)

Now beginning on the left (south side of the whole façade), and reading straight across without ever entering the porches except for the quatrefoils paired with the statues that concern us.

17. Hosea:

A. 'So I bought her for myself, for fifteen pieces of silver.' (III. 2.)

B. 'So will I be also for you.' (III. 3.)

18. Joel:

A. The sun and the moon without light. (II. 10.)

B. The fig tree and the vine without leaves. (I. 7.)

19. Amos:

*On the front*

A. 'The Lord will cry from Zion.' (I. 2.)

B. 'The dwellings of the shepherds will mourn.' (I. 2.)

*On the inside of the porch*

C. The Lord with the mason's line. (VII. 8.)

D. The place where it did not rain. (IV. 6.)

20. Obadiah:

*On the inside of the porch*

A. 'I hid them in a cave.' (I. *Kings* XVIII. 13.)

B. 'He fell on his face.' (I. *Kings* XVIII. 7.)

*On the front*

C. The captain of fifty.

D. The messenger.

21. Jonah:

A. Escaped to the sea.

B. Under the gourd.

22. Micah:

*On the front*

A. The tower of the flock. (IV. 8.)

B. Each rests and 'nobody will frighten them.' (IV. 4.)

*On the inside of the porch*

C. 'Swords into ploughshares.' (IV. 3.)

D. 'Spears into pruning hooks.' (IV. 3.)

23. Nahum:

*On the inside of the porch*

A. 'Nobody will look back.' (II. 8.)

B. 'Prophecy against Nineveh.' (I. 1.)

*On the front*

C. Your princes and your leaders. (III. 17.)

D. Precocious figs. (III. 12.)

24. Habakkuk:

A. 'I will watch to see what he will say.' (II. 1.)

B. The ministry to Daniel.

25. Zephaniah:

*On the front*

A. The Lord strikes Ethiopia. (II. 12.)

B. The beasts in Nineveh. (II. 15.)

*On the inside of the porch*

C. The Lord visits Jerusalem. (I. 12.)

D. The cormorant and the lout.[228] (II. 14.)

26. Haggai:

*On the inside of the porch*

A. The houses of the princes *ornamented with panelling*[229] (I. 4.)

B. 'The sky retaining its dew.' (I. 10.)

*On the front*

C. The temple of the Lord is desolate. (I. 4.)

D. 'Thus said the Lord of armies.' (I. 7.)

27. Zachariah:

A. Iniquity takes flight. (V. 6-9.)

B. 'The angel who spoke to me.' (IV. 1.)

28. Malachi:

A. 'You have offended the Lord.' (II. 17.)

B. 'This commandment is for you.' (II. 1.)

Having thus put the sequence of the statues and their quatrefoils briefly before the eyes of the spectator (in case of the pressure of train times, it may be charitable to make him aware that, going from the east end of the cathedral the road that goes south, *rue St Denis*, is the shortest route to the station) I will begin again with St Peter and will interpret the sculptures in the quatrefoils a little more completely.

Keeping for the quatrefoils the numerals adopted for the statues, the quatrefoils of St Peter will be designated 1A and 1B, and those for Malachi 28A and 28B.

1A *Courage*, with a leopard[230] on his shield; the French and English being in agreement in the reading of this symbol down to the time of the Black Prince's leopard coinage, in Aquitaine.

1B *Cowardice* – A man frightened by an animal darting out of a thicket, while a bird continues to sing. The coward does not have the courage of a thrush.[231]

2A *Patience* having a bull on its shield (never retreating).[232]

2B *Anger*[233] – A woman stabbing a man with a sword. Anger is essentially a feminine vice. A man, worthy of being called a man, can be driven to fury or madness by *indignation* (see the Black Prince of Limoges), but not by anger. So he can be fiendish enough – 'Incensed with indignation, Satan remained *fearless*' – but in this last word is the difference, there being as much fear in anger as there is in hatred.

3A *Sweetness* carries a lamb[234] on its shield.

3B *Vulgarity*, again a woman, kicking over her cupbearer. The final forms of extreme French vulgarity being in the feminine gestures of the cancan; see the favourite fashionable prints in the shops of Paris.

4A *Love*, divine, not human love: 'I in them and you in me.' Her shield supports a tree[235] with many branches grafted on to its cut-off stem. 'In these days the Messiah will be cut off, but not for himself.'

4B *Discord* – A husband and wife quarrelling. She has dropped her distaff (Amiens wool manufactures, see later – 9A).[236]

5A *Obedience* carries a shield with a camel. Actually the most disobedient of all the beasts than can be of service to man, which has the worst character, yet passing his life in the most painful service. I do not know how far his character has been understood by the northern sculptor; but I believe he has been taken as a kind of bearer of burdens which has neither joy nor sympathy, like the horse, nor power to demonstrate anger, like the bull.[237] His bite is bad enough (see Mr Palgrave's account of him), but probably little known at Amiens, even by crusaders who would always ride their own warhorses, or nothing.[238]

5B *Rebellion* – A man snapping his fingers before his bishop.[239] As Henry VIII before the Pope, and the modern French and English cockneys before all the priests, no matter who they are.

6A *Perseverance*, the great spiritual form of virtue commonly called Fortitude.

Usually taming or cutting to pieces a lion; here caressing one and holding her crown.'Hold fast to what you have[240] so that no man will take your crown.'[241]

6B *Atheism*, leaving his shoes at the church door. The foolish infidel is always represented with bare feet in the manuscripts of the twelfth and thirteenth centuries, the Christian having 'as shoes for his feet the preparation of the Gospel of Peace'.[242] Compare: 'How beautiful your feet are with shoes, *O prince's daughter*!'[243]

7A *Faith*, holding a chalice with a cross above it,[244] which was universally accepted in ancient Egypt as being the symbol of faith. It is also an enduring symbol for, leaving aside all differences of church, the words 'unless you eat the flesh of the son of man and drink his blood, you have no life in you,'[245] remain in their mystery to be understood only by those who have learned the sacred character of food,[246] in all times and all countries, and the laws of life and spirit, which depend on its acceptance, refusal and distribution.

7B *Idolatry*, kneeling before a monster. The *contrary* of faith – not the *lack* of faith. Idolatry is faith in false gods and quite distinct from faith in nothing at all (6B), the *Dixit incipiens*.[247] Very wise men can be idolaters, but they cannot be atheists.

8A *Hope* with gonfalon standard[248] and a crown before it, at a distance;[249] as opposed to the crown which fortitude holds in her hands with constancy (6A).

The gonfalon (Gund, war; fahr, standard, according to Poitevin's dictionary) is the flag which in battle means: forward; essentially sacred; hence the name gonfallonier always given to the standard-bearers in the armies of the Italian republics.

He is in the hand of hope, because she fights always before her, going towards her goal, or at least having the joy of seeing it draw nearer. Faith and fortitude wait, as St John in prison, but without being offended.

Hope is however placed below St James because of the seventh and eighth verses of his last chapter ending thus: 'Strengthen your hearts, for the coming of the Lord approaches.' It is he who interrogates Dante on the nature of hope (*Par.*, C.XXV., and see Cary's notes).

8B *Despair* stabbing himself.[250] Suicide is not considered heroic or sentimental in the thirteenth century and there is no Gothic morgue built beside the Somme.

9A *Charity* carrying on her shield a woolly ram and giving a coat to a naked beggar. The old wood manufacture of Amiens had this notion of its purpose, namely, to clothe the poor first, the rich afterwards. In those times no nonsense was talked about the evil consequences of indiscriminate charity.[251]

9B *Avarice* with a coffer and money. The modern notion common to the English and the Amiénois of the divine consummation of the manufacture of wool.

10A *Chastity*, shield with the Phoenix.[252]
10B *Lust*, a too ardent kiss.[253]

11A *Wisdom*, on her shield an edible root, I think;[254] signifying temperance, as the beginning of wisdom.

11B *Folly*,[255] the ordinary type used in all the early psalters, of a glutton armed with a club. This virtue and this vice are the earthly wisdom and folly completing the spiritual wisdom and the corresponding folly (under St Matthew). Temperance, the complement of obedience, and covetousness with violence, that of atheism.

12A *Humility*, on her shield a dove.

12B *Pride*, falling from his horse.

### 42

All these quatrefoils are rather symbolic than representational; and, as their purpose was sufficiently achieved if their symbol was understood, they had been entrusted to an inferior workman compared to the one who sculpted than those we are going to review and which are placed under the statues of the prophets.

The subject of most of these quatrefoils is either a historical fact or a scene spoken of by the prophet as having effectively assisted in a vision. And it is the ablest hands that the architect has in general charged with their execution. In interpreting them, I recall for each of them the name of the prophet whose life or prophecy they illustrate.[256]

13A '*Isaiah* – I saw the Lord seated on a throne.' (VI. I.)[257]

The vision of the throne 'high and elevated' between the seraphim.

13B 'See, this has touched your lips.' (VI. 7.)

The angel is standing before the prophet and holds, or rather held, the coal with tongs which had been artistically sculpted but are now broken.

Only a fragment remains in his hand.[258]

14A *Jeremiah*.[259] The burial of the belt. (XIII. 4, 5.)

The prophet is digging on the shores of the Euphrates, represented by vertical furrows[260] which wind down towards the middle of the bas-relief. Note that the translation should be 'hole in the ground,' and not in the 'rock'.

14B *The breaking of the yoke.* (XXVIII. 10.)

From the neck of the prophet Jeremiah; it is represented here by a doubled and redoubled chain.

15A *Ezekiel.*[261] The wheel within a wheel. (I. 16.)

The prophet is seated; in front of him two wheels of equal size, one locked in the circumference of the other.

15B 'Son of man, turn your face towards Jerusalem.' (XXI. 2.)

The prophet before the gate of Jerusalem.

16 *Daniel*

16A 'He has shut the lions' mouths.' (VI. 22.)

Daniel holding a book; the lions are treated as heraldic supporters. The subject is given more life in the series that we will find further on (24B).

16B 'At the same moment the fingers of a man's hand came out.' (V. 5.)

Belshazzar's feast represented by the king alone, seated at a small oblong table. Next to him the young Daniel looking only fifteen or sixteen years old, gracious and sweet, interprets the drawn characters. Beside the quatrefoil, coming out of the small cloud wreath comes a small bent hand, writing, as if with an upside-down pen, on a fragment of Gothic wall.[262]

For modern bombast as opposed to old simplicity, compare Belshazzar's feast by John Martin.[263]

43

The following subject begins the series of minor prophets.

17 *Hosea.*[264]

17A 'So I bought her for me for fifteen pieces of silver and a quantity of barley.' (III. 2.)

The prophet pouring the grain and the silver into the lap of the woman 'beloved of her friend'.[265] The sculpted pieces of silver each carry a cross with an inscription consistent with money of the time.

17B 'So will I also be for you.' (III. 3.)

He puts a ring on her finger.

18 *Joel*.[266]

18A 'The sun and the moon without light.' (II. 10.)

The sun and the moon as two little flat balls high in the external moulding.

18B 'The debarked fig tree and the vine stripped of its fruit.' (I. 7.)

Note the continual insistence on the blight of vegetation as a sign of divine punishment (19D).

19 *Amos. On the front.*

19A 'The Lord will cry of Zion.' (I. 2.)

Christ appears with a little cross on his halo.

19B 'The lodgings of the shepherds will mourn.' (I. 2.)

Amos with the hooked or knotted staff of the shepherds, and a bottle in a wicker basket, before his tent (the architecture of the right foil is restored).

*On the inside of the porch.*

19C 'The Lord with the mason's line.' (VII. 8.)

Christ again this time, and always from now on, with a little cross in his halo, has a large trowel in his hand which he lays on the top of a half-built wall. There appears to be a line twisted around its handle.

19D 'The place where it was not raining.' (IV. 7.)

Amos is gathering the leaves of the vine without fruit to feed his sheep who find no grass. It is one of the most beautiful pieces of sculpture.

20 *Obadiah*[267] *(on the inside of the porch)*.

20A 'I hid them in a cave.' (I. *Kings*, XVIII. 13.)

Three prophets at the mouth of a well, to whom Obadiah brings loaves.

20B 'He fell on his face.' (XVIII. 7.)

He kneels before Elijah who wears a shaggy coat.[268]

*On the front*

20C The captain of fifty.[269]

Elijah(?) speaking to an armed man under a tree.

20D *The messenger*. A messenger on his knees before a king. I cannot explain these two scenes 20C and 20D.

The uppermost may signify the dialogue of Elijah with the captains (II. *Kings*. I. 9.) and the lower one the return of the messengers[270] (II. *Kings*. I. 5.)

21 *Jonah*[271]

21A Escaped from the sea.

21B Under the ground. A small beast resembling a grasshopper gnawing the stem of a gourd. I would like to know what insects attack the gourds of Amiens.[272] This could be an entomological study for anyone who is so inclined.

22 *Micah*.

*On the front*

22A 'The tower of the flock.' (IV. 8.)

The tower is wrapped in clouds and God appears above it.

22B Each will rest, and 'nobody will frighten them'. (VI. 4.)

A man and his wife 'under his vine and his fig trees'.

*Inside the porch*

22C 'Swords into ploughshares.' (IV. 3.) – Nevertheless, two hundred years after these medallions were cut, the manufacture of swords had become one of the principal industries of Amiens! Not to her advantage.

22D 'Spears into pruning hooks.'[273]

23 *Nahum*

*On the inside of the porch*.

23A 'Nobody will look back.' (I. 8)

23B 'The burden of Nineveh.'[274] (I. 1.)

*On the front*

23C 'The princes and the great men.' (III. 17.)

23A, B and C are none of them susceptible to certain interpretation. The prophet in A is pointing, near the base of the quatrefoil, to a hill which the Père Rozé says is covered with grasshoppers. I can only copy what he says of them.

23D 'The precocious figs.' (III. 12.)

Three people beneath a fig tree catch its falling fruit in their mouths.

24 *Habakkuk*

24A 'I will wake up so as to see what he says to me.' (II. 1.)

The prophet is writing on his tablet what Christ dictates to him.

24B 'The ministry to Daniel.'

The traditional visit to Daniel. An angel carries Habakkuk by his hair, the prophet has a loaf of bread in each hand. They break through the roof of the cave. Daniel is stroking the back of a young lion; the head of another is held carelessly under his arm. Another is gnawing bones at the bottom of the cave.[275]

25 *Zephaniah*.[276]

*On the front*

25A 'The Lord strikes Ethiopia.' (II. 12.)

Christ striking a city with a sword. Note that in these bas-reliefs all violent actions are expressed in a feeble and ridiculous way; calm actions always well expressed.

25B 'The beasts in Nineveh.' (II. 15)

Very fine. All kinds of crawling beasts among the tottering walls, and coming out of their cracks and crannies. A monkey squatting and turning into a demon reverses the Darwinian theory.

*On the inside of the porch*

25C 'The Lord visits Jerusalem.' (I. 12.)

Christ passing through the streets of Jerusalem with a lantern in each hand.

25D 'The hedgehog and bittern.'[277] (III. 14.)

With a singing bird in a cage at the window.

26 *Haggai*

*On the inside of the porch*

26A 'The houses of the princes *ornamented with panelling.*'[278] (I. 4.)

A perfectly built house of square stones gloomily solid; the grating (of a prison?) on the front of the sub-basement.

26 'The sky retains its dew.' (I. 4.)

The skies as a projecting mass, with stars, sun and moon on the surface. Underneath, two withered trees.

*On the front*

26C 'The Lord's temple desolate.' (I. 4.)

The falling of the temple, 'not one stone left on another,' majestically empty. More square stones. Examine the text. (I. 6.)

26D 'Thus said the Lord of the Armies.' (I. 7.)

Christ pointing to his ruined temple.

27 *Zechariah*

27A 'Iniquity in flight.' (§§ 6 to 9.)

Wickedness in the Ephah.[279]

27B 'The angel who spoke to me.' (IV. 1.)

The prophet almost reclining, a glorious winged angel flying out of the cloud.

28 *Malachi*

28A 'You have wounded the Lord.' (II. 17.)

The priests thrust Christ through with a barbed lance whose point comes out through his back.

28B 'This commandment is for you.' (II. 1.)

In these panels, the one placed at the base is often an introduction to the one above, its explanation. It is perhaps chapter 1 verse 6 of the indicated titles that the image of Christ may be alluding to here.

44

With this bas-relief terminates the series of sculptures designed to illustrate the apostolic and prophetic teaching which constitutes what I mean by the 'Bible' of Amiens. But the two lateral porches contain supplementary subjects which are necessary for the completion of the pastoral and traditional teaching addressed to her people in these days.

The northern porch consecrated to St Firmin, who is the first missionary of Amiens, has on its central pier the statue of the saint; above, on the back of the arch, the story of the discovery of his body; on the sides of the porch his companions, the saints and the angels, in the following order:

Central statue: St Firmin

> South side (left):
> 41. St Firmin the confessor.
> 42. St Domice.
> 43. St Honoré.
> 44. St Salve.
> 45. St Quentin.
> 46. St Gentian
> North side (right):
> 47. St Geoffroy.
> 48. An angel.
> 49. St Fuscien, martyr.
> 50. St Victoric, martyr.
> 51. An angel.
> 52. St Ulpha.

45

Of these saints, with the exception of St Firmin and St Honoré, of whom I have already spoken,[280] St Geoffroy[281] is more real for us than the others; he was born in the year of the battle of Hastings, at Molincourt in the Soissonais and was Bishop of Amiens from 1104 to 1150. A man of entirely simple, pure and just life: one of the most severe of the ascetics, but not in the least sombre – always sweet and merciful. A great number of miracles are attributed to him, but all indicating a life which was above all miraculous by its justice and peace.

Consecrated at Rheims and accompanied to his diocese by a procession of other bishops and nobles, he dismounts from his horse at St Acheul, the place of St Firmin's first tomb, and walks barefoot from Amiens to Picquigny to ask the vidame of Amiens for the freedom of the chatelain Adam. He defended the privileges of the inhabitants of the town, with the help of Louis le Gros against the count of Amiens, defeated him and razed his castle; nevertheless, the people not obeying him enough in the discipline of their lives, he blames his own weakness rather than theirs and retires to the grande-chartreuse, not finding himself capable of being their bishop. The superior questioning him on the reasons for his retirement, and asking him if he had ever sold the offices of the Church, the bishop answered: 'My father, my hands are pure of simony, but I have a thousand times allowed myself to be seduced by praise.'

46

St Firmin the confessor was the son of a Roman senator who received the body of St Firmin himself. He piously maintained the tomb of the martyr in his father's garden and eventually built a church over it dedicated to our Lady of martyrs, which was the first episcopal seat of Amiens, at St Acheul, and of which we have spoken above.

St Ulpha was an Amiénoise girl who lived in a chalk cave above the marshes of the Somme; if ever Mr Murray provides you with a comic guide for a visit to Amiens, no doubt this enlightened author will be able to count much on your enjoyment of this saint being disturbed in her devotions by the frogs, and keeping them quiet by the strength of prayers. You are, of course, now absolutely above such extravagances and are sure that God cannot or will not so much as shut a frog's mouth for you. Remember, therefore, that as he also now leaves open the mouth of the liar, the blasphemer and the traitor, you must shut your own ears to their voices, as far as you are able.

From her name comes St Wolf – or Guelph – see again Miss Yonge's Christian names. Our tower of Wolf's stone, Ulverstone, and the church of Ulpha are ignorant, I believe, of their Picard relatives.

47

The other saints, in this porch, are all similarly provincial, as it were personal friends of the Amiénois;[282] and under them the quatrefoils represent the charming order of the year which they protect and sanctify, with the signs of the zodiac above, and the labours of the months below; little differing from the way they are always represented – except for May: see below. The Libra also is quite rare in the woman who holds the scales; the lion particularly good-humoured, and the harvest, one of the most beautiful pieces in the whole series of sculptures; several of the others particularly fine and detailed.[283]

41. *December.* – Killing and heating the pig.[284] Above, Capricorn with a tail that tapers quickly; I cannot decipher the accessories.

42. *January.* – Two headed,[285] with a sad expression. Aquarius weaker than most of the bas-reliefs of this series.

43. *February.* – Very fine, warming his feet and putting coals on the fire. The fish above, elaborate but uninteresting.

44. *March.* – At work in vine furrows.[286] Aries careful but fairly ugly.

45. *April.* – Feeding his falcon; very pretty.

Above, Taurus with charming leaves for pasture.

46. *May.* – Very peculiar, a middle-aged man is sitting under the trees listening to the birds singing and Gemini above, a bridegroom and a bride.

This quatrefoil rejoins those of the interior angle at Zephaniah.

52. *June*. – Opposite rejoining the interior angle where Haggai is. Mowing. Note the charming flowers sculpted all across the grass. Above, Cancer with his shells superbly modelled.

51. *July*. – The harvest. Very beautiful. The smiling lion completes the demonstration that all the seasons and all the signs are regarded as an equal benediction and providentially kind.

50. *August*. – Threshing.[287] Virgo above, holding a flower, her drapery very modern and confused for a work of the thirteenth century.

49. *September*. – I am not sure of his action, whether he is pruning or gathering fruit in some way from the tree full of leaves.[288] Libra above; charming.

48. *October*. – Treading grapes.[289] Scorpio a very traditional and sweet figure with a forked tail, it is true, but without sting.

47. *November*. – Sowing, with Sagittarius; half hidden when this photograph was taken thanks to the beautiful arrangements which go on now without interruption, whether it be for one work or another, in the French cathedrals; they never can let them alone for ten minutes.

48

And now, finally, if you care to see it, we will enter the Madonna's porch – only, if you come, good female protestant reader, come civilly; and please remember – if you have in known history, things to remember – if you cannot remember, be solemnly assured of this – that the cult of the Madonna, or the cult of any Lady, dead or alive, never did any human creature any harm – but that the cult of money, the cult of the wig, of the cocked hat and feathers, the cult of plates, the cult of the pot and the cult of the pipe, have done, and are doing a great deal of evil and that all of them offend millions of times more the God of heaven and earth and of the stars, than all the most absurd and most charming errors committed by the generations of his simple children, about what the

Virgin-mother could, or would, or might do, or experience for them.

### 49

And next, please observe this simple historical fact about the three sorts of Madonnas. First, the sorrowful Madonna – the Byzantine type, and Cimabue's. It is the noblest of all, and the most ancient to have had a popular, recognisable influence.[290]

Secondly, the queenly Madonna who is essentially the Frank and Norman Madonna, crowned, calm, full of power and gentleness. It is the one who is represented in the porch.

Thirdly, the nurturing Madonna who is the Raphaelesque[291] and generally most recent and decadent one, she is seen here in a good French style in the south porch, as we have already noted.

You will find in Mr Viollet-le-Duc (the article *Virgin* in his *Dictionary*, is altogether deserving of the most attentive study) an admirable comparison between this statue of the queenly Madonna of the southern porch and the nurturing Madonna of the transept. I will perhaps be able to obtain a photograph of these two drawings, side by side but, if I can, the reader will please observe that he has a little flattered the queen and a little coarsened the nurturer, which is not fair. The statue in this porch, in the thirteenth century style, is very beautiful, but there is no reason otherwise to give it any importance, the more ancient Byzantine types having a lot more grandeur.

### 50

The story of the Madonna, in its principal events, is told in the series of statues around the porch and in the quatrefoils placed below them. Several of them refer however to a legend about the Magi that I have not been able to fathom and I am not sure of their interpretation.

The large statues on the left, reading outwards as usual, are:
  29. The Angel Gabriel.

30. Virgin Annunciate.

31. Virgin Visitant.

32. St Elizabeth.

33. The presentation of the Virgin.

34. St Simeon.

On the right, reading outwards:

35, 36, 37. The three Kings.

38. Herod.

39. Solomon.

40. The Queen of Sheba.

51

I am not sure of rightly understanding what these last two statues are doing here; but I think that the idea of their creator[292] was that essentially the Queen Mary visited Herod when she sent, or had sent for her, the Magi to announce to him her presence at Bethlehem; and the contrast between Solomon's reception of the Queen of Sheba, and Herod's driving out the Madonna into Egypt is emphatically described all along this side of the porch, with the various consequences for the two kings and for the world.

The quatrefoils under the two great statues run in the following order:

29. Under Gabriel.

A. Daniel seeing the stone cut out without hands.[293]

B. Moses and the burning bush.[294]

30. Under the Virgin Annunciate.

A. Gideon and the dew on the fleece.[295]

B. Moses retiring with the tables of the law. Aaron, dominant, points to his burgeoning rod.[296]

31. Under the Virgin Visitant.

A. The message to Zacharias: 'Do not fear, for your prayer is heard.'[297]

B. The dream of Joseph: 'Do not be afraid of taking Mary for your wife.'[298]

32. Under St Elizabeth:

A. The silence of Zacharias: 'They perceived that he had had a vision in the temple.'[299]

B. There is none of your relatives who is called by this name.[300] 'He wrote saying his name is John.'[301]

33. Under the presentation of the Virgin.

A. Flight into Egypt.

B. Christ with the Doctors.

34. Under St Simeon.

A. Fall of the Idols in Egypt.[302]

B. The return to Nazareth.

These two last quatrefoils rejoin those of Amos which are so beautiful (C. and D.).

Then on the opposite side, under the Queen of Sheba and rejoining the A and B of Obadiah.

40. A. Solomon entertains the Queen of Sheba. The Grace cup.

B. Solomon teaches the Queen of Sheba: 'God is above.'

39. Under Solomon:

A. Solomon on his Judge's throne.

B. Solomon praying before the gate of his temple.

38. Under Herod:[303]

A. Massacre of the Innocents.

B. Herod orders the ship of the Kings to be burned.[304]

37. Under the third King:

A. Herod questioning the Kings.

B. Burning of the ship.

36. Under the second King:

A. Adoration in Bethlehem? Not certain.

B. The voyage of the Kings.

35. Under the first King:

A. The Star in the East.

B. 'Being warned in a dream that they must not return to Herod.'[305]

Doubtless I will one day find out the real sequence of these subjects, but that matters little, this group of quatrefoils being of less interest than the rest, and that of the massacre of the innocents curiously illustrative of the sculptor's inability to express strong action or violent passion.

But I do not wish to enter here into questions respecting the art of these bas-reliefs. The have never had any other object than that of being symbols, or guides to thought. And if the reader lets himself be quietly guided by them, he can create himself more beautiful pictures in his heart; and at all events he may recognise the following general truths as their message to all people.

## 52

First, that throughout the sermon on the Amiens mount, Christ never appears as the crucified, nor is he for a moment thought of as dead; but as the incarnate word, as the present friend – as the prince of peace on the earth[306] – and as the eternal king in heaven. What his life *is*, what his commandments *are*, and what his judgement will be are the things taught here; not what he once did, not what he once suffered, but what he is doing at present, what he requires us to do. This is the pure, joyous, beautiful lesson of Christianity; and the reasons for falling from his faith and all the corruptions of its sterile practices can be summarised briefly thus: the habitual contemplation of Christ's death, instead of his life, meditation on his past sufferings substituting for our present duty.[307]

## 53

Then secondly, although Christ does not carry his cross, the afflicted prophets, the persecuted apostles, the martyred disciples, do carry theirs. For if it is salutary for you to remember what your immortal creator has done for you, it is no less well for you to remember what our dying fellow creatures have done for us as well. You may at your pleasure deny or defy Christ, but the martyr you can only forget: deny him, you cannot. Every stone of this edifice has been cemented with his blood and there is no groove of its pillars that has not been worked with his suffering.

### 54

Keeping then these things in your heart, return now to the central statue of Christ, listen to his message and understand it. He holds the book of the eternal law in his left hand; with his right he blesses, but blesses on condition: '*Do* this, and you will live,' [308] or rather in a stricter and more rigorous sense: 'Be this, and you will live.' To show pity is nothing, you must also be pure in your heart.

And with this word of the unabolished law. 'This, if you do not, this, if you are not, you will die.'

### 55

Die – whatever idea you have of death – totally and irrevocably. There is no talk of the pardon in the theology of the thirteenth century (in our modern sense) of sins, nor is there any talk of purgatory. Above this image of Christ with us, of Christ our friend, is placed the image of Christ above us. Of Christ, our judge. For this present life – here is his helpful presence. After this life – here is his coming to take account of our deeds and of the intentions of our deeds; and the separating of the obedient, of the loving from the mean, with no hope given to any recourse, any reconciliation. I do not know what suffering commentaries were added subsequently and written in frightened minuscule by the hand of the fathers, or limited in hesitant murmurs by the prelates of the modern Church. But I know that the language of every sculpted stone, of every glowing window, of these things that were daily seen and universally understood by the people, was absolutely and uniquely the teaching of Moses at Sinai as well as of St John at Patmos, from the beginning as at the end of the revelation of the Lord to Israel.

It was thus, simply – severely – and without interruption for the three great centuries of Christianity in her strength (eleventh, twelfth and thirteenth centuries), and in the whole extent of her empire, from Iona to Cyrene and from Calpe to Jerusalem. At what time the doctrine of purgatory was openly accepted by the Catholic doctors, I neither know nor care to know. It was formulated for the first time by Dante, but was never for a moment accepted by the sacred artist teachers of his time or by those of any great school, at any time whatsoever.[309]

### 56

I do not know nor do I care to know – at what time the notion of justification by faith in the modern sense found itself clearly fixed in the minds of the heretical sects and schools of the North. In reality, its strength was sealed by its first authors on an asceticism which differed from monastic rule in that it was only apt to destroy, never to build, which forced itself to impose on everybody what severity it thought proper for itself on everybody else also, and thus struggled to make of the world a monastery without art, without letters and without pity.[310]

Its violent effort broke down in the middle of furies of reactionary dissoluteness and unbelief and remains now the most despicable of popular bandages and plasters for every broken condition of the law and bruising of the conscience that interest can provoke or hypocrisy disguise.

### 57

From the quarrels that followed between the two great sects of the corrupted Church on the subject of prayers for the dead and indulgences for the living, of papal supremacy or popular liberties, no man, woman or child need take the trouble to study the history of Christianity. They are nothing but the quarrels of men, and the laughter of demons among the ruins. Its life, gospel and power are entirely written in the great works of its true believers: in Normandy and Sicily, on the islets of the rivers of France and on the lawns sloping down to the English rivers, on the rocks of Orvieto and by the sands of the Arno.

But of all the works, the simplest, most complete and most imposing in its lessons to the active mind of northern Europe is that built on the foundation stones of Amiens.[311]

58

Believe what it teaches you, reader, or believe it not as you wish: understand only how thoroughly it was once believed, and that all beautiful things were made, and all noble acts done,[312] when this faith still had strength, before what we may call 'the present time' came, in which the question of knowing if religion has any effect on morality is gravely discussed by people who have essentially no idea what either one of these words may mean.

Concerning which debate you may perhaps have the patience to read what follows, as the spire of Amiens fades in the distance and your carriage rushes towards the Isle of France which today exhibits the most admired patterns of European art, intelligence and life.

59

All human creatures, in all times and places of the world, who have ardent affections, common sense, and self-control have been and are naturally moral. Human nature in its fullness is necessarily moral – without love it is inhuman – without sense,[313] inhuman – without discipline, inhuman. In the exact proportion in which men are born capable of these things, in which they are taught to love, to think, to endure suffering, they are noble, live happily, die calmly and are remembered with perpetual honour and goodwill by their race. All wise men know and have known these things since the form of man was separated from the dust; the knowledge and enforcement of these laws have nothing to do with religion:[314] a good and wise man differs from a wicked and idiotic one, simply as a good dog from an aggressive one, and as every breed of dog from a wolf or a weasel. And if you are to believe in, or preach without believing in, faith in a spiritual world or law, only in the hope that whatever you do, or anybody else does, that is stupid or undignified, may be thanks to these doctrines mended and patched, and pardoned, and entirely renewed, the less you believe in a spiritual world and above all, the less you talk about it, the better it will be.

60

But if, loving the creatures that are like yourself, you feel that you would love still more dearly creatures better than yourself, if they were revealed to you; if striving with all your might to improve what is evil, near you and around you, you would like to think of the day when the judge of all the earth will wholly do right[315] and when the little hills will rejoice on every side;[316] if, separating yourself from the companions who have given you all the best joy you have had on earth, you keep the desire to meet their eyes again and shake their hands, where eyes will not be dim and hands will not be weak; if, preparing yourself to lie down beneath the grass in silence and solitude without seeing beauty again, without feeling joy again, you would care for the promise that was made to you of a time when you should see God's light again and know the things you aspire to know, and walk in the peace of eternal love – *then* the hope of these things for you is religion; their substance in your life is faith. And in their virtue it is promised to us that the kingdoms of this world will become one day the kingdoms of our Lord and of his Christ.[317]

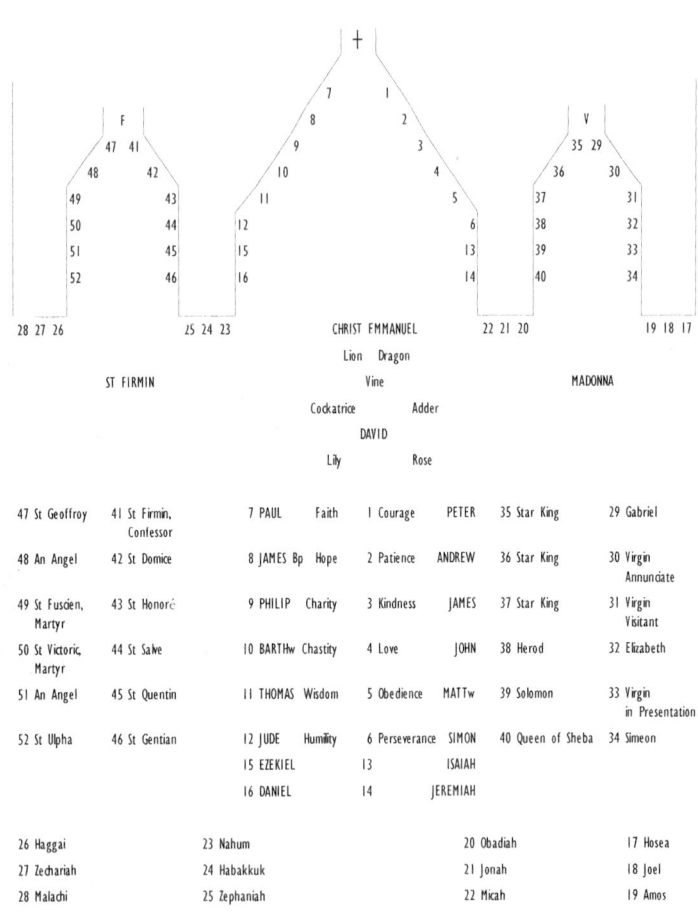

AMIENS

Plan of West Porches

## Appendix I

Chronological list of the main events referred to in *The Bible of Amiens*

A.D.

- 250   Origin of the Franks
- 301   St Firmin comes to Amiens
- 332   St Martin
- 345   Birth of St Jerome
- 350   First church of Amiens built on the grave of St Firmin
- 358   Franks conquered by Julian near Strasbourg
- 405   St Jerome's Bible
- 420   Death of St Jerome
- 421   Birth of St Genevieve – Foundation of Venice
- 445   The Franks cross the Rhine and take Amiens
- 447   Mérovée king at Amiens
- 451   Battle of Châlons – Attila defeated by Aëtius
- 457   Death of Mérovée – Childeric king at Amiens
- 466   Birth of Clovis
- 476   End of Roman Empire in Italy, under Odoacer
- 481   End of Roman Empire in France
        Clovis crowned at Amiens
        Birth of St Benedictine
- 485   Battle of Soissons – Clovis defeats Syagrius
- 486   Syagrius dies at the court of Alaric
- 489   Battle of Verona – Theodoric defeats Odoacer
- 493   Clovis marries Clotilde

| | |
|---|---|
| 496 | Battle of Tolbiac – Clovis routs the Alemanni |
| | Clovis crowned at Rheims by St Rémy |
| | Clovis baptised by St Rémy |
| 508 | Battle of Poitiers – Clovis conquers the Visigoths under Alaric – Death of Alaric |

## Appendix II

General plan of *Our Fathers Have Told Us*[318]

The first part of Our Fathers Have Told Us, now submitted to the public, is enough to show the plan and tendencies of the work; contrary to my usual custom, I have recourse to subscription before publication, because the degree to which I can increase its usefulness by illustrating it with engravings will greatly depend on the number of those who will support its expenses.

I do not find in the present state of my health any reason to fear a weakening of my general faculties, whether in conception or ability to work, other than the natural and enforced cooling down of an old man's enthusiasm; of which, however, enough remains in me to guarantee my readers against the abandonment of a project that I have been nourishing already for twenty years.

The work, if I live to complete it, will consist of ten parts, each limited to a local aspect of Christian history, and all combining at the end to illustrate the influence of the Church in the thirteenth century.[319]

The present volume completes the first part, which describes the beginnings of Frank power and the artistic heights which it reached with the cathedral of Amiens.

The second part, *Ponte della Pietra*, will I hope do more for Theodoric and Verona than I have been able to do for Clovis and the first capital of France.

The third, *Ara Coeli*, will trace the foundations of Papal power.

The fourth, *Ponte-a-Mare*, and the fifth, *Ponte Vecchio*, will only gather with much difficulty into brief form what I possess of sparse materials relative to Pisa and Florence.

The sixth, *Valle Crucis*, will concern itself with the monastic architecture of England and Wales.[320]

The seventh, *The Sources of the Eure*, will be entirely dedicated to the cathedral of Chartres.

The eighth, *Domrémy*, to that of Rouen and the schools of architecture which it represents.

The ninth, *The Bay of Uri*, to the pastoral forms of Catholicism, up to the present time.

And the tenth, *The Bells of Cluse*, to the pastoral Protestantism of Savoy, Geneva, and the Scottish border.[321]

Each part will consist of four sections only; and one of them, the fourth, will generally be descriptive of a historic city or cathedral considered as resulting in – and tracing – the religious influence studied in the preparatory chapters.

There will be at least one illustration per chapter; for the remainder there will be drawings which will be placed at once in Sheffield museums for public reference, and they will be engraved if I am provided support or the opportunity to bind them into the completed work.

As in the case of Chapter IV of this first part, a small edition of the descriptive chapters will be printed in reduced form for travellers and non-subscribers; but otherwise, my intention is that this work be reserved exclusively for subscribers.

# Notes

**1.** This part of the introduction was dedicated in the *Mercure de France*, where it first appeared in the form of an article, to Mr Leon Daudet. I am happy to be able to renew for him here the testimony of my deep gratitude and of my admiring friendship.

**2.** Here, according to Mr Collingwood, are the circumstances under which Ruskin wrote this book:

'Mr Ruskin had not been abroad since the spring of 1877, but in August 1880, he felt able to travel again. He left to make a tour of the northern French cathedrals, staying at his old haunts, Abbeville, Amiens, Beauvais, Chartres, Rouen, and then returned with Mr A Severn and Mr Brabanson to Amiens, where he spent the greater part of October. He was writing a new book *The Bible of Amiens*, destined to be for the *Seven Lamps* what *St Mark's Rest* was to *The Stones of Venice*. He did not feel able to lecture to strangers at Chesterfield, but he visited old friends at Eton, on 6 November 1880, to give a lecture on Amiens. For once he forgot his notes, but the lecture was no less brilliant and interesting. It was in fact the first chapter of his new work *The Bible of Amiens*, itself conceived as the first volume of *Our Fathers*, etc. *Sketches on the History of Christianity*, etc.

'The distinctly religious tone of the work was noted as marking, if not a change, then at least a strong development of a tendency that had been strengthening for some time past. He had passed from the phase of doubt to an acknowledgement of the powerful and salutary influence of serious religion; he had come to an attitude of mind in which, without unsaying anything he had said against narrowness of creed and inconsistency of practice, without stating any definite doctrine of the afterlife or adopting any sectarian dogma, he regarded the fear of God and the revelation of the Divine Spirit as great facts and motives not to be neglected in the study of history, as the groundwork of civilisation and the guide of progress.' (Collingwood, *The Life and Work of John Ruskin*, II, pp. 206 and following). With regard to the subtitle of *The Bible of Amiens*, which Mr Collingwood recalls *(Sketches of the History of Christianity for the Boys and Girls who Have Been Held at its Fonts)*, I will point out how much it resembles other subtitles of Ruskin, as for example *Mornings in Florence: Simple Studies of Christian Art for English Travellers*, and even more so *St Mark's Rest: The History of Venice, for the Rare Travellers who still Care for Her Monuments*.

**3.** The heart of Shelley, snatched from the flames in front of Lord Byron by Hunt, during the cremation. Mr André Lebey (himself author of a sonnet on the death of Shelley) sent me an interesting correction on this subject. It was not Hunt but Trelawney who took Shelley's heart out of the furnace, not without seriously burning his hand. I regret not being able to publish here Mr Lebey's curious letter. It reproduces in particular this passage from Trelawney's memoirs: 'Byron asked me to preserve the scull for him, but remembering that he had formerly used one as a drinking cup, I did not want Shelley's to be subjected to this profanation.' The day before, while Williams's corpse was being identified, Byron told Trelawney: 'Let me see the jaw, I can recognise anyone I have talked to by their teeth.' But, taking into account Trelawney's reports and without even considering the hardness Childe Harold willingly affected in front of the Corsair, one must remember that, a few lines further on, Trelawney recounting Shelley's cremation, declares: 'Byron could not bear this spectacle and swam off to the Bolivar.'

**4.** See the admirable portrait of St Martin in Book I of *The Bible of Amiens*. 'He voluntarily accepts the loving cup, he is the patron of honest drinking. The stuffing of your Martinmas goose is fragrant in his nostrils and sacred for him are the last rays of departing summer.'

**5.** You will therefore perhaps have a chance as I did (even if you do not find the route indicated by Ruskin) to see the cathedral, which at a distance seems to be made only of stone, suddenly transformed, and – the sun passing through its interior, making visible and volatilising its windows, on which there are no paintings – standing up towards the sky, between its stone pillars, giant and immaterial apparitions of gold, green and flame. You will also be able near the slaughterhouses to look for the view from which the engraving *Amiens on All Souls' Day* was taken.

**6.** The beauties of the cathedral of Amiens and of Ruskin's book do not require the shadow of a notion of architecture to be felt, and so that this article may be sufficient in itself, I have used only the most up to date technical terms that everybody knows, and only when precision and conciseness made them necessary. At all events, to respond to readers who are modest and would say, like Mr Jourdain, 'Do as if I did not know it', I remind them that the main façade of a cathedral always faces west. The doorway of the west façade, or west porch, generally consists of three porches, a main one and two secondary ones. The opposite end of the cathedral, that is to say the east part, does not have a porch and is called the apse. The south porch and the north porch are the porches of the south and north façades. The passage that forms the arms of the cross in cruciform churches is called the transept. A trumeau, says Viollet-le-Duc, is a pillar dividing a main doorway into two bays. The same Viollet-le-Duc calls a 'quatrefoil' an architectural member consisting of four circular lobes.

**7.** *The Bible of Amiens*, IV, §§6, 7 and 8.

**8.** Mr Paul Desjardins has put it much better by speaking of stones that have remained intact longer than hearts.

**9.** And looked at by them: I can at this moment even see the men hurrying towards the Somme swollen by the tide, passing in front of the porch they have known for so long and raising their eyes towards the 'Star of the Sea'.

**10.** Begun on 3 July 1508 the 120 stalls were completed in 1522, on St John's Day. The beadle, Mr Regnault, will let you walk around in the middle of the life of all these people who in the colour of their frames, the lives of their gestures, their worn-out coats, the solidity of their build, continue to uncover the essence of the wood, to show its strength, and to sing of its softness. You will see Joseph travelling on the balustrade, Pharaoh sleeping on the crest where the shape of his dreams unfolds, while on the lower misericords the soothsayers are engaged in interpreting. He will let you pinch with no risk of damage to them the long ropes of wood and you will hear them produce a sound like a musical instrument which seems to say, and which proves, in effect, how indestructible and fine they are.

**11.** Miss Marie Nordlinger, the eminent English artist, has brought to my attention a letter from Ruskin in which Victor Hugo's *Notre-Dame de Paris* is adjudged the dregs of French literature.

**12.** *The Cathedral of Rouen at Different Hours of the Day* by Claude Monet (Camondo Collection). For 'interiors' of cathedrals, I am aware only of those, so beautiful, by the great painter Helleu.

**13.** *The Bible of Amiens*, III, §§50, 51, 52, 53, 54 (dated Avallon, 28 August 1882).

**14.** Mr Huysmans says: 'The Gospels insist that St Jude not be confused with Judas, and yet he was; and because of the similarity of his name with that of the traitor, during the Middle Ages Christians denied him ... He emerges from his silence only to ask Christ a question on Predestination, and Jesus' answer is beside the point or, to put it bluntly, he does not answer him at all,' and he goes on to speak of 'the deplorable reputation he owes to his namesake Judas' (*La Cathédrale*, pp. 454-455).

**15.** *The Bible of Amiens*, IV, §§30-36.

**16.** *Ezekiel* 1:16.

**17.** *Daniel* 6:22.

**18.** *Joel* 1:7 and 2:10.

**19.** *Amos* 4:7.

**20.** *Habakkuk* 2:1.

**21.** *Zephaniah* 1:12; 2:14; 2:15.

**22.** Arriving at this door, Ruskin says: 'If you come, good Protestant female reader, come civilly, and please recall that no cult of the female of any sort, whether of the dead or the living, ever did any human creature any harm – but that the cult of money, the cult of the wig, the cult of the tricorn hat and feathers, have done and are doing a great deal of harm, and that any of these, and all of them, are quite a million times more offensive to the God of Heaven, of the Earth and of the Stars than all the most absurd and most charming mistakes made by the generations of his simple children about what the Virgin Mother could, or would, or might experience for them.'

**23.** And the castings of several statues referred to here and also the choir stalls.

**24.** *The Bible of Amiens*, IV, §§52 and following.

**25.** Mr André Michel, who did us the honour of mentioning this study in an artistic discussion of the *Journal des Débats*, seems to have seen in these last lines a kind of regret at not finding the statue of Ruskin in front of the cathedral, almost a desire to see it there and, in short, seems already to be coming up with a plan to ask for it to be placed there some day. Nothing was further from our mind. It is enough for us, and pleases us more, to meet Ruskin every time we go to Amiens in the guise of the 'Mysterious Traveller' with whom Renan talked in the Holy Land. But after all, since so many statues are put up (and since Mr André Michel gives us the idea which would never have occurred to us), let us admit that a statue of Ruskin in Amiens would at least have the advantage over another statue of actually meaning something. We see him very well, on one of the squares of Amiens 'as a stranger come to town', as Mr Boislèves says of the bronze of Alfred de Vigny.

**26.** Title of a painting by Gustave Moreau which is in the Gustave Moreau Museum.

**27.** At Sheffield.

**28.** This part of the preface appeared first in the *Gazette des Beaux-Arts*.

**29.** Among the writers who have spoken of Ruskin, Milsand was one of the first, both in order of time and by the force of his thinking. He has been a sort of forerunner, an inspired and incomplete prophet, who did not live long enough to see the development of the work he had in effect foretold.

**30.** The Ruskin of Mr de la Sizeranne. Ruskin has been considered to this day, and with just claim, as the personal preserve of Mr de la Sizeranne and, if at times I try to venture on his terrain, it certainly will not be to underestimate him or usurp his right, which is not the first occupant's alone. As I enter this subject dominated on all sides by the magnificent monument he has erected to Ruskin, I must thus render homage and pay tribute to him.

**31.** Since these lines were written, Mr Bardoux and Mr Brunhes have published, one a considerable work, the other a small volume on Ruskin. I recently had the opportunity to say how much I admired these two books, but too briefly not to wish to come back to them. All I can say here is that my very high esteem for Mr Bardoux's beautiful effort does not prevent me from thinking that Mr de la Sizeranne's book was too perfect within the limits the author had set for himself to have anything to lose from this competition and emulation that seems to be generated on the subject of Ruskin, and to which we owe, among other things, some curious pages by Mr Gabriel Mourey, and some definitive words by Mr André Beaunier. Messrs Bardoux and Brunhes have changed the point of view and thereby renewed the horizon. This is what, with all due respect, I tried to do here myself a little earlier.

**32.** To be more exact, Saint-Urbain is mentioned once in *The Seven Lamps* and Amiens once also (but only in the preface to the second edition), while there are mentions of Abbeville, Avranches, Bayeux, Beauvais, Bourges, Caen, Caudebec, Chartres, Coutances, Falaise, Lisieux, Paris, Rheims, Rouen, Saint-Lô, to speak only of France.

**33.** In *St Mark's Rest*, he goes so far as to say there was just one Greek art from the battle of Marathon down to the day of doge Selvo (compare the pages of *The Bible of Amiens*, in which he makes the builders who dug the ancient labyrinth of Amiens descend from Daedalus, 'the first sculptor who gave a moving representation of human life'); and in the mosaics of the baptistery of St Mark's he recognises a harpy in a cherub, a canephora in a Herodias, a Greek vase in a golden dome, etc.

**34.** In an admirable study published by the *Gazette des Beaux-Arts*. Since Fromentin, no painter, we believe, has shown greater mastery as a writer. These lines had already appeared while Mr Ary Renan was still alive. Now that he is dead, I wonder if I did not understate the truth. It now seems to me that he was superior to Fromentin.

**35.** 'To such an insignificant degree,' he says, 'that I believe no interpretations of Greek religion have ever been so affectionate, none of Roman religion so reverent, as those which are at the base of my teaching.'

**36.** Compare Chateaubriand, preface to the first edition of *Atala*. 'The muses are celestial women who do not disfigure their features by grimacing; when they cry, it is with the secret design of embellishing themselves.'

**37.** *Praeterita*, I, chapter 2.

**38.** What an interesting collection one could make with landscapes of France seen through English eyes: *The Rivers of France* by Turner; *Versailles* by Bonnington; *Auxerre* or *Valenciennes*, *Vézelay* or *Amiens* by Walter Pater; *Fontainebleau* by Stevenson and so many others!

**39.** *The Seven Lamps of Architecture.*

**40.** This sentence of Ruskin's applies better to idolatry as I understand it taken out of context than where it is found in *Lectures on Art*. I have moreover given the beginning of the development further on in note 307.

**41.** How could Mr Barrès omit Ruskin when, in an abominable chapter of his later book, he was electing an ideal senate for Venice? Was he not more worthy to sit in it than Léopold Robert or Théophile Gautier, and would he not have been well placed between Byron and Barrès, between Goethe and Chateaubriand?

**42.** *The Stones of Venice*, I, IV, LXXI. Throughout this volume the references to *The Stones of Venice* are given with the numbers (volumes, chapters and paragraphs) of the *Traveller's Edition*. This verse is taken from *Ecclesiastes*, XII, 9.

**43.** Chapter III, §27.

**44.** I do not have the time today to make myself clear on this defect, but it seems to me that through my translation, dull though it may be, the reader will be able to perceive, as through the rough but suddenly illuminated glass of an aquarium, the rapid but visible abduction of the thought by the sentence, and the immediate loss the thought undergoes as a result.

**45.** Throughout *The Bible of Amiens*, the reader will often find similar formulas.

**46.** Renan.

**47.** I was still not quite sure of the perfect justice of this idea, but my mind was soon relieved by the only means that exists for the verification of our ideas, I mean the chance encounter with a great mind. In fact, almost at the moment I had written these lines there appeared in the *Revue des Deux Mondes* the verses of the countess de Noailles given below. One will see that I had unknowingly, as Mr Barrès said at Combourg, 'followed in the footsteps of genius':

> Children, take a good look at all the rounded plains;
> The nasturtium surrounded by its bees;
> Take a good look at the pond, the fields, before love;
> For, after, one never again sees anything of the world.
> After, one only sees one's heart before oneself;
> One only sees a bit of flame on the road;
> One hears nothing, one knows nothing, and one listens
> To the feet of sad love which owns or sits.

**48.** Compare, in *Arrows of the Chace*, the response Ruskin gave his students and which was quoted by Mr de la Sizeranne: 'If you had ever read ten lines of my work and understood it, you would know that I care no more for Mr Disraeli and Mr Gladstone than for two old bagpipes, but that I hate all liberalism as I hate Beelzebub, and that I stand with Carlyle, alone henceforth in England, for God and the Queen!' – (Translator's note.)

**49.** Compare, in *Unto This Last*, the words used to describe King Solomon, 'a Jewish merchant, having major interests in business with the Gold Coast and known for having made one of the most considerable fortunes of his time, famous also for his great practical wisdom'. (*Unto This Last*, III, §42.) – (Translator's note.)

**50.** *The Laws of Fiesole*, I, 1-6. Compare the commentary and final dedication of these words at the end of *Modern Painters*:

'All the substance of these passionate words of my youth were condensed later in this aphorism given twenty years afterwards in my inaugural Oxford lecture: "All great art is praise" and on this aphorism, the even bolder maxim founded, "So far from art's being immoral, nothing is moral except art in its ultimate power. Life without work is sin, work without art is brutality" (I forget the words, but that is their import); and now, writing beneath the cloudless peace of Chamonix, what must really be the supreme words of this book which their beauty inspired and their strength guided, I am able with yet happier and calmer heart than ever before to confirm the essential article of its faith: that is to say that the knowledge of what is beautiful leads on and is the first step towards the knowledge of the things that deserve to be loved, and that the laws, the life and the joy of beauty in the material world of God are as eternal and sacred parts of his creation as, in the world of spirits, virtue, and in the world of angels, praise' (Chamonix, Sunday, 16 September 1888, *Modern Painters*: vol. V, *Epilogue*, p. 390). – (Translator's note.)

**51.** Allusion to I *Corinthians*, XIII, 6. – (Translator's note.)

**52.** The eminent scholar, Mr Charles Newton Scott, has kindly written to me that he sees in the title *By the Rivers of Waters* a quotation from the *Song of Songs*, V, 2 '(Your eyes are as doves) on the bank of the stream.' – (Translator's note.)

**53.** Compare with *Praeterita*:
'Towards the moment in the afternoon when the fashionable modern traveller, having left by the morning train from Charing Cross for Paris, Nice and Monte Carlo, has to put up with some seasickness from the crossing and some irritation at having to struggle to find seats at Boulogne, and begins to look at his watch to see how far he is from the buffet at Amiens, he is exposed to the disappointment and annoyance at a useless train stop at an unimportant station where he reads the name: "Abbeville".

'Just when the train starts off again, he will be able to see, if he cares to raise his eyes for a moment from his newspaper, two square towers dominated by the poplars and willows of the marshy ground that he is crossing. He would probably never want to pay any more attention to them than by this glance; and I scarcely know how to impress upon even the most sympathetic reader the influence they have had on my own life.

'I must here tell the reader in advance that there have been in sum three centres of thought to my life: Rouen, Geneva and Pisa.

'It was in 1835 that I saw Rouen and Venice for the first time – Pisa only in 1840 – and I was able to understand the complete power of any of these great sights only much later. But, for Abbeville, which is like the preface to and interpretation of Rouen, I was already then in a position to understand it and I felt that it provided for me immediate access to healthy work and joy.

'… I knew my most intensely happy moments in the mountains. But for joyful and unmitigated pleasure, seeing Abbeville come into view on a beautiful summer's afternoon, getting off in the courtyard of the Hotel Europe and running down the road to see St Wulfram before the sun had left its towers, are things for which the past has to be cherished until the end. Of Rouen and its cathedral what I have to say will be found, if I live long enough, in *Our Fathers Have Told Us*.' (*Praeterita*, I, IX, §§177, 180, 181.) – (Translator's note.)

**54.** Compare *Praeterita*, the impression of slow tidal currents rising and falling along the steps of the Hotel Danielli. – (Translator's note.)

**55.** Isaac Walton, famous fisherman of the Dove, born in 1593 at Stratford, died in 1683, best-known for writing *The Compleat Angler* (London,

1653). – (Translator's note.)

**56.** Already in *Modern Painters* he mentions 'the serene simplicity of the grace of the poplars of Amiens' (*Modern Painters*, IV, V, 20). The fourth volume of *Modern Painters* was published in 1855. – (Translator's note.)

**57.** M H Dusevel, *History of the Town of Amiens*, Amiens, Caron and Lambert, 1848, p. 305. – (Author's note.)

**58.** When Carpaccio wants to give the impression of great splendour, he has recourse to the draperies hung out of the windows when representing a festival in a town scene. – (Author's note.)

I have never found this remark in any of the great studies Ruskin devoted to Carpaccio (*Guide to the Fine Arts Academy at Venice* and in *St Mark's Rest*, *Altar of the Slaves*. This supports what I said in the introduction to this volume on pages 43 and 44. Nor do I recall ever seeing mention of it in the pages of *Fors Clavigera* devoted to Carpaccio (*Fors Clavigera*, letter 71.) – (Translator's note.)

**59.** The name of Penelope, evoked here in connection with a woman from Picardy, is evoked in *The Story of Arachné* in connection with a female worker from Normandy. 'Arachné was a Lydian girl from a poor family. And as all girls had to, she had learned to spin and weave, and not just weave and knit good strong clothes but to cover them with images, as you know Penelope is said to have woven, or as those which the queen of our own William the Conqueror embroidered. Of which the only ones remaining are those of Bayeux in Normandy, known the world over under the name of *The Bayeux Tapestry*.' (*Verona and Other Lectures*, II, *The Story of Arachné*, §18.) – (Translator's note.)

**60.** 'Your factory chimneys, how much higher and better loved than the cathedral spires' (*Crown of Wild Olive*, Eleventh Lecture). – (Translator's note.)

**61.** *St John*, III, 29. – (Translator's note.)

**62.** Compare with the description of the church tower at Calais (*Modern Painters*, V, 1, §§2 and 3.) – (Translator's note.)

**63.** Compare with *Queen of the Air* (I, II), Proserpina called the Queen of Destiny. – (Translator's note.)

**64.** In reality Ruskin will not speak any more of this exterior chancel wall except by way of simple allusion in the fourth chapter. But you could read a superb description of it on pages 400 and 401 in *The Cathedral* by Mr Huysmans. Unfortunately we do not have the space to reproduce it here. Mr Huysmans who has confessed a quite extraordinary devotion to Our Lady of Chartres nevertheless recognises that the chancel wall is much more beautiful at Amiens than at Chartres. – (Translator's note.)

**65.** The first fixed and established footsteps; wandering tribes called the Franks had swept over the country and recoiled again and again. But *this* invasion of the so-called Salian Franks, will never retreat again. – (Author's note.)

**66.** See the note at the end of the chapter for allusions to the battle of Soissons. – (Author's note.)

**67.** The first four figures of this illustration are explained in the text. The fifth represents the relations of Normandy, Maine, Anjou and Aquitaine. See Viollet-le-Duc, *Dictionary of Architecture*, Vol. 1, p. 136. – (Author's note.)

Here I will describe what appears on the first four maps of France which we have not represented here. The first is simply a physical map of France. In the second there are in the north up to the Somme two small ranges of fleurs de lys, that is to say the Franks. From the Somme to the Loire, a space left blank which I believe is the Roman domination. Brittany is covered with diagonal hatch marks descending from left to right which signify the Bretons; Burgundy, with diagonal hatch marks descending from right to left which signify the Burgundians; the South of France from the Loire to the Pyrenees is covered with horizontal hatch marks which indicate the Visigoths. In maps 3 and 4, Brittany and Burgundy will stay covered with Bretons and Burgundians respectively. But they are the only parts of France to remain unchanged. In fact, in map 3 which shows the results of the battle of Soissons, the space that was white just now between the Seine and the Loire is now covered with fleurs de lys (i.e., Franks). And in map 4, the map of France after the battle of Poitiers, the fleurs de lys have replaced the horizontal hatch marks (the Visigoths) everywhere from the Loire to the Pyrenees, except in the part between the Garonne and the sea. – (Translator's note.)

**68.** Diagonal hatch marks descending from left to right.

**69.** Diagonal hatch marks descending from right to left.

**70.** Horizontal hatch marks.

**71.** More exactly his knight's cloak, in all likelihood the trabea with red and white stripes, the same garment as worn by the kings of Rome and chiefly by Romulus. – (Author's note.)

**72.** Mrs Jameson, *Legendary Art*, Vol. II, p. 721. – (Author's note.)

**73.** Character from the *Pilgrim's Progress* by John Bunyan. – (Translator's note.)

**74.** Mrs Jameson, Vol. II, p. 722. – (Author's note.)

**75.** Ruskin is not the only one, it seems to me, who likes using these characteristics to represent a saint. The best of George Eliot's clergymen and Carlyle's prophets are no more 'preaching saints' than they are 'saints like John the Baptist'. They 'do not spend a breath in disagreeable exhortation'. They are as kind 'to the clown as to the king' and also like 'an honest drink'.

First, in Carlyle see Knox: 'What I like about this Knox is that he had an amusing side to him. He was a man with heart, honest, brotherly, brother to the great, brother also to the little, sincere in his sympathy for both; he had his Bordeaux pipe in his Edinburgh home, he was a gay and sociable man. Those who think this Knox was a dark fanatic, subject to fits of rage, are making a big mistake. Not at all: he was one of the most solid of men. Practical, prudent, patient, etc.' Again, Burns 'was habitually witty and gay, a companion of infinite joy, laughter, sense and heart. He is not a lugubrious man; he has the most gracious expressions of courtesy, the noisiest flights of gaiety, etc.' This is now Mohamed: 'Sincere, serious, but also amiable, cordial, sociable, fun even, and a good laugh besides.' And similarly Carlyle likes to speak of Luther's laughter. (Carlyle, *The Heroes*, translation by Izoulet, pp. 85, 237, 298, 299, etc.)

And in George Eliot, see Mr Irwine in *Adam Bede*, Mr Gilfil in *Scenes of Clerical Life*, Mr Farebrother in *Middlemarch*, etc.

'I am obliged to recognise that Mr Gilfil did not ask Mrs Fripp why she had not been in church and made not the least effort towards her spiritual education. But the following day he sent her a generous piece of lard, etc. You may conclude from that that this vicar did not shine in the spiritual functions of his position and, to be honest, what I can say about him to the good is that he applied himself to fulfil his functions with speed and brevity.' He forgot to take off his spurs when going up to the rostrum and essentially made no sermons. But never was a vicar so well loved by his flock nor had a better influence on it. 'The farmers especially enjoyed the company of Mr Gilfil, for not only would he smoke his pipe with them but also season the details of parish business with plenty of jokes, etc. Riding his horse was the chief entertainment of the old man now that his hunting days were over. It was not just to the farmers of Shepperton that Mr Gilfil's company was agreeable, he was a welcome guest to the best houses in this part of the country. If you had seen him conduct Lady Sitwell to the dining room (as just now St Martin the Empress of Germany) and you had heard him speak to her with his fine and gracious gallantry, etc.' 'But very frequently he would stay to smoke his pipe while drinking gin and water. Here I find myself drawn to speak to you of another of the vicar's weaknesses, etc.' (*Mr Gilfil's Love Story*, translated by Albert-Durade, pp. 116, 117, 121, 124, 125, 126.) 'As for the minister, Mr Gilfil, old gentleman who smoked very long pipes and preached very short sermons.' (*Tribulations of the Revd Amos Barton*, same translation, p.4). 'Mr Irwine in effect had no elevated tendencies, nor religious enthusiasm and considered a true waste of time talking doctrine and Christian awakening to old father Taft and Cranage, the blacksmith. He was not hard-working, nor self-sacrificing, nor very generous with alms and even his belief was fairly broad. His intellectual tastes were rather pagan, etc. But he had this Christian charity which is often lacking in men of illustrious virtue. He was indulgent for the faults of his neighbour and little inclined to suppose evil, etc. If you had met him mounted on his grey mare, his dogs running at his side, with a smile of good humour, etc. The influence of Mr Irwine in his parish was more useful than that of Mr Ryde who insisted strongly on the doctrines of the Reformation, and severely condemned the covetousness of the flesh, etc., and was very learned. Mr Irwine was as different from that as possible, but he was so penetrating; he understood what one meant in a flash, he conducted himself as a gentleman with the farmers, etc. He was not a famous preacher, but he said nothing that would not make you wiser if you could remember what it was.' (*Adam Bede*, same translation, pp. 84, 85, 226, 227, 228, 230.) – (Translator's note.)

**76.** *Modern Painters*, Plate 73. – (Author's note.)

**77.** Words falsely attributed to Foulon, Minister of War, and for which he had his throat cut (July 1789). – (Translator's note.)

**78.** This method is not followed in the following chapters. – (Author's note.)

**79.** Name of the goddess Kâli, one of the incarnations of Shiva, given by extension to the temple and to the town of Puri on the coast of Orissa (Coromandel). – (Translator's note.)

**80.** Capital of Tibet. The Dalai Lama lives in a monastery in the vicinity of Llasa. It is an extremely well-frequented place of pilgrimage. – (Translator's note.)

**81.** On St Benedict, see in *Verona and Other Lectures* the two chapters which should have formed part of *Our Fathers Have Told Us*, in the sixth volume *Valle Crucis*, on England. And notably pp. 124-128 of *Verona*. – (Translator's note.)

**82.** Character from the tales of chivalry, introduced by Tennyson in *Idylls of the King*. – (Translator's note.)

**83.** Miss Ingelow. – (Author's note.)

**84.** After inquiry, I find it is in the plain between Paris and Sèvres. – (Author's note.)

**85.** They appear again at Nanterre under the names St Genevieve's Park and St Genevieve's Close (Abbé Vidieu, *St Genevieve, Patron Saint of Paris*). – (Translator's note.)

**86.** Allusion to *Micah*, IV, 8. – (Translator's note.)

**87.** See generally all the descriptions Carlyle has had occasion to give of Prussian and Polish land, or of the edge of the Baltic shores. – (Author's note.)

**88.** Gigantic – and not yet fossilised!. See Gibbon's note on the death of Theodebert: 'The king pointed his spear – the bull *overturned a tree on its head* – he died the same day' (VII, 255). The horn of Uri and her shield surmounted with high crests of the German helm attest the terror that these auroch herds inspired. – (Author's note.)

**89.** Claudius, Aurelain, Probus, Constantius; and after the division of the empire, to the East, Justinian. 'The Emperor Justinian was born of an obscure race of Barbarians, the inhabitants of a wild and desolate country, to which the names of Dardania, Dacia and Bulgaria have been successively applied. The names of these Dardanian peasants are Gothic, and almost English. Justinian is a translation of Uprauder (upright); his father Sabatius (in Greco-barbarous language, Stipes) was called in his village "Istock" (Stock).' (Gibbon, beginning of Chapter XI and note.) – (Author's note.)

**90.** Character from *The Antiquary*. – (Translator's note.)

**91.** See *Childe Harold* by Byron. – (Translator's note.)

**92.** On the confluence of the Tees and the Greta, see the pages of *Modern Painters* where the verses of Walter Scott are quoted (*Modern Painters*, III, IV, 16, §§36 and 37. On the Greta by Turner, see *Lectures on Art*, §170). – (Translator's note.)

**93.** Gibbon grasps the subject more closely in a sentence of his twenty-second chapter: 'The independent warriors of Germany *who considered sincerity as the noblest of their virtues* and freedom as the most precious of their possessions.' He is speaking especially of the Frank tribes of the Attuarii against whom the Emperor Julian had to refortify the Rhine from Cleves to Basle. But the first letters of the Emperor Jovian, after Julian's death, 'delegated the military command of Gaul and Illyrium (we shall see later what a vast command it was) to Malarich, *a brave and faithful officer* of the nations of the Franks'; and they remain the loyal allies of Rome in her last struggle with Alaric. Apparently for the sole pleasure of varying his language in a captivating way and, in any case, without intimating that there was any cause for such a great change in the national character, we see Mr Gibbon in his next volume suddenly adopting the abusive epithets of Procopius and calling the Franks 'a light and perfidious nation' (VII, 251). The only discernible motive for this unexpected definition of them is that they refuse to be bribed into friendship or allegiance with Rome and Ravenna; and that in his invasion of Italy the grandson of Clovis did not previously send direct warning of the route that he proposed to take, nor even entirely signify his intentions until he had secured the Po at Pavia; subsequently declaring his plan with sufficient clarity by 'attacking almost at the same instant the hostile camps of the Goths and Romans who, instead of uniting their arms, fled with equal precipitation'. – (Author's note.)

**94.** For a detailed illustration of this word, see *Val d'Arno*, Lecture VIII; *Fors Clavigera*, Letters XLVI, 231, LXXVII, 137; and Chaucer, *Romaunt of the Rose* (1212). Next to him (the knight Arthur) 'dansed dame Franchise'. The English verses are quoted and commented on in the first lecture on

*Ariadne Florentina* (§26):

> 'After all of them was Franchise
> Who was neither brown nor dusky of hue
> But white as new falling snow
> *She was courteous, joyous and frank*
> Her nose was long and pointed
> Her eyes were glad and laughing; her eyebrows soft
> Her hair was blonde and long
> She was as simple as the doves in the trees
> Her heart sweet and debonair
> *She did not dare to speak or act*
> *Nor did she have to do anything.*'

And I hope my female readers will no longer confuse Franchise with Liberty. – (Author's note.)

**95.** Their first mischievous assault into Alsace had been provoked by the Romans themselves (or at least by Constantius in his jealousy of Julian) who had used 'presents and promises, the hope of booty and the perpetual concession of all the territories they were capable of conquering' (Gibbon, Chapter IX, 3-208). By any other historian than Gibbon (who has really no fixed opinion on any character or question, but holding to the general truism that the worst men sometimes behave well, and the best often do wrong, praises when he needs to round off a sentence and blames when he cannot, without doing so, end another one), we might have been surprised to be told here of the nation 'which deserved, assumed and maintained the honourable name of freemen', that 'these undisciplined robbers treated as their natural enemies all the subjects of the empire who possessed any property which they were desirous of acquiring'. The first campaign of Julian which throws back the Franks and Germans across the Rhine, but grants the Salian Franks, under solemn oath, the territories situated in the Netherlands, will be traced at another time. – (Author's note.)

**96.** Ronsard is in fact intended. – (Translator's note.)

**97.** Recounts – in quarters. – (Translator's note.)

**98.** It is for Ruskin characteristic of bad writers. Compare 'Never think that Milton uses epithets to fill out his verse, as would a shallow writer. He needs all of them, and not one more than he uses.' (*Sesame and Lilies, Of*

*Kings' Treasuries*, 21). See also later on. – (Translator's note.)

**99.** Allusion to the *Epistle to the Ephesians*: 'Have for your reins truth for a girdle' (*St Paul, Epistle to the Ephesians*, VI, 14). St Paul in effect does nothing more here than pick up an image from *Isaiah*. 'And justice will be the girdle for his reins' (*Isaiah*, XI, 5). See also *St Peter*: 'Come, then, having girdled the reins of your spirit.' (*First Epistle*, I, 13.) – (Translator's note.)

**100.** Compare *Val d'Arno* relative to a statue in Chartres Cathedral and a painting in Westminster Abbey: 'At Chartres and at Westminster … the highest rank has as a distinctive symbol the flowing hair, etc. If you do not know how to read these symbols you have nothing before you but a stiff and uninteresting figure' (*Val d'Arno*, VIII, 212). There is here besides a lot more than that – and one can love without knowing how to read these symbols – in these statues of Chartres. And Ruskin has demonstrated it himself in admirable pages (*The Two Paths*, I, 33 and following) that I have quoted later, in note 190. – (Translator's note.)

**101.** One will enter further into the thinking behind this sentence when approaching it from the end of Chapter II in *Seven Lamps of Architecture* (*Lamp of Truth*, p. 139 from the Elwall translation): 'The architecture of the Middle Ages crumbled because it had lost its strength and lost all strength of resistance, by disobeying its own laws, in sacrificing a single truth. It is good for us to remember this as we tread on the bare ground of its foundations and stumble over its scattered stones. These broken skeletons of pierced walls through which our sea breezes moan and murmur, strewing them piece by piece and bone by bone, along the bleak promontories on which previously the houses of prayer took the place of pharos lights – these grey arches and quiet naves under which the sheep of our valleys feed and rest on the grass that has buried the altars – these shapeless heaps, which are not of the earth, which lift our fields into strange banks of flowers, or stay the course of our torrents with stones that are not their own, have other thoughts to ask from us than those of mourning for the rage that despoiled or the fear that forsook them. It was not the robber, nor the fanatic, nor the blasphemer who sealed the destruction they had wrought; war, wrath, terror might have marked their worst, and the strong walls would have risen and the slim columns would have started up again from under the land of the destroyer. But they could not rise from the ruins of their own violated truth.' – (Translator's note.)

**102.** 'Do not let the sun go down on your anger' (*St Paul, Epistle to the Ephesians*, IV, 26). – (Translator's note.)

**103.** Read Mr Plimsoll's article on coal mines for instance. – (Author's note.)

**104.** Beheaded in 1535, on the order of Henry VIII, for having refused to preach the sermon on supremacy. – (Translator's note.)

**105.** In the whole of this portrait of Clovis, Ruskin reveals a tendency not to give too unfavourable a moral interpretation of hardness, a tendency that exists also in Carlyle, it seems to me (see in Carlyle, *Cromwell*, etc.) In this, there are I believe, two things. First, a sort of historical or sociological gift that knows how to discover a different moral intention in apparently identical actions, according to the time and the civilisation, and to connect the extremely diverse forms which the same morality or immorality assumes through the ages. This gift exists to a very high degree in writers such as Ruskin, and still more in George Eliot. It exists also in Mr Tarde. Secondly, a literary man with a certain kind of imagination may naturally appreciate a wild lack of education. At times, even in Ruskin's letters, this taste is recognised by a certain affectation of hardness and non-conformity. Read in Mr de la Sizeranne's book, p. 61, Ruskin's answer to a vicar in debt: 'You should try begging first; I would not forbid you from stealing if that was necessary. But don't buy things you can't pay for. And of all kinds of debtors, pious people building churches they can't pay for are, in my opinion, the most detestable fools. And you are, of all people, the most absurd, etc., etc.' – (Translator's note.)

**106.** The legend later picked upon this comparison and the walls of Angoulême, after the battle of Poitiers, are said to have fallen at the sound of Clovis's trumpets. 'A miracle,' says Gibbon, 'which may be reduced to the supposition that some clerical engineer had secretly undermined the foundations of the rampart.' I cannot too often warn our honest readers against the modern habit of reducing all history whatever to the 'supposition that', etc. The legend is, without doubt, the natural and faithful expansion of a metaphor. – (Author's note.)

**107.** Robert d'Humières tells me this is an allusion to this English proverb: 'The Ethiopian can no more change his skin than the leopard his spots.' – (Translator's note.)

**108.** Augustin Thierry, according to Grimm's grammar of the Germanic languages, gave: 'Hlodo-wig, famous warrior, Hildebert, amazing in battle, Hlodo-mir, famous chief.' – (Translator's note.)

**109.** When? For this tradition, like that of the vase, implies that Clovis and St Rémy were friends, and that the king had a peculiar respect for the Christians of Gaul, even though he himself had not yet been converted. – (Author's note.)

**110.** It is a curious proof of the absence in mediocre historians of the slightest sense of a true interest in anything they recount that not in Gibbon, nor in Messrs Bussey and Gaspey, nor in the knowledgeable *History of the Towns of France* can I find, in the most conscientious research that my writer's morning allows, what town was at this time the capital of Burgundy or at least in which of its four nominal capitals – Dijon, Besançon, Geneva and Vienne – Clotilde was brought up. The probability appears to me in favour of Vienne (called always by Messrs B and G 'Vienna' with the hope of what profit for the minds of their less geographical readers I cannot say) above all because it is said that Clotilde's mother was 'thrown into the Rhône with a stone around her neck'. The author of the introduction to *Burgundy* in the *History of the Towns* is so impatient to give his little snarl against anything that smacks of religion that he entirely forgets the existence of the first queen of France, never names her nor as such the place of her birth, but contributes only to the knowledge of the young students this beneficial snippet, that Gondeband, 'more political than a warrior, found in the heart of his theological controversies with Avitus, bishop of *Vienne*, the time to have his three brothers murdered and collect their inheritance'.

The one great fact that my readers will find it well to remember is that Burgundy, at that time, by whatever king or victorious tribe its inhabitants may be subdued, comprises exactly the whole of French Switzerland, and even German Switzerland, as far east as Vindonissa, the Reuss, from Vindonissa through Lucerne to the St Gothard being its effective eastern boundary; that to the west, it meant all Jura, and the plains of the Saône, and to the south comprised all of Savoy and Dauphiné. According to the author of *Historic Switzerland*, Clovis's messenger was first sent to Clotilde disguised as a beggar, while she distributed alms at the gate of St Peter at Geneva, and it is from Dijon that she departed and fled into France pursued by the emissaries of her uncle. – (Author's note.)

**111.** Clovis and Theodoric. – (Translator's note.)

**112.** The basilica of St Peter and St Paul. See Abbé Vidieu, *St Genevieve, Patron Saint of Paris*. – (Translator's note.)

**113.** 'You have been taught that, since you have carpets ... "kickshaws" instead of beef for your food, sewers instead of sacred wells for your thirst, you are the cream of creation and each of you a Solomon' (*Pleasures of England*, p. 49, quoted by Mr Bardoux, p. 237). – (Translator's note.)

**114.** Taking the San branch of the upper Vistula. – (Author's note.)

**115.** Note, however, generally that the strength of a river, *ceteris paribus*, must be estimated by its straight course, flats (which almost always give rise to meanders) not being able to provide tributaries. – (Author's note.)

**116.** The considerations on the Vistula and the Dniester, river-ditches of Europe, are taken up in *Candida Casa* (§22), the fourth lecture in the *Verona* collection and the first chapter of *Valle Crucis*. *Valle Crucis* should have been included in *Our Fathers Have Told Us*. By the way, this part of *Candida Casa* is very reminiscent of *Drachenfels* in its historical and geographical views and in its ironic quotations from Gibbon. – (Translator's note.)

**117.** 'They (the seven churches of Ephesus, Smyrna, Pergamon, Thyatira, Sardis, Philadelphia and Laodicea) are built along hills, and through the plains of Lydia, drawing a large curve like a flight of birds or a swirl of clouds, all in Lydia itself or on its border, all of an essentially Lydian character, the most enriched with gold, the most delicately luxurious, the most sweetly musical, the most tenderly sculpted of the churches of those days. In them were united the talents and the felicities of the Asiatic and the Greek. If the last message of Christ had been addressed to the churches of Greece, it would have been only for Europe and for a limited time. If it had been addressed to the churches of Syria, it would have been only for Asia and for a limited time. Addressed to Lydia, it is addressed to the universe and for always' (*Fors Clavigera*, letter LXXXIV). This message of Christ to the seven churches – which is commented on at length in the rest of the letter – is contained, as is well known, in the first three chapters of the *Gospel according to St John* or more exactly in the second and third chapters. In the first, Jesus orders St John to write to the angels of the seven churches. See also the beautiful book of Mr de Voguë on the churches of Asia Minor. – (Translator's note.)

**118.** Then taking up the word, you will say before the Eternal your God: 'My father was a poor Syrian ready to die and he went down into Egypt with a small number of men and he stayed there and became there a great and powerful nation which multiplied itself greatly.' (*Deuteronomy*, XXVI, 5.)

– (Translator's note.)

**119.** Sir F Palgrave, *Arabia*, vol. II, p. 155. I gratefully adopt in the following paragraph his division of the Asiatic nations (p. 160). – (Author's note.)

**120.** Gibbon's fifty-sixth chapter begins with a sentence which may be taken as the epitome of the entire history we have to investigate. 'The three great nations of the world, the Greeks, the Saracens and the Franks encountered each other on the theatre of Italy.'

I use the more general word Goths instead of Franks and the more precise word Arab for Saracen, but otherwise the reader will observe that the division is the same as mine. Gibbon does not recognise the Roman people as a nation, but only the Roman power as an empire. – (Author's note.)

**121.** Recent events have shown the force of these words (Note from the May 1885 revision.) – (Author's note.)

**122.** But the angel of the eternal found her by a fountain of water in the desert, near the fountain which is on the way to Shur. And he said: 'Hagar, servant of Sarai, where have you come from?', etc. (*Genesis*, XVI, 7 and 8) – (Translator's note.)

**123.** *Genesis*, XII, 1. – (Translator's note.)

**124.** Compare: 'There never was only one Greek art, from the days of Homer to those of the doge Selvo' (*St Mark's Rest*, VIII, §92). – (Translator's note.)

**125.** In *The Crown of Wild Olive*, Cincinnatus also symbolised the strength of Rome. 'It was (agriculture) the source of all the strength of Rome and, of all its tenderness, the pride of Cincinnatus and the inspiration of Virgil (*The Crown of Wild Olive*, p. 196) – (Translator's note.)

**126.** Milman, *History of Christianity*, Volume III, p. 36. – (Author's note.)

**127.** I find the same generalisation expressed to the modern student in the term 'Balkan Peninsula' which extinguishes every ray and trace of past history at once. – (Author's note.)

**128.** Gibbon says more clearly: 'From the coast or the extremity of Caithness and Ulster, the memory of Celtic origin was distinctly preserved in the perpetual resemblance of the language, religion and manners, and the peculiar character of the British tribes can be naturally ascribed to the influence of accidental and local circumstances.' The Lowland Scots, 'wheat eaters' or wanderers, and the Irish are positively identified by Gibbon at the time our own history begins. 'It is *certain*' (italics are his, not mine) 'that in the declining age of the Roman Empire, Caledonia, Ireland and the Isle of Man were inhabited by the Scots' (Chapter XXV, Vol. IV, p. 279).

The higher civilisation and feebler courage of the Lowland *English* made them either the victims of Scotland or the grateful subjects of Rome. The mountaineers, Picts in the Grampians, or of their own colour in Cornwall and Wales, have never been either instructed or subdued and remain to this day the uncultivated and fearless strength of the British race. – (Author's note.)

**129.** 'The Phoenix is, from the highest Christian antiquity, the symbol of immortality' (Émile Mâle, *History of Religious Art in the Thirteenth Century*). – (Translator's note.)

**130.** See, in *On the Old Road*, the hope of the resurrection, necessary condition of the song for the Christians. Even in antiquity the song of Orpheus, the song of Philomela, the swan's song, the song of Alcyon are inspired by an obscure hope of resurrection (*On the Old Road*, II, §§45 and 46). – (Translator's note.)

**131.** Allusion to the verse in *Genesis* which precedes Jacob's dream: 'Then he took stones from the place and made of them his bed and lay down in the same place' (*Genesis*, XXVIII, 11). – (Translator's note.)

**132.** Allusion to the Bible – 'Then Moses said: "I will turn away now and see this great vision and why the drink does not consume itself"' (*Exodus*, III, 3). – (Translator's note.)

**133.** I *Samuel*, XVII, 28. – (Translator's note.)

**134.** *St Luke*, I, 80. It concerns St John the Baptist. – (Translator's note.)

**135.** I should myself mark as particularly fatal in the decline of the Roman Empire the hour when Julian rejected the counsel of the augurs. 'For the last time the Etruscan Haruspices accompanied a Roman Emperor, but by a singular fatality their unfavourable interpretation by the signs of heaven was disclaimed, and Julian followed the advice of the philosophers who coloured their predictions with the bright hues of the Emperor's ambition.' (Milman, *History of Christianity*, Chapter VI.) – (Author's note.)

**136.** 'I am alone, to my belief, in still thinking with Herodotus.' Anyone with a mind keen enough to be struck by the characteristic qualities of a writer's personality, and disregarding whatever he may have been told about Ruskin, that he was a prophet, a seer, a protestant and other things that make no sense, will feel that such traits, although certainly secondary, are nevertheless very 'Ruskinian'. Ruskin lives in a kind of fraternal society with all the great minds of all times, and as he is interested in them only so far as they can answer eternal questions, there are for him neither ancients nor moderns, and he can speak about Herodotus as he would of a contemporary. As the ancients have no value for him except in so far as they are 'current' and can serve as illustrations for our daily meditations, he does not treat them at all as ancients. Then again all their words, not suffering from the passage of time and no longer considered as relating to a given period, are of greater importance to him, keeping in a way the scientific value they might have had, but which they had lost as time passed. From the way Horace speaks at the fountain of Bandusia, Ruskin deduces that he was pious 'in the manner of Milton'. And already at eleven years old, learning the odes of Anacreon for his own pleasure, he learned 'with certainty, what was very useful to me in my later study of Greek art, that the Greeks liked doves, swallows and roses just as tenderly as I did' (*Praeterita*, §81). For an Emerson, 'culture' evidently has the same value. But even without stopping at profound differences, let us first note, to emphasise the particular traits of Ruskin's character, that in his eyes science and art were no different (see the Preface, pp. 37 - 41), he speaks of the ancients as scholars with the same reverence as of the ancients as artists. He invokes the one hundred and fourth psalm when discussing discoveries in the natural sciences, he sides with Herodotus (and would willingly oppose his opinion to that of a contemporary scholar) in a question of religious history, he admires a painting by Carpaccio as an important contribution to the descriptive history of parrots (*St Mark's Rest: The Shrine of the Slaves*). Evidently here we would quickly rejoin the idea of classical sacred art (see notes 164 and 314 further on): 'There is but one Greek art, etc., St Jerome and Hercules,' etc., each of these ideas leading to the others. But for the moment we only have a Ruskin tenderly loving his library, making no distinction between science and art, therefore thinking that a scientific theory may remain true as a work of art may remain beautiful (he never expresses this idea explicitly, but it secretly governs all the others and, alone, could make them possible), and asking of an ancient ode or a mediaeval bas-relief for some information on natural history or critical philosophy, persuaded that it is more useful to consult all wise men of all times and of all countries than the fools of today. Naturally this inclination is repressed by a critical sense so just that we can trust him entirely, and he exaggerates it only for the pleasure of making little jokes on 'the entomology of the thirteenth century', etc., etc. – (Translator's note.)

**137.** Even the best catholic historians have too often closed their eyes to the inescapable connection between monastic virtue and the Benedictine rule of agricultural labour. – (Author's note to the 1885 revision.)

**138.** Robert d'Humières tells me that there is here an allusion to the mountains of Switzerland, such as the Matterhorn, etc. – (Translator's note.)

**139.** Gibbon's hypothetical conclusion relative to the effects of mortification and his following historical statement must be noted as already containing all the systems of modern philosophies and politics which have since changed the monasteries of Italy into barracks and the churches of France into magazines. 'This voluntary martyrdom must have gradually destroyed the sensibility, both of mind and body; nor *can it be assumed* that the fanatics who torment themselves are capable of any lively affection for the rest of mankind. *A sort of cruel sensibility has characterised the monks of every age and country.*' – (Author's note.)

How much penetration and judgement this sentence exhibits I hope will appear to the reader as I unfold before him the actual history of his faith; but being, I suppose, one of the last surviving witnesses of the character of the reclusive life as it still existed at the beginning of this century, I can point to the portrait of it given by Scott in the introduction to *The Monastery* as one perfect and trustworthy in the letter and spirit; and for myself I can say that the most gentle, refined and in the deepest sense amiable kinds of character I have ever known, have been either those of monks, or those of servants trained in the Catholic faith. And when I formulated this judgement I did not know of Miss Alexander's *Edwige* (note to the 1885 revision). – (Author's note.)

**140.** The habit of assuming, for the conduct of men of sense and feeling, motives intelligible to the foolish, and probable to those with base souls, prevails with all vulgar historians, partly for the satisfaction of it and partly because of pride; and it is horrible to contemplate the quality of false witness against their neighbours which mediocre writers commit, simply to round their superficial judgements and give them more force. 'Jerome admits, in effect, with specious but doubtful humility, the inferiority of the unordained monk to the ordained priest,' says Dean Milman in his eleventh chapter, following up his gratuitous doubt of Jerome's humility with no less gratuitous affirmation of the ambition of his opponents. 'The clergy, no doubt, had the wisdom to foresee the dangerous rival, as to influence and authority, which was appearing in Christian society.' – (Author's note.)

**141.** The best place to read this chapter is in the church of San Giorgio dei Schiavoni in Venice. One takes a gondola and, in a quiet canal, a little before reaching the shimmering, sparkling infinity of the lagoon, one comes upon this 'Shrine of Slaves' where one can see (when the sun illuminates them) the paintings of Carpaccio devoted to St Jerome. One must bring *Saint Mark's Rest* and read the entire chapter of which I give here an important extract, not because it is one of Ruskin's best, but because it was clearly written under the influence of the same preoccupations as Chapter III of *The Bible of Amiens* – and to give to *The Lion Tamer* an illustration in which one sees 'The Lion'. Ruskin had gone to Venice to study Carpaccio from September 1876 to May 1877, that is to say, two or three years before beginning *The Bible of Amiens*. Here is the passage from *Saint Mark's Rest*:

'But the next picture! How was such a thing ever permitted to be put in a church? Nothing surely could be more perfect in comic art; St Jerome, in truth, introducing his novice lion to monastic life, with the resulting effect on the vulgar monastic mind.

'Do not imagine for an instant that Carpaccio does not see the comical in all this, as well as you do, perhaps even a little better. "Ask after him tomorrow, believe me, and you will find him a serious man."

'But today Mercutio himself is not more fantastic nor Shakespeare himself more gay in his fantasy of "the gentle animal and of a good conscience" than here the painter as he drew his delicately smiling lion with his head on one side like a Perugino's saint, and his left paw raised, partly to show the thorn wound, partly in a sign of prayer:

'For if I must, as lion come in struggle
Into this place, it would be pity for my life.'

'The fleeing monks are hardly at first intelligible except as white and blue oblique masses; and there was much debate between Mr Murray and me, as he sketched the picture for the Sheffield Museum, whether the actions of flight were in fact well rendered or not; he maintaining that the monks were really running like Olympic archers ... I on the contrary estimating that Carpaccio had failed, having no gift for representing rapid movement. We are probably both right, I do not doubt that the running action, if Mr Murray says so, is well drawn; but at this time Venetian painters had been trained to represent only slow and dignified motion, and not till fifty years later, under classic influence, came the impetuous power of Veronese and Tintoretto.

'But there are many deeper questions respecting this subject of St Jerome than that of artistic skill. The picture is in effect a joke; but is it just a joke? Is the tradition itself a joke? Or is it only by our own fault and perhaps Carpaccio's that we make it so?

'In the first place then, you will please remember, as I have often told you, Carpaccio is not responsible himself for this circumstance. He begins to think of his subject, intending doubtless to execute it very seriously. But his mind no sooner fastens on it than the vision of it comes to him as a joke, and he is forced to paint it as such. Forced by the fates ... We must ask Atropos and not Carpaccio why this picture makes us laugh; and why the tradition it records has become for us a dream and an object of mirth. Now that I approach the sunset of my life, not a day passes without leaving me more doubtful of all our cherished contempts and more anxious to discover what root there was for the stories of good men, which are now a goldmine for the mocker.

'And I need to read a good *Life of St Jerome*. And if I go to Mr Ongania I shall find, I suppose, the autobiography of George Sand, and the life of Mr Sterling perhaps; and of Mr Werner, written by my own master and which indeed I have read, but forget now who either Mr Sterling or Mr Werner were; and perhaps also I shall find in religious literature the lives of Mr Wilberforce and Mrs Fry; but not the smallest scrap of information on St Jerome. To whom nevertheless all the charity of George Sand, and all the ingenuity of Mr Sterling, and all the benevolence of Mr Wilberforce, and a great quantity, if we knew it, of the daily comfort and peace of our own little lives every day, are veritably owing, as to a charming old pair of spiritual spectacles, without which we would never have read a word of the Protestant Bible. It is of no use, however, to begin a life of St Jerome now, and of little use to look at these pictures without a life of St Jerome, but you only have to be clear of knowing this much about him, as not in the least doubtful or mythical, but entirely true, and the beginning of facts quite limitlessly important for all modern Europe – namely, that he was born of a good or at least a rich family, in Dalmatia, that is to say midway between the east and the west; that he made the great eastern book, the Bible legible for the west, that he was the first great teacher of the nobility of ascetic scholarship and courtesy, as opposed to barbarous asceticism; the founder, properly speaking, of the well-arranged cell and tended garden, where before there had been only desert and wild wood – and that he died in the monastery he had founded at Bethlehem.

'It is this union of a gentle and refined life with noble continence, this love and imagination illuminating the mountain cave into a frescoed cloister, training its savage beasts to become domestic friends, which Carpaccio has been ordered to paint for us, and with an unceasing refinement of exquisite imagination he fills these three canvases with incidents which mean, as I believe, the story of all monastic life, and death, and the spiritual life for all time: the power of this great and wise and kind spirit reigning in the perpetual future over all domestic culture; and the help rendered by the companion souls of the lower creatures to the highest intelligence and virtue of man. And if at the last picture – St Jerome working while his white dog' [in *Praeterita* (III, 11) Ruskin says that his dog Wisie was exactly like St Jerome's dog in Carpaccio] 'watches his face with a satisfied look – you will compare in your memory a hunting piece by Rubens or Snyders in which the disembowelled dogs roll on the ground in their blood, you may perhaps begin to feel that there is something more serious in this kaleidoscope of St George's Chapel than you at first believed. And if you now care to continue to follow it with me, let us think over this ludicrous subject a little more quietly.

'What account are we given here, voluntarily or involuntarily, of monastic life, by a man of the keenest perception, living in the midst of it? That all the monks who have caught sight of the lion are terrified out of their wits. What a curious proof of the timidity of monasticism! Here are men who profess to prefer heaven to earth – preparing themselves to pass from one to the other – as a reward for all their present sacrifice! And this is the way they receive the first chance that is offered them to accomplish this change of state.

'Evidently Carpaccio's impression of monks must be that they were not more brave or better than other men but that they liked books and gardens and peace, and were afraid of death, consequently recoiling before the forms of danger that were the business of chivalric warriors, somewhat egoistically and meanly.

'He clearly looks at them in their role as knights. What he may afterwards tell us of good concerning them will not be from a witness prejudiced in their favour. Some good he tells us, however, even here. The arrangement, agreeable in its wildness, of the trees; the buildings for agricultural and religious use set down as if in an American clearing here and there, as the ground was prepared for them; the perfect grace of joyous, pure, illuminating art, filling every little cornice cusp of the chapel with a portrait of a saint,* last and chiefly the perfect kindness to and fondness for all the animals. Are you not, when you contemplate this happy spectacle, better able to understand what sort of men they were who first secured from the tumult of war the sweet corners of meadow beside your own mountain streams, at Bolton and Fountains, Furness and Tintern? But of the saint himself Carpaccio has nothing but good to tell you. The common monks were at least inoffensive creatures, but here is a strong and benevolent one. "Calm, before the lion!" says the guide with his usual perspicacity, as if, alone, the saint had the courage to confront the raging beast – a Daniel in the lions' den! They might as well say of Carpaccio's beauty that she is calm before the lapdog. The saint is leading in his new pet as he would a lamb, and he vainly exhorts his brethren not to be ridiculous.

'The grass on which they have dropped their books is ornamented with flowers; there is no sign of trouble or asceticism on the old man's face, he is evidently altogether happy, his life being complete and the entire scene one of ideal simplicity and security of heavenly wisdom:

"Her ways are ways of pleasantness and all her paths are peace."' – (Translator's note.)

The biblical verse which ends this quotation is taken from *Proverbs* (III, 17).

*See the part of the monastery visible in the distance, in the lion picture, with its fragments of fresco on the wall, its door covered with ivy, and its illuminated cornice.

**142.** Milman, *History of Christianity*, Vol. III, p. 162. Note the sentence in italics, for it relates the true origin of the papacy. – (Author's note.)

**143.** *St Matthew*, X, 37. Compare *Fors Clavigera*: 'There comes a time for all his true disciples when these words of Christ must enter into their hearts: "He who loves his father and mother more than me is not worthy of me." Leave the house in which you are at home, be in contention with those who are dear to you: that is it – if Christ's words mean anything – that is just what will be asked of his true disciples.' – (Translator's note.)

**144.** *Sesame and Lilies, Of Kings' Treasuries*, 17: 'What singular and salutary effect it would have on us who are used to taking the accepted use of a word for its true sense, if we kept the Greek form *biblos* or *biblion* as the correct word for "book", instead of using it only for the special case when we wanted to give it the dignity of the idea and translated it into English everywhere else we met it. For example, we would translate *The Acts of the Apostles* (XIX, 19) "Many of those who practised the magic arts brought their bibles together and burned them in front of all the men, and worked out their value and found it to be fifty thousand pieces of silver." And if, on the contrary, we were to translate that according to our usual custom, and speak always of the Holy Book instead of the Holy Bible,' etc. – (Translator's note.)

**145.** This sort of ignorance deep in their souls is at the base of Ruskin's idea of all the prophets, that is to say of all men truly inspired. Speaking of himself, he says: 'Thus, year by year, I have been led to speak, knowing no more, when I unfolded the scroll where my message was contained, what next would be written there, than a blade of grass knows what the form of its first fruit will be' *Fors Clavigera*, IV, letter LXXVIII, p. 121) and speaking of the last days of Moses: 'The whole history of those forty years was unfolded before him, and the mystery of his own ministries revealed to him' (*Modern Painters*, IV, V, XX, 46, quoted by Mr Brunhes). But this future that men do not see is already contained in their hearts. And it seems to me that Ruskin never expressed it in a more mysterious and beautiful way than in this sentence on Giotto as a child, when he saw Florence for the first time: 'He saw at his feet the innumerable towers of the city of lilies, the depths of his own heart yet hiding the fairest of them all (the Campanile)' (p. 320 of the American edition of *The Poetry of Architecture; Giotto and his Work in Padua*). – (Translator's note.)

**146.** *St Luke*, XVI, 31. – (Translator's note.)

**147.** Gibbon, Chapter XV (II, 277). – (Author's note.)

**148.** *Ibid.*, II, 283. – His expression 'the best educated and wealthiest' must be retained and confirmation of this fact, which constantly appears in Christianity, that minds modest in their conceptions and lives little concerned with gain are the most likely to receive what there is of the eternal in Christian principles. – (Author's note.)

**149.** *St Paul, Ephesians*, II, 2 and V, 16; – *Colossians*, III, 6. – (Translator's note.)

**150.** *St Matthew*, XVI, 24; – *St Mark*, VIII, 34 and X, 21. See in the postscript of my introduction a sentence from *Lectures on Art* in which these words of Matthew are beautifully interpreted. – (Translator's note.)

**151.** One of the most curious aspects of modern evangelical thought is the pleasing connection established between the truth of the Gospel and the extension of lucrative commerce! – (Author's note.)

**152.** 'Take also the helmet of salvation and the sword of the Spirit, which is the word of God' (*St Paul, Ephesians*, VI, 17). St Paul develops the image in the *Epistle to the Hebrews* (IV, 12). – (Translator's note.)

**153.** See the passage from *Praeterita* (III, 34, 39) quoted by Mr Bardoux, where Ruskin discusses the Bible with a protestant 'who did not trust himself to interpret all the possible feelings of men and angels' and where at Turin he enters a temple in which a sermon is preached to fifteen old women 'who are, at Turin, the only children of God'. – (Translator's note.)

**154.** Ruskin had said previously (1856) with a somewhat different feeling: 'This art of drawing which is of more importance for the human race than the art of writing, for people have difficulty drawing something without being of some use to others and themselves and have difficulty writing something without wasting their time and that of other people.' (*Modern Painters*, IV, XVII, 31, quoted by Mr de la Sizeranne.) – (Translator's note.)

**155.** *Commentaries on the Galatians*, Chapter III. – (Author's note.)

**156.** A typically Ruskinian allusion to the etymology of the word: Sophia; here it is hardly a pun, but the reader has been able to see in the previous chapter just how far Ruskin's etymological enthusiasm could take him, in the case of the meaning delicately 'saline' of the word *salique* and in the puns with 'salted' and 'salient'. But taking into consideration the above passage only (Sophia – Wisdom), it finds its explanation (and with it, all of Ruskin's plays on words, even the most tiresome) in the following lines of *Sesame and Lilies, Of Kings' Treasuries*, 15: 'A well-educated gentleman is learned in the peerage of words; knows the words of true descent and ancient blood, at a glance, from words of modern slang; remembers all their ancestry, their inter-marriages, distant relationships, and the extent to which they were admitted, and the offices they held, among the national nobility of words at any time, and in any country,' etc. I have not the time to show that here again there is a form of idolatry, and one of those to which the temptation of a man of taste has the most difficulty not to succumb. – (Translator's note.)

**157.** 'Every Sunday, if not more often, the greatest number of right thinking people in England gratefully receive, from their masters, a blessing formulated thus: "The grace of our Lord Jesus Christ, the love of God and the communion of the Holy Spirit be with you." Now I do not know what sense is attributed in the English public mind to these expressions. But what I have to say to you positively is that the three things exist in a real and actual way, can be known by you, if you want to know them, and possessed by you if you want to possess them.'

Follow the commentary on these three words (*Lectures on Art*, IV, §125). – (Translator's note.)

**158.** See the last paragraph of page 45 of *The Shrine of the Slaves*. Strangely, as I revise this page for the printers, a clipping from the newspaper *The Christian* is sent to me, in which a comment by the orthodox evangelical editor could in the future serve to define for us the heresy of his sect; in his extreme audacity, he actually *opposes* the power of the Holy Spirit to the work of Christ (I only wish I had been at Matlock and heard the kind doctor's sermon).

'An interesting and somewhat unusual sight was witnessed last Saturday in Derbyshire; two old fashioned friends – dressed in original Quaker garb – preaching at the roadside to a large and attentive audience in Matlock. One of them, who as a doctor has a good practice in the county and goes by the name of Dr Charles A Fox, made an energetic appeal to his listeners, pressing them to see to it that each of them was living quietly in the light of the Holy Spirit within. Christ within was the hope of glory, and it was as he was followed in the ministry of the Spirit that we were saved by him, who became thus to each the beginning and the end of the law. He recommended to his listeners that they not build their house on the sand by believing in the free and easy Gospel so commonly preached to the wayside hearers, as if we were saved by believing this or that. Nothing short of the work of the Holy Spirit in the soul of each one of us could save us, and to preach anything short of this was simply to delude the simple and unwary in the most terrible manner.

*'It would be disloyal to criticise an address after such a short extract, but we must express the conviction of our knowledge that it is the obedience of Christ unto death, the death on the cross, rather than the action of the Holy Spirit in us, which constitutes the good news for sinners. Ed.'*

Regarding this editorial piece of modern English press theology, I will simply place the fourth, sixth and thirteenth verses of *Romans* (putting into italics the expressions which are of the greatest importance and which are always neglected): 'that the justice of the LAW might be fulfilled *in us*, who walk not according to the flesh but according to the spirit … for to have the spirit *turned* to things of the flesh, is death, but to things of the spirit, is life, and peace … For if you live for the flesh, you will die; but if *it is through the spirit* that you mortify the *deeds* of the body, you will live.'

It would be well for Christianity that the baptismal service explained what it professes to abjure. – (Author's note.)

**159.** Compare: 'You are perhaps surprised to hear Horace spoken of as a pious person. Wise men know he is wise, sincere men know he is sincere. But pious men, for want of attention, do not always know he is pious. One great obstacle to your understanding of him is that you were made to construct Latin verses with the required introduction of the word Jupiter when you were in need of a dactyl. And you always feel Horace only used it when he needed a dactyl. Note the assurance that he gives us of his piety: *Dis, pietas mea, et musa, cordi est*, etc. (*Val d'Arno*, Chapter IX, §§218, 219, 220, 221 and following). See also: 'Horace is as exactly sincere in his religious faith as Wordsworth, but all the ability to understand the honest classic poets has been taken away from most of our gentlemen by the mechanical exercise of versification at school. Throughout the whole of their lives, they never can rid themselves of this idea that all verses were written as exercises and that Minerva was just a convenient word to put last but one in a hexameter and Jupiter as the last. Nothing is more fallacious … Horace dedicates his favourite pine to Diana, sings his autumnal hymn to Faunus, guides the noble youth of Rome in his hymn to Apollo, and tells the farmer's young daughter that the Gods will love her although she has only a handful of salt and flour to give them – just as seriously as ever an English gentleman taught the Christian faith to the youth of England, in England's truest days' (*The Queen of the Air*, I, 47, 48). And finally: 'The faith of Horace in the spirit of the fountain of Brundisium, in the faun of his hillside, and in the protection of the great gods is constant, deep and effective' (*Fors Clavigera*, Letter XCII, 111). – (Translator's note.)

**160.** See *Praeterita*, I. – (Translator's note.)

**161.** Compare *Praeterita*, I, XII: 'I admire what I could have been if at that moment love had been with me instead of against me, if I had had the joy of a permitted love and the incalculable encouragement of its sympathy and admiration.' It is always the same idea as sorrow, doubtless because it is a form of egoism and an obstacle to the full exercise of our faculties. Just as earlier: 'All the adversities, which reside in *temptation* or in *distress*,' and in the preface to *Arrows of the Chace*: 'I have said to my country words of which not one has been altered by interest or weakened by pain.' And in the text which occupies us *sorrow* is compared to *fault*, as in these passages temptation is compared to pain and interest to distress. 'Nothing is so frivolous as the dying,' said Emerson. For another point of view, that of Ruskin's sensibility, the quotation from *Praeterita*: 'What would I have become if love had been with me instead of against me,' should be compared to this letter from Ruskin to Rossetti, given by Mr Bardoux: 'If you are told that I am hard and cold, be assured that is not true. I have no friendships and no loves, in effect; but for all that I cannot read the epitaph of the Spartans to the people of Thermopylae without my eyes filling with tears, and there is still, in one of my drawers, an old glove that has been there for eighteen years and which is still today full of meaning to me. But if on the other hand you ever feel yourself disposed to think me particularly good, you would be as wrong as those who have the opposite opinion of me. My only pleasures consist of seeing, thinking, reading and making other men happy to the extent possible, without harming my own good.' – (Translator's note.)

**162.** Compare: 'How much have I loved – and not to egoistic ends – the morning light is still visible to me on these hills, and you who read me, you can believe in my thoughts and in my words, in the books I will write for you, and you will then be happy at having believed me' (*The Queen of the Air*, III). – (Translator's note.)

**163.** Compare: 'Every great symbol and oracle of paganism is already understood in the Middle Ages and, at the gate of Avallon which is of the twelfth century, we see on one side Herodias and his daughter and on the other Nessus and Deianire' (*Verona and Other Lectures*, IV, *Mending of the Sieve*, §14). – (Translator's note.)

**164.** Similarly in *Val d'Arno*, the lion of St Mark descends directly from the lion of Nemea, and the crest which crowns him is that which one sees on the head of Hercules of Carnarina (*Val d'Arno*, I, §16, p.13) with this difference indicated elsewhere in the same work (*Val d'Arno*, VIII, §203, p.169) 'that Heracles kills the beast and makes a helmet and cloak of his skin, while the Greek St Mark converts the beast, and makes an evangelist of him.'

It is not in order to find another sacred genealogy for the lion of Nemea that we have quoted this passage, but to insist on the entire thinking at the end of this chapter of *The Bible of Amiens* 'that there is a sacred classic literature'. Ruskin did not want (*Val d'Arno*) Greek to be opposed to Christian, but to Gothic (p.161), 'for St Mark is Greek like Heracles'. We are touching here on one of Ruskin's most important ideas or, more exactly, one of his most original feelings towards the contemplation and study of Greek and Christian works of art, and it is necessary, to make it well understood, to quote a passage from *St Mark's Rest* which, in our opinion, is one of those in the works of Ruskin where that particular disposition of mind is better shown and better seen at work, which made him take no heed of the coming of Christianity, recognise an already Christian beauty in pagan works, and follow the persistence of a Hellenic ideal in the works of the Middle Ages. That this disposition of mind, which we believe to be wholly aesthetic, at least logically in its essence if not chronologically in its origin, was systematised in Ruskin's mind and that he extended it to historical and religious criticism is certain indeed. But even when Ruskin compares Greek royalty and Frank royalty (*Val d'Arno, Franchise*), when he declares in *The Bible of Amiens* that 'Christianity has brought no great change to the human ideal of virtue and happiness,' when, as we saw on the previous page, he speaks of the religion of Horace, he simply draws theoretical conclusions from the aesthetic pleasure he experienced upon recognising a canephora in Herodias' daughter, a harpy in a cherub, a Greek vase in a Byzantine dome. Here is the passage from *St Mark's Rest*: 'And this is true, not of Byzantine art only, but of the whole of Greek art. There is but one Greek art, from Homer's day down to the doge Selvo's (we could say from Theognis to the countess Mathieu de Noailles), 'and these St Mark's mosaics are as truly wrought in the power of Daedalus, with the Greek instinct for building, and in the power of Athena, with the Greek religious soul, as ever chest of Cypselus or shaft of Erechtheum.'

Then Ruskin enters the baptistery of St Mark's and says: 'Over the door is Herod's feast. Herodias' daughter dances with the head of John the Baptist in a basket on her head; it is simply the translation of any Greek girl on a Greek vase, bearing a pitcher on her head … Let us pass now into the farther chapel under the darker dome. Very dark, for my old eyes hardly decipherable, for yours, if they are young and bright, it should be beautiful, for it is indeed the origin of all those gold-domed backgrounds of Bellini and Cimabue and Carpaccio; itself a Greek vase, but with new Gods. The ten-winged cherub which is in the recess behind the altar has written on the circle in its breast 'Fullness of Wisdom'. It symbolises the breadth of the Spirit, but it was once no more than a Greek harpy and on its limbs very little flesh barely dissimulates the claws of birds that they were. Above, Christ himself ascends, borne in a whirlwind of angels and, as the vaults of Bellini and Carpaccio are only the amplification of the harpy, so the paradise of Tintoretto is only the final realisation of the thought contained in this narrow cupola.

'… These mosaics are not earlier than the nineteenth century. And yet they are still absolutely Greek in all the modes of thought and forms of tradition. The fountains of fire and water are pure forms of the Chimera and the Siren, and the dancing girl, though a princess of the thirteenth century in sleeves of ermine, is still the phantom of some sweet girl carrying water from a fountain in Arcadia.'

For me, this page has not only the charm of having been read in the baptistery of St Mark's, in those blessed days when, with some other disciples 'in spirit and in truth' of the master, we would go about Venice in a gondola, listening to the teachings by the water's edge, and landing at each one of the temples that seemed to spring up from the sea to offer us the object of his descriptions and the very image of his thought, to give life to his books, whose immortal reflection shines in them today. But if these churches are the life of Ruskin's books, they are also their spirit. (The line repeated by Fantasio: 'You call me your life, call me your soul' never had a more appropriate application.) Undoubtedly, Ruskin's books have retained something of the beauty of these places. Undoubtedly, if Ruskin's books had not first created in us a kind of fever and desire that, in our imagination, gave to Venice and Amiens a beauty which, once in their presence, we did not find in them at first, the shimmering sun of the canal or the golden cold of a French autumn morning on which they were read has given these pages a charm we only feel later, less fascinating than when they were first read, but deeper perhaps and which they will keep indelibly as if they had been dipped in some chemical preparation which leaves beautiful, verdant reflections on the pages, and which, here, is nothing but the special colour of the past. Indeed, if this page from *St Mark's Rest* had no other charm, we would not have to quote it here. But it seems to us that commenting on this ending of the chapter from *The Bible of Amiens* will make you understand its profound meaning and its uniquely 'Ruskinian' character. And compared with similar pages (see notes 136 and 314), it will enable the reader to discover an aspect of Ruskin's thought which, even if he has read all that has been written to date on Ruskin, will have for him the charm, or at least the merit, of being shown, it seems to me, for the first time. – (Translator's note.)

**165.** 'The Greek himself put Hercules cutting the lions' throats on his pottery or amphorae' (*The Crown of Wild Olive*, Elwall translation, p. 44). – (Translator's note.)

**166.** Allusion to the fourteenth book of *Judges* in which Samson tears apart a young lion 'as if he had ripped up a kid with his bare hands'. 'And here, several days later, he had in the body of the lion a swarm of bees and honey … And he said to them: "From that which devoured comes nourishment, and sweetness exudes from that which is strong"' (*Judges*, XIV, 5-20). – (Translator's note.)

**167.** Against a lion (I *Samuel*, XVII, 34-38). – (Translator's note.)

**168.** Daniel. (See *Daniel*, Chapter VI.) – (Translator's note.)

**169.** Probably an allusion to Virgil: 'Nec magnos metuent armenta leones.' (*Eclogues*, IV, 22.) – (Translator's note.)

**170.** 'They shall not hurt nor destroy in all my holy mountain' (*Isaiah*, XI, 9). – (Translator's note.)

**171.** 'But no man knows of that day and hour' (*St Matthew*, XXIV, 36). – (Translator's note.)

**172.** See the same idea in Renan, *Life of Jesus*, and notably pages 201 and 295. Renan claims that this idea is expressed by Jesus and relies on *St Matthew*, VI, 10, 33; *St Mark*, XII, 34; *St Luke*, XI, 2; XII, 31; XVII, 20, 21. But the texts are rather vague, except perhaps for *St Mark*, XII, 34 and *St Luke*, XVII, 21. – (Translator's note.)

**173.** Compare Bossuet, *Elevations on the Mysteries*, IV, 8: 'Let us contain the lively projections of our wandering thoughts, by this means we will in some fashion command the birds of the sky. Let us prevent our thoughts from creeping as do the reptiles of the earth ... This will be to tame lions as to subjugate our impetuous anger.' – (Translator's note.)

**174.** The spire of Amiens is a carpenter's spire (see Viollet-le-Duc, article *Spire*). – (Translator's note.)

**175.** See *Lectures on Art*, 62-65. The passage quoted above from *The Two Paths* has more relevance to sculpture. – (Translator's note.)

**176.** More exactly, *Of French Architecture*, at least in the place quoted: *Dictionary of Architecture*, Vol. I, p. 71. But in the article *Cathedral*, it is called (Vol. II, p. 336) the quintessential *ogival* church. – (Author's note.)
Ruskin is confused here. In Volume I (p.71) Viollet-le-Duc calls, not the cathedral of Amiens, but the choir of Beauvais the Parthenon of French architecture. – (Translator's note.)

**177.** See the development of these ideas in *Miscellaneous* by Walter Pater (article on 'Notre-Dame d'Amiens'). I do not know why Ruskin's name is not mentioned in it a single time. – (Translator's note.)

**178.** It was a numerical principle with the French architects of the great ages to use the stones of their quarries as they lay in the bed; if the beds were thick, the stones were used in their full thickness, if they were thin, in their inevitable thinness and adjusted with beautiful care to directions of thrust and weight. The natural blocks were never sawn, only squared* into fitting, the whole native strength and crystallisation of the stone being thus kept unflawed – 'never dividing a stone into two. This method is excellent, it keeps in the stone all its natural force, all its means of resistance' (see Mr Viollet-le-Duc, article, *Building (Materials)*, Vol. IV, p. 129). He adds the very notable fact that, to this day, there are seventy departments of France in which the use of the stone-saw is unknown.** – (Author's note.)

On stones used in the direction of the grain or against the grain, see Ruskin, *Val d'Arno*, Chapter VII, §169. Essentially, for Ruskin who establishes no dividing line between nature and art, between art and science, an uncut stone is already a scientific document, that is to say in his eyes, a work of art which must not be mutilated. 'A history is written in them, and in their veins and their zones, and their broken lines, their colours write various legends, never untrue, of the former political states of the mountain kingdom to which this marble belonged, of its infirmities and energies, convulsions and consolidations, from the beginning of time' (*Stones of Venice*, III, 1, 42, quoted by Mr de la Sizeranne.) – (Translator's note.)

*Squaring a stone consists of removing from its two beds the portions of limestone which have preceded or followed the complete geological formation, thereby removing the parts that are susceptible of decomposition (Viollet-le-Duc). – (Translator's note.)

** And Viollet-le-Duc assures us that these are the ones with the best buildings. – (Translator's note.)

**179.** *Psalms* (XI, 4). – (Translator's note.)

**180.** *St Matthew*, XVIII, 20. – (Translator's note.)

**181.** 'For you are the temple of God living as God has said: "I will live in the midst of them and walk there; I will be their God and they will be my people" ' (II *Corinthians*, VI, 16). – (Translator's note.)

**182.** Compare the contrary idea in Léon Brunschwig's beautiful book, *Introduction to the Life of the Mind*, Chapter III: 'In order to experience an aesthetic joy, to appreciate the edifice, no longer as well built but as truly beautiful, one must … feel it in harmony, no longer with some external purpose, but with the intimate state of actual consciousness. That is why ancient monuments that no longer serve the purpose for which they were built or whose purpose fades more quickly from our memory lend themselves so easily and so completely to aesthetic contemplation. *A cathedral is a work of art when one no longer sees in it the instrument of salvation, the centre of social life in a city*; for the believer who sees it another way, it is something else' (page 97). And page 112: 'The cathedrals of the Middle Ages ... may have for some people a certain charm their authors did not suspect.' The sentence in italics is not in italics in the text. But I wanted to isolate it because it seems to me that it is the very counterpart of *The Bible of Amiens* and, more generally, of all Ruskin's studies on religious art in general. – (Translator's note.)

**183.** Compare the related passage from *Lectures on Art* in which the old French expression 'lodger of the Good God' is recalled (*Lectures on Art*, II, §60 and following). – (Translator's note.)

**184.** See note 64 above on these sculptures. – (Translator's note.)

**185.** Compare: 'The work of the carpenter, doubtless the first occupation to be engaged in by the founder of our religion' (*Lectures on Art*, II, §31) – (Translator's note.)

**186.** The philosophical reader is quite welcome to 'detect' and 'expose' as many carnal motives as he pleases, besides the good ones – competition with neighbour Beauvais – comfort for sleepy heads – solace to fat sides, and the like. He will find at last that no quantity of competition or comfort-seeking will procure anything close to the equal of this sculpture; still less his own philosophy, whatever system he adheres to; and that it was indeed the little mustard seed of faith in the heart, with a very notable quantity of honesty besides in the habit and disposition, that made all the rest grown together for good. – (Author's note.)

**187.** Arnold Boulin, master-joiner at Amiens, solicited the enterprise, and obtained it in the first months of the year 1508. A contract was drawn up and an agreement made with him for the construction of one hundred and twenty stalls with historical subjects, high backs and pyramidal canopies. It was agreed that the principal executor should have seven Tournay sous (a little less than the French sou) a day, for himself and his apprentice (threepence a day for the two of them, that is to say a shilling a week for the master, and sixpence a week for the worker), and for the superintendence of the whole work, twelve crowns a year, at the rate of twenty-four sous to the crown (that is to say twelve shillings a year). The salary of the simple workman was only to be three sous a day. For the sculptures of the stalls and the historical subjects they were to deal with, the bargain was made separately with Antoine Avernier, image cutter, residing at Amiens, at the rate of thirty-two sous (sixteen pence) the piece. Most of the wood came from Clermont-en-Beauvoisis, near Amiens; the finest, for the bas-reliefs, from Holland, via St Valery and Abbeville.

The Chapter appointed four of its own members to superintend the work: Jean Dumas, Jean Fabres, Pierre Vuaille and Jean Lenglaché, to whom my authors (canons both) attribute the choice of subjects, the placing of them, and the initiation of workmen 'in the true or highest sense of the Bible or of the legends and having at the same time the simple know-how of the workman up to the height of genius of the theologian'.

Without pretending to apportion the credit for know-how and theology in the business, we have only to observe that the whole company, master, apprentices, workmen, image-cutter, and four canons got stuck in and started work on 3 July 1508, in the great hall of the bishopric, which was to be the workshop and studio throughout the whole time of the business. In the following year, another carpenter, Alexander Huet, was associated with the body, to carry on the stalls on the right hand side of the choir, while Arnold Boulin continued with those on the left. Arnold, leaving his new associate in command for a time, went to Beauvais and St Riquier to see the woodwork there; and in July 1511 both masters went to Rouen together 'to study the pulpits of the cathedral'.

The year before, also, two Franciscans, monks of Abbeville 'expert and renowned in working in wood, had been called by the Amiens Chapter to give their opinion on work in progress, and had each earned twenty sous for his opinion, and travelling expenses'.

In 1516, another name and an important one appears on the accounts, that of Jean Trupin 'a simple workman at the wages of three sous a day', but doubtless a good and spirited sculptor, whose true portrait it is without doubt, and by his own hand, that forms the elbow-rest of the eighty-fifth stall (on the right, nearest the apse) beneath which is cut his name Jhan Trupin, and again under the ninety-second stall, with the added wish, 'Jan Trupin, God provide'.

The entire work was finished on St John's Day, 1522, without (as far as we know) any manner of interruption by dissension, death, dishonesty or incapacity among its fellow-workmen, master or servant.

And the accounts being audited by four members of the Chapter, it was established that the total outlay was 9,488 livres, 11 sous, and 3 obols (décimes), or 474 napoleons, 11 sous, 3 décimes of modern French money, or roughly 400 pounds sterling in English money.

For which sum, you perceive, a company of probably six or eight good workmen, old and young, had been kept happy and busy for fourteen years; and this, that you see, left as a substantial result and gift for you.

I have not examined the carvings so as to assign, with any decision, the several masters' work; but in general the flower and leaf design in the traceries will be by the two head carpenters and their apprentices: the elaborate Scripture histories by Avernier, brightened up here and there with varied oddities by Trupin, and the joining and fitting by the common workmen. No nails are used, all is mortised, and so beautifully that the joints have not moved to this day, and are still almost imperceptible. The four terminal pyramids 'you might take for giant pines forgotten for six centuries on the soil where the church was built, they might be looked on at first as a wild luxury of sculpture and hollow traceries, but seen and analysed close up, they are marvels of systematic order in construction, uniting all the lightness, strength and grace of the most famous spires in the last epoch of the Middle Ages'.

The above particulars are all extracted or simply translated from the excellent description of the *Stalls and External Walls of the Choir of the Cathedral of Amiens*, by Canons Jourdain and Duval (Amiens, Alfred Caron, 1867). The accompanying lithographic sketches are exceedingly good, and the reader will find the entire series of subjects indicated with precision and brevity, both for the woodwork and the external wall of the choir, of which I have no room to speak in this traveller's summary. – (Author's note.)

**188.** The strongest and last to be defended part of the earliest city was on this height. – (Author's note.)

**189.** The cathedral. – (Translator's note.)

**190.** Compare with *The Two Paths*: 'These statues (of the west porch of Chartres) have been long and justly considered as representative of the highest skill of the twelfth or earliest part of the thirteenth century in France; and they indeed possess a dignity and delicate charm, which are for the most part lacking in later works. It is owing partly to real nobility of feature, but chiefly to the grace, mingled with severity, of the falling lines of excessively *thin* drapery; as well as to a most studied finish in composition, every part of the ornamentation tenderly harmonising with the rest. To the extent that their power over certain tones of the religious mind is owing to a palpable degree of non-naturalism in them, I do not praise it: the exaggerated thinness of body and stiffness of attitude are faults; but they are noble faults, and give the statues a strange look of forming part of the very building itself and sustaining it, not like the Greek caryatid, without effort, or like the Renaissance caryatid, by a painful or impossible effort, but as if all that was silent and stern, and withdrawn apart, and stiffened with a chill of heart in the terror of earth, had passed into a shape of eternal marble; and thus the Spirit had given, to bear up the pillars of the church on earth, all the patient and expectant nature that is needed no more in heaven. This is the transcendental view of the meaning of these sculptures.

'I do not insist on it. What I do rely on is their purely naturalistic and vital power. They are all portraits – most of them unknown, I believe – but palpably and unmistakenly portraits, if not taken from the actual person for whom the statue stands, at all events studied from some living person whose features might fairly represent those of the king or saint intended. Several of them I believe to be authentic; there is one of a queen who has evidently, while she lived, been notable for her bright black eyes. The sculptor has cut the iris deep into the stone, and her dark eyes are still suggested with her smile.

'There is something else that I would like you to note particularly in these statues: the way that the floral moulding is connected to the vertical lines of the statue.

'You have thus the supreme complexity and richness of curves side by side with the pure and delicate parallel lines, and the two features gain in interest and beauty; but there is a deeper meaning in this than a simple compositional effect; a meaning that was not denied by the sculptor, but which has so much greater value for being unintentional. I mean the intimate association of the beauty of lower nature in animals and flowers with the higher beauty of nature in the human form. You never have this in Greek work. Greek statues are always isolated; white surfaces of stone, or depths of shadow, bring out the form of the statue while the world of lower nature which they despised was withdrawn from their heart in the darkness. Here the clothed statue seems the type of the Christian spirit, in every respect, weaker and more contracted but purer; reclothed in white robes and its crown, and with the wealth of all creation by its side.

'The first degree of change will be put before you in a moment, simply by comparing this statue from the west front of Chartres with that of the Madonna from the door of the south transept of Amiens.

'This Madonna, with the sculpture that surrounds her, represents the culmination of Gothic art of the thirteenth century. Sculpture has progressed continuously in the interval; progressed simply because it becomes every day more sincere and more tender and more suggestive. Making its way, the old device of Douglas: "Tender and true" can however be taken up again by all of us for ourselves, no less in art than in other things. Believe me, the primary universal characteristic of all great art is tenderness, as the second is truth. I find this every day to be more and more true; an infinity of tenderness is the quintessential gift and heritage of all truly great men. It surely implies in them a relative intensity of disdain for low things, and gives to them a severe and arrogant appearance in the eyes of all hard, stupid and vulgar people, completely terrifying for those who are capable of terror and hateful for those who are incapable of anything more elevated than hatred. The spirit of Dante is the archetype of this class of spirit. I say that the *primary* heritage is tenderness – the *second* is truth; because tenderness is in the nature of the creature, truth in its habits and acquired knowledge; besides, love comes first, as well in order of dignity as that of time, and is always pure and complete: what truth has which is better is that it is perfect.

'To come back to our statue, you will note that the arrangement of the sculpture is exactly the same as at Chartres. A severe falling drapery enhanced at the sides by a rich floral ornament; but the statue is now completely animated; she is no longer immovable like a rigid pillar, but she leans out of her nook and the floral ornament, instead of being a conventional garland, is an exquisite arrangement of hawthorns. The work taken as a whole, although perfectly characteristic of the progress of the age in its style and intention, is in certain more subtle respects inferior to that of Chartres. Individually the sculptor, although belonging to a more advanced school of art, was himself a man with a quality of soul inferior to the one who worked at Chartres. But I do not have the time to indicate to you the more subtle characteristics in which I recognise this.

'So this statue marks the culmination of Gothic art because, before this time, the eyes of its artists had been firmly fixed on natural truth; they had been progressing from flower to flower, from form to form, from face to face, gaining perpetually in knowledge and truth, perpetually, as a result, in power and grace. But having arrived at this point a fatal change was made to their ideal. From the statue, they began to turn their attention principally to the niche of the statue, and from the floral ornament to the mouldings which surrounded it.' (*The Two Paths*, §§33-39). – (Translator's note.)

**191.** Less delightful than the one at Bourges. Bourges is the cathedral of hawthorn. Compare Ruskin, *The Stones of Venice*: 'The architect of Bourges cathedral liked hawthorns; so he covered his porch with hawthorn. It is a perfect Niobe of May. Never was such hawthorn. You would gather it immediately but for the fear of being pricked' (*The Stones of Venice*, III, 13-15). – (Translator's note.)

**192.** Compare: 'Note that calm is the attribute of the highest art.' *Connections between Michaelangelo and Tintoretto*, §219, relative to comparison between the angels of Della Robbia and Donatello 'paying attention to what they are singing, or even transported by it – the angels of Bernadino Luini, full of a fearful conscience – and the angels of Bellini which, on the contrary, even the youngest, sing with as much calm as the Fates while spinning.' – (Translator's note.)

**193.** See, however, pages 32 and 130 (§§112-114) of the octavo edition of *The Two Paths*. – (Author's note.)

**194.** The same shade of meaning (knitted or embroidered) reappears in *Verona and Other Lectures*, p. 47. – (Translator's note.)

**195.** Compare on the apparent and real height of cathedrals and mountains, *The Seven Lamps of Architecture*, Chapter III, §4. – (Translator's note.)

**196.** Compare 'I have seen this inscription engraved above the porch of a good many churches: "Here is the house of God and the gate of heaven"' (*The Crown of Wild Olive*, II). – (Translator's note.)

**197.** Article *Meneau*. – (Translator's note.)

**198.** Against too great perfection in art, see particularly *The Stones of Venice*, II, Chapter III, §§23, 24 and 25; against finish in performance, *The Stones of Venice*, II, Chapter VI, §§20 and 21; against excessive precision, *Elements of Drawing*, II, §104. – (Translator's note.)

**199.** At St Acheul. See the first chapter of this book and the *Historical Description of the Cathedral of Amiens* by A P M Gilbert, octavo, Amiens 1833, pp. 3-7. – (Author's note.)

**200.** Feud, Saxon faedh, low Latin Faida (Scottish 'fae', English 'foe', derivative), Johnson. Remember also that the rest of Feud, in its Norman sense of land allotment, is *foi*, not *fee*, which Johnson, old Tory that he was, did not observe – neither in general does the modern anti-feudalist. – (Author's note.)

**201.**   'Tu quoque magnam
　　　　Partem opere in tanto, sineret dolor, Icare, haberes,
　　　　Bis conatus erat casus effingere in auro –
　　　　Bis patriae cecidere manus.'

There is, advisedly, no pathos allowed in primary sculpture. Its heroes conquer without exultation, and die without sorrow. – (Author's note.)

**202.** See *Fors Clavigera*, Letter LXI, p. 22. – (Author's note.)

**203.** Thus, the command to the children of Israel 'that they go forward' is addressed to their own wills. They obeying, the sea retreats, *but not before* they dare to advance into it. *Then*, the waters make a wall on their right hand and their left. – (Author's note.)

**204.** The original is written in Latin only. 'Supplico tibi, Domine, Pater et Dux rationis nostrae, ut nostrae Nobilitatis recordemur, qua tu nos ornasti: et ut tu nobis presto sis, ut iis qui per sese moventur; ut et a Corporis contagio, Butorumque affectuum repurgemur, eosque superemus, atque regamus; et, sicut decet, pro instrumentis iis utamur. Deinde, ut nobis adjuncto sis; ad accuratam rationis nostrae correctionem, et conjunctionem cum iis qui vere sunt, per lucem veritatis. Et tertium, Salvatori supplex oro, ut ab oculis animorum nostrorum caliginem prorsus abstergas; ut norimus bene, qui Deus, aut Mortalis habendus. Amen.' – (Author's note.)

**205.** Viollet-le-Duc, Vol. VIII, p. 256. He adds: 'One of them is like art' (meaning the general art of sculpture), 'a monument of the first order'; but this is only partially true; also I find a note in Mr Gilbert's account of them, p. 126: 'The two missing fingers on the right hand of Bishop Gaudefroi appear to be a defect that occurred during the casting.' See further, on these monuments, and those of the children of St Louis, Viollet-le-Duc, Vol. IX, pp. 61 and 62. – (Author's note.)

**206.** I steal again from the Abbé Rozé the two inscriptions with his introductory notice of the evilly inspired interference with them.

'The tomb of Évrard de Fouilloy (died in 1222), poured in bronze in full relief, was supported according to custom by enlisted monsters in masonry filling the lower part of the monument, to indicate that this bishop had laid the foundations of the cathedral. An evilly inspired architect has dared to tear down the masonry so that the hand of the founding prelate is no longer visible at the base of the building.

'We read along the edge the following inscription in fine thirteenth century characters:

'Qui populum pavit, qui fundamenta locavit
Huius structure, cuius fuit urbs data cure

> Hic redolens nardus, fama requiescit Ewardus,
> Vir pius afflictis, viduis futela, relictis
> Custos, quos poterat recreabat numere; vbis,
> Mitib agnus erat, tumidis leo, lima supbis.'

Geoffroy d'Eu (died in 1237) is represented as is his predecessor in episcopal habit, but the lower part of the bronze supported by Chimaera is hollowed out, this prelate having raised the building to its vaulting. Here is the legend engraved on the edge:

> 'Ecce premunt humile Gaufridi membra cubile.
> Seu minus aut simile nobis parat omnibus ille;
> Quem laurus gemina decoraverat, in medicina
> Lege qū divina, decuerunt cornua bina;
> Clare vir Augensis, quo sedes Ambianensis
> Crevit in imensis; in cœlis auctus, Amen, sis.'

There is a lot to study in these two monuments; everything is of great interest, from the design, to the sculpture, to the arrangement of the ornaments and the draperies.'

In saying above that Geoffroy d'Eu gave thanks in the cathedral for its completion, I meant only that he had brought the choir into condition for service: 'To its arches' may or may not mean that the vaulting was closed. – (Author's note.)

**207.** In French in the text. – (Translator's note.)

**208.** Compare *Sesame and Lilies*: II. *Of Kings' Treasuries*, 22: 'A "pastor" is a person who *feeds*, a "bishop" is a person who *sees*. The function of the bishop is not to rule, ruling is the function of the king; the function of the bishop is to watch over his flock, to count it sheep by sheep, to be always ready to give a complete account of it. At the end of this road, Bill and Nancy knock each other's teeth out. Does the bishop know all about it? Can he explain in detail how Bill has got into the habit of hitting Nancy, etc. But this is not the idea that we have of a bishop. Perhaps not, but it was St Paul's and Milton's.' – (Translator's note.)

**209.** Allusion to *St Matthew*: 'Now all that happened so that what God had said through the prophet would be accomplished: A virgin will be pregnant and she will give birth to a son and he will be called Emmanuel, which means: God with us' (I, 23). The prophet of whom St Matthew speaks is Isaiah (III, 14). – (Translator's note.)

**210.** See now the plan at the end of this chapter. – (Author's note.)

**211.** *St John*, 14, 60. – (Translator's note.)

**212.** *St Matthew*, XXII, 5. – (Translator's note.)

**213.** *St Matthew*, XXI, 7. – (Translator's note.)

**214.** To distinguish these different lilies better, refer to the beautiful passages in *The Queen of the Air* and *Val d'Arno*: 'Consider what each of these five tribes (of the Drosidae) has been for the spirit of man. First in their nobility; the lilies gave the lily of the Annunciation, the asphodels the flower of the Elysian fields, the iris, the fleur de lys of chivalry; and the amaryllids, Christ's lily of the field, while the rush, trodden always under foot, became the emblem of humility. Then take each of these tribes and continue to follow the extent of their influence. "The crown imperial, lilies of all kinds" of Perdita are the first tribe; which, giving the type of perfect purity in the Madonna's lily, have by their charming form influenced the entire decorative design of Italian sacred art; while the ornament of war was continually enriched by the curve of the triple petals of the Florentine "giglio" and the French fleur de lys; so that it is impossible to count their influence for good in the Middle Ages, partly as a symbol of the female character, and partly of the utmost brightness and refinement in the city which was the flower of cities.' (*The Queen of the Air*, II, §82).

In *Val d'Arno*, in the lecture entitled *Fleur de Lys*, one should note (§251) the recollection of Cora and Triptolemus concerning the Florentine fleur de lys and Hera's crown which typifies the form of the purple iris, or the flower mentioned by Pindar when he describes the birth of Iamus, and which is also found near Oxford. The note Ruskin gives on page 211 of *Val d'Arno* points out that Florentine artists generally place the true white lily in the hands of the angel of the Annunciation, but on the front of Orvieto, it is the 'fleur de lys' that is given to him by Giovanni Pisano, etc., etc., and the whole lecture ends with the beautiful sentence on lilies which I quoted in the preface, page 50. – (Translator's note.)

**215.** 'O Proserpine, have I not here the flowers which in your fright you dropped from Pluto's chariot, the asphodels which come out before the nightingale dares, the dark violets, the pale primroses, the hardy primula and the crown imperial, the irises of every species, and among others the fleur de lys!' (*Winter's Tale*, scene XI, translation by François-Victor Hugo).

– (Translator's note.)

**216.** *Song of Songs*, II, 1. – (Translator's note.)

**217.** *St John*, XV, 1. – (Translator's note.)

**218.** According to Mr Émile Mâle, the sculptor of Amiens was inspired here by a passage from Honorius of Autun. Here is the passage (Mâle, p. 61): 'The asp is a species of dragon which can be charmed with songs. But it is on guard against charmers when it hears them; it is said to stick one ear against the ground and stop up the other with its tail, so that it can hear nothing and evade the incantation. The asp is the picture of the sinner who closes his ears to the meaning of life.' Mr Mâle concludes thus: 'The Christ of Amiens who is commonly called Christ the teacher is in fact something more; he is Christ the conqueror. He triumphs by his word over the devil, sin and death. The idea is beautiful and the sculptor has realised it magnificently. But let us not forget that the *Speculum Ecclesiae* has provided him with the primary concept for his work and has dictated orders to him. At the source of one of the most beautiful works of the thirteenth century we find the book of Honorius of Autun.' (*Religious Art of the Thirteenth Century*, p. 62.) – (Translator's note.)

**219.** 'You will step on the asp and on the serpent and you will trample under your feet the lion and the dragon.' (Psalm XCI, 13.) – (Translator's note.)

**220.** See my summary of the history of Barbarossa and Alexander, in *Fiction, Fair and Foul*, *Nineteenth Century*, November 1880, pp. 752 and following ... See *On the Old Road*, Vol. II, p. 3. – (Author's note.)

**221.** Compare first chapter, §33, of this volume, 'until the same sign is read the wrong way by a degenerate throne.' – (Translator's note.)

**222.** See what Viollet-le-Duc says and the very precise drawings of it in his article *Christ*, *Dictionary of Architecture*, III, 245. – (Author's note.)

See also earlier, page 55, Huysmans' opinion on this statue. – (Translator's note.)

**223.** Psalm XXIV. – (Translator's note.)

**224.** See the circle of the powers of the heavens in the Byzantine interpretations: I. Wisdom; II. Thrones; III. Dominatons; IV. Angels; V.

Archangels; VI. Virtues; VII. Potentates; VIII. Princes; IX. Seraphim. In the Georgian order (Dante, §XXVIII, Cary's note), the angels and archangels are separated, giving altogether nine orders, but not nine ranks. Note that in the Byzantine circle the cherubim are first, and that is the strength of the Virtues which call on the dead to rise (*St Mark's Rest*, p. 97 and pp. 158 & 159). – (Author's note.)

**225.** *St Luke*, X, 5. – (Translator's note.)

**226.** Today the slang word for a priest, among the mob in France, is a *pax vobiscum* or a *vobiscum* for short. – (Author's note.)

**227.** It is there (in the *De orte et obita Patrum*, attributed to Isodora of Seville), says Mr Mâle, that we learn that Isaiah was cut in two with a saw, in the reign of Manassus (Émile Mâle, *History of Religious Art in the Thirteenth Century*, p. 214). At the St Honoré Gate in Amiens, Isaiah is represented with his head split open. – (Translator's note.)

**228.** See the Septuagint version. – (Author's note.)

**229.** In French (ornées de lambris) in the text. – (Translator's note.)

**230.** According to Mr Mâle it is a lion. – (Translator's note.)

**231.** Interpreted differently by Mr Mâle: 'Our artists have represented cowardice at Paris, at Amiens, at Chartres and at Rheims by a scene full of popular good-naturedness. A knight gripped by panic throws down his sword and flees as fast as his legs will carry him from a hare which pursues him; doubtless it is right, for an owl perched on a tree seems to give its lugubrious cry. One could say it is an old proverb or some fable. I would willingly believe that the anecdote of the soldier pursued by a hare was one of a number of little stories that the preachers like to tell their flocks. There is, in *King Somme* by Brother Lorens, something that has a strong resemblance to our bas-relief' (*History of Religious Art*, pp. 166 & 167). See the description of the Patience of the Doge's Palace, from the fourth face of the seventh capital (*The Stones of Venice*, I, V, §LXXI). – (Translator's note.)

**232.** In the cathedral of Laon there is a pretty compliment paid to the oxen which carried the stones of its tower to the hilltop it stands on. The tradition is that they harnessed themselves, but tradition does not say how an ox can harness itself* even if it had a mind. Probably the first form of the story was only that they went joyfully, 'lowing as they went'. But at all events their statues are carved on the height of the tower, eight, colossal, looking from its galleries across the plains of France. See drawing in Viollet-le-Duc, under article *Steeple*. – (Author's note.)

*See Chapter III above: 'The life of Jerome does not start like that of a monk of Palestine. Dean Milman has not explained to us how any man's life could.' – See in Mâle (page 77) a story of Guibert of Nogent related to the oxen of Laon. – (Translator's note.)

**233.** Compare *The Stones of Venice*, I, V, LXXXVIII.

**234.** Symbol of sweetness according to the theologians because he lets the things most precious to him be taken without a fight, namely his milk and his wool (see Mâle). – (Translator's note.)

**235.** The olive branch of concord (see Mâle, p. 170). – (Translator's note.)

**236.** See the Discord of the Doge's Palace (third face of the seventh capital) with Spencer's quotation *The Stones of Venice*, I, V, §LXXI. – (Translator's note.)

**237.** Compare Volney: 'Finally nature has visibly predestined it (the camel) to slavery in refusing it all defences against its enemies. Deprived of the horns of the bull, the hoofs of the horse, the tooth of the elephant and the lightness of the stag, what can the camel do?' (*Travels in Egypt and Syria*). – (Translator's note.)

**238.** Compare the Obedience of the Doge's Palace (sixth face of the seventh capital) and the comparison with the Obedience of Spencer and that of Giotto at Assisi. *The Stones of Venice*, I, V, §LXXXIII. – (Translator's note.)

**239.** 'Rebellion appears in the Middle Ages under a single guise only, disobedience to the church ... The rose window in Notre-Dame de Paris' (these little scenes are almost identical at Paris, Chartres, Amiens and Rheims) 'offers a curious detail: the man who revolts against the bishop wears the conical hat of the Jews ... The Jew who for so many centuries refused to hear the word of the church seems to be the very symbol of revolt and obstinacy' (Mâle, p. 172). – (Translator's note.)

**240.** *Apocalypse*, III, 2. – (Translator's note.)

**241.** Compare the Constancy of the Doge's Palace (second face of the seventh capital): *Constantia sum, nil timens*, and the comparison with Giotto at the *Pilgrim's Progress* (*The Stones of Venice*, I, V, §LXIX). – (Translator's note.)

**242.** *Ephesians*, VI, 15. – (Translator's note.)

**243.** *Song of Songs*, VII, 1. – (Translator's note.)

**244.** At Paris a cross, at Chartres a chalice. At the Doge's Palace (first face of the ninth capital) its motto is: *Fides optima in Deo*. The faith of Giotto holds a cross in her right hand, in the left an amulet, she has a key at her belt and tramples on cabalistic books. On the faith of Spencer (*Fidelia*), see *The Stones of Venice*, I, V, §LXXVII. – (Translator's note.)

**245.** *St John*, VI, 53. – (Translator's note.)

**246.** In this passage it was for me, not the words of Christ, but the words of Ruskin that for many years 'remained in their mystery'. I always thought, however, that what was meant here was the sacred character of food in its most general and material sense and that, in speaking of the laws of life and of the spirit as linked to its acceptance and to its refusal, Ruskin meant to signify the indispensable and constant sustenance that food gives to thought and life, any partial refusal of food translating itself by a modification of the state of mind, as for instance in asceticism. As to the distribution of food, it seems to me that the laws of the spirit and of life are also linked to it in that they depend, if one takes the subjective viewpoint of he who gives (that is to say, the moral viewpoint), upon the charity of the heart and, if one takes the viewpoint of those who receive, and even of those who give (considered objectively, from the political viewpoint), upon strong social order. – But I had no certainty, for I did not find in any of Ruskin's books the same ideas or the same expressions I had in mind. And the works of a great writer are the only dictionary in which one might verify with certainty the meaning of the words he uses. However, this same idea, being Ruskin's, had to be found again in Ruskin. We do not think of an idea once only. We like an idea for a certain time, we come back to it several times, even if it is only to abandon it forever. If you have met in the company of some person a man who is very fickle, I do not say in his friendships, but in his acquaintances, no doubt during the year that follows this meeting you would, if you were his doorman, see entering his house the friend or a letter from the friend you met or, if you were his own memory, you would see, passing by, the image of his ephemeral friend. So with an intellect, should you wish to see again one of its ideas, even if it were only a passing idea and favoured only for a while, you must do as fishermen do: cast an attentive net, move it from one place to another (from one time period to another) according to its catch, even if this must be constantly repeated. If the mesh of the net is tight and fine enough, it would be surprising if you did not stop in passing one of these beautiful creatures we call ideas, which delight in the waters of thought, given birth there by what seems to be spontaneous generation, and where those who love to stroll on the edges of thought are sure to see them one day, if only they have a little patience and a little love. The other day, while reading in *Verona and Other Lectures* the chapter entitled *The Story of Arachné* and having come to a passage (§§25 & 26) on cookery, a key science and the basis of the happiness of states, I was struck by the final sentence. 'Now you are likely to laugh when I say this; and I am happy that you laugh, provided only that you understand only that I am not laughing, but am absolutely and entirely serious, stating to you what I believe to be necessary for the prosperity of this and every other nation: namely, first, diligent purification and kindly *distribution of food*, so that we should be able, and not only on Sundays, but after the day's work which, if it is rightly understood, is a constantly recurring and daily divine service – that we should be able, I say, then to eat the fat meat and drink the sweet liquors, and send portions of them for whom nothing is prepared. (This last sentence is from *Nehemiah*, VIII, 10.) Some day I shall perhaps find a precise commentary on the words 'acceptance' and 'refusal'. But I believe that for 'food' and 'distribution' this passage verifies absolutely my hypothesis. – (Translator's note.)

**247.** 'The fool has said in his heart, there is no God' (Psalm XIV).

The *Dixit incipiens* reappears often in Ruskin. I quote from memory from *The Queen of the Air*: 'It is the task of the divine to condemn the errors of antiquity and that of philosophy to take account of them. I ask you only to read with a sympathetic humanity the thoughts of men who lived, without our being able to blame them, in a darkness that it was not in their power to dispel and to remind you that some accusation of folly can justly be attached to the affirmation: "There is no God." The folly is prouder, deeper and less pardonable which professes: "There is no God except for me" (*The Queen of the Air*, I), and in *The Stones of Venice*:

'As it is written: "He who trusts in his own heart is a fool," and it is also written: "The fool has said in his heart: there is no God." And self-adulation led gradually to forgetting everything except oneself and to a failure of belief all the more fatal in that it still kept the form and language of faith' (*The Stones of Venice*, II, IV, XCII) and also *The Stones of*

*Venice*, I, V, 56, etc., etc. – (Translator's note.)

**248.** According to Mr Mâle, symbol of resurrection, for the cross ornamented with a standard is the symbol of Jesus Christ coming out of the tomb. We shall have our crown, our recompense, on the day of the resurrection. – (Translator's note.)

**249.** The hope of Giotto has wings, an angel before her carries a crown. The hope of Spencer is attached to an anchor. See *The Stones of Venice*, I, V, §LXXXIV. – (Translator's note.)

**250.** Before the thirteenth century, it is anger which stabs itself. From the thirteenth century, it is despair. The transition is visible at Lyon where despair is opposed by patience (Mâle). – (Translator's note.)

**251.** Speaking of the realistic and practical character of Christianity in the north, Ruskin again evokes this figure of the charity of Amiens in *Pleasures of England*: 'While the ideal charity of Giotto at Padua presents her heart in her hand to God, and tramples at the same instant on bags of gold, the treasures of the world, and gives only corn and flowers: that on the west porch at Amiens is content to clothe a beggar with a piece of the staple manufacture of the town' (*Pleasures of England*, IV).

The same comparison (certainly a fortuitous encounter) has also occurred to Mr Mâle, and he has expressed it particularly well.

'The Charity which presents God with its passionate heart is of the country of St Francis of Assisi. The Charity which gives its coat to the poor is of the country of St Vincent de Paul.'

Ruskin again compares different interpretations of Charity in *The Stones of Venice* (chapter on the Doge's Palace): 'Charity is represented in the fifth capital. A woman, loaves of bread on her knees, gives one of them to a child who reaches out her arms towards her across an opening in the foliage of the capital. Very inferior to Giotto's symbol of this virtue. At the chapel of the Arena she distinguishes herself from all the other virtues by the circular glory that surrounds her head and by her fiery cross. She is crowned with flowers, holds in her right hand a vase of corn and flowers, and in her left receives a treasure from Christ who appears above her to give her the means to fulfil her office of charity unceasingly, while she tramples underfoot the treasures of the earth. The beauty proper to most of the Italian conceptions of charity is that they subordinate beneficence to the ardour of her love, always represented by flames; here they take the form of a cross, around her head; in the chapel of Orcagna at Florence they come out of a censer that she has in her hand;

and, in Dante, they set her completely ablaze, to such an extent that in the blaze of her clear flames she can no longer be distinguished. Spencer represents her as a mother surrounded by happy children, a conception which has since been trivialised and vulgarised by the English painters and sculptors' (*The Stones of Venice*, I, V, §LXXXI). See in paragraph LXVIII of the same chapter how the Venetian sculptor has distinguished liberality from charity. – (Translator's note.)

**252.** To ascertain how its once glorious religion is profaned and misread by the modern French mind, it is worth the reader's while to ask at Mr Goyer's (Place St Denis) for the *Journal of St Nicholas* for 1880 and look at the Phoenix as drawn on page 610. The story is meant to be moral, and the Phoenix there represents avarice, but the entire destruction of all sacred and poetical tradition in a child's mind by such a picture is an immorality which would neutralise a year's preaching.

To make it worth Mr Goyer's while to show you the number, buy the one with 'the conclusions of Jeannie' (p. 337): The church scene (with dialogue) in the text is lovely. – (Author's note.)

Mr Mâle is not far from believing that the artist who represented chastity at Notre-Dame de Paris (rose window) intended to portray on its shield a salamander, symbol of chastity because it lives in flames, even has the ability to extinguish them, and is sexless. But the artist having erred and transformed the salamander into a bird, his error was copied at Amiens and at Chartres. – (Translator's note.)

**253.** But chaste nonetheless: 'There we are far from the terrible figures of luxury sculpted on the gate of the Roman churches; at Moissac, at Toulouse, toads devouring the sex of a woman and hanging from her breasts' (Mâle). – (Translator's note.)

**254.** 'Its shield is decorated with a serpent which, at times, coils around a stick. No shield is nobler, since it was Jesus himself who gave it to prudence: "Be prudent," he said, "like the serpents"' (Mâle).

Giotto gives prudence the double face of Janus and a mirror (*The Stones of Venice*, I, V, §LXXXIII). See in this chapter of *The Stones of Venice* the definition of the words temperance, σϱϕϕοσύυη, μαυία, ΰβϕις (§LXXIX). – (Translator's note.)

**255.** Folly, which is the opposite of prudence, deserves to detain us longer. We see her at Paris, at Amiens, on the two portals of Chartres, on the rose window of Auxerre and of Notre-Dame de Paris,* in the guise of a scantily clad man armed with a stick who walks in the middle of stones and sometimes receives a pebble on the head. Almost always he carries a shapeless object in his mouth. That is obviously the image of a fool whom invisible urchins seem to be pursuing while throwing stones. The curious thing is that such a lively figure, who seems to be borrowed from everyday reality, has a literary origin. It is born from the combination of two passages in the *Old Testament*. One reads in effect in *Psalms*: 'The fool has thrown a stone at God, but the stone has fallen on his own head. He put a rock in the road so that his brother would run into it but he will fall over it himself.' There you have the fool of Amiens. He walks on pebbles which seem to roll beneath his feet and a stone comes to hit him on the head.

But what is the object he carries in his mouth? A later passage from *Psalms* explains it to us. Whoever has leafed through some miniature psalters from the thirteenth century has noted that the illustrations, few though they may be, never vary. At the head of Psalm LIII is a drawing of a fool entirely similar to the character sculpted on the portal of our cathedrals. He is armed with a stick and is getting ready to eat a round object which is quite simply, when one looks a little closer, a piece of bread. One reads in effect in the text: "The fool has said in his heart: there is no God. The fool accomplishes abominable iniquities ... *he devours my people as he would a piece of bread.*" One cannot doubt, I believe, that the artist has tried to render this passage. Thus can one explain the so complex figure of folly who, like so many others, has been imagined first by the miniaturists, and adopted subsequently by the sculptors and the glass painters' (Mâle). – (Translator's note.)

\*The figure of folly at the gate of Notre-Dame de Paris has been retouched. A comet that the fool is blowing has replaced the object that he seemed to be eating, and the stick has become a kind of torch.

**256.** Usually the prophecies are written on pennants rather than given on bas-reliefs, as at Amiens. To complete with Ruskinian images the picture that Ruskin provides here, we shall stop quoting only Mr Mâle and compare the prophecies given at Amiens to those inscribed on the baptistery of St Mark's. Readers know that these mosaics are described in *St Mark's Rest*, in the chapter *Sanctus, Sanctus, Sanctus*. And the baptistery of St Mark's, the dazzling freshness of which is so sweet during Venice's burning afternoons, is in its way a kind of Ruskinian Holy of Holies. Mr Collingwood, Ruskin's favourite disciple, to whom we owe, in short, the finest book ever written about him, has said that *St Mark's Rest* was to *The Stones of Venice* what *The Bible of Amiens* was to *The Seven Lamps of Architecture*. I think he means that both subjects were chosen by Ruskin as historical examples, intended to illustrate the laws set forth in his theoretical works. This is the moment when, as Alphonse Daudet would say, 'the teacher goes to the blackboard'. And, in effect, in many respects nothing is closer to *The Bible of Amiens* than this *Gospel of Venice*. But *St Mark's Rest* is Ruskin no longer at his best. In the chapter quoted above entitled *The Requiem* he himself says very movingly: 'Pass on now into the farther chapel under the darker dome. Darker, and very dark; to my old eyes, scarcely decipherable; to yours, if young and bright, it should be beautiful, for it is indeed the origin of all these golden-domed backgrounds of Bellini, and Cimabue, and Carpaccio, etc.' But after all it was to try and see what these 'old eyes' had seen that we went every day to shut ourselves up in this dark and dazzling baptistery. And we can say of them what he said of Turner's eyes: 'Through these eyes, now filled with dust, generations yet unborn will learn to behold the light of nature.' – (Translator's note.)

**257.** Ruskin in a moment of discouragement applied this verse from Isaiah to himself: 'Woe is me,' he cries out in *Fors Clavigera*, 'for I am a man with impure lips, and I am a lost man because my eyes have seen the king, the lord of armies' (*Fors Clavigera*, III, LVIII). – (Translator's note.)

**258.** At the baptistery of St Mark's, as at the Arena of Padua and at the west porch of the cathedral of Verona, the prophecy recalled on Isaiah's amulet is: *Ecce virgo concipiet et pariet filium et vocabitur nomen ejus Emmanuel* (*Isaiah*, VI, 14). And this is the way the inscription appears (being more evocative of Byzantine mosaics for those who happen to have seen them):

```
       ECCE V
        IRGO
       CIPIET
       ET PAR
       IET FILI
       UM ET V
       OCABIT
       UR NOM
```

And these inscriptions, and these brilliant colours alongside the grey allegories of Amiens make one think of the page from *The Stones of Venice* that we quoted above, pages 59 and 60. – (Translator's note.)

**259.** At the baptistery of St Mark's the text from Jeremiah is: *Hic est Deus noster et non extimabitur alius.* – (Translator's note.)

**260.** On the manner of representing rivers see in particular *Giotto and his Work in Padua* in the *Baptism of Christ*. – (Translator's note.)

**261.** 'How are we to believe that the sculptor of Amiens who represented Ezekiel, head in hand before a mean little wheel, had the ambition to illustrate this passage of the prophet: "I looked at the animals and there were wheels on the ground near the animals. From their vantage point ... the wheels seemed to be made of golden stone ... each wheel appeared to be in the middle of another stone. They had a horrifying circumference and height and the four wheels were completely filled with eyes. When the animals walked, the wheels went along beside them. Above was a crystal clear resplendent sky." The total religious horror of such a vision disappears the instant one tries to represent it. These small images inscribed in the quatrefoils are as charming as the clear figures which decorate the French books of hours. But they have retained nothing of the grandeur of the originals which they sought to translate' (Émile Mâle, p. 216, *passim*). – (Translator's note.)

**262.** I am afraid this hand has been broken since I described it, at all events, it is indistinguishably shapeless in the photograph. – (Author's note.)

**263.** English painter (1789-1854). His *Belshazzar's Feast* is from 1821. – (Translator's note.)

**264.** At the baptistery of St Mark's: *Venite et reveramur ad dominum quia ipse capit et sana (bit nos)*. (*Hosea*, VI, 1.) – (Translator's note.)

**265.** Allusion to the verse: 'After that the Lord said to me: "Go then and love a woman beloved of her friend and an adulteress, as the Lord loves the children of Israel who look to other gods and love flagons of wine"' (*Hosea*, III, 1).
And then the prophecy adds: 'So I bought that woman for myself for fifteen pieces of silver and a homer of barley and half a homer of barley.' – (Translator's note.)

**266.** To St Mark: *Super servos meos et super ancillas effundam de spiritu meo*. (*Joel*, II, 29). – (Translator's note.)

**267.** To St Mark: *Ecce parvulum dedit te in gentibus* (*Obadiah*, 2). – (Translator's note.)

**268.** 'They answered him: he was a hairy man ... and Ahaziah replied to them: "It is Elijah the Tishbite"' (II *Kings*, I, 8). This hairy coat was one more similarity between Elijah and St John the Baptist who was believed to be the reincarnation of Elijah (see Renan, *The Life of Jesus*). – (Translator's note.)

**269.** 'He sent to him a captain of fifty with his fifty men' (II *Kings*, I, 9). – (Translator's note.)

**270.** Relates to Ahaziah who had sent them to consult Beelzebub, god of Ekron. – (Translator's note.)

**271.** At St Mark's: *Clamavi ad dominum et exandivit me de tribulatione mea*. – (Translator's note.)

**272.** Compare earlier, on the knowledge one could have of camels at Amiens. – (Translator's note.)

**273.** 'The nations will forge their swords into hoes and their lances into billhooks.' This verse is found in *Isaiah* (II, 4) and in *Joel* (III, 10). After having analysed this passage in *The Bible of Amiens* and isolated the biblical verse that forms its basis, let us reverse the operation, and starting from this verse, let us show how it enters the composition of other pages of Ruskin. We read for example in *The Two Paths*: 'It is not in supporting the sufferings of others but in making an offering of our own that we approach the great change which must come for the iron of the earth: when men forge their swords into ploughshares and their lances into billhooks we will learn how not to make war.' (*The Two Paths*, 196)

And in *Lectures on Art*: 'And Christian art, as it was born out of chivalry, was only possible as long as chivalry forced kings and knights to take care of the people. And it will not be possible again until, literally, *swords are forged into ploughshares*, when your St George of England will justify his name, and when Christian art will make itself known as the Lord made it, when breaking bread.' (IV, 126.) – (Translator's note.)

**274.** The statue of the prophet, at the back, is the most magnificent of the entire series; note especially the 'diadem' of his luxuriant hair, plaited like a girl's, indicating the Achillean strength of this most terrible of the prophets (See *Fors Clavigera*, letter LXV, p. 157). For the rest, this long flowing hair was always one of the insignia of the Frankish kings, and their way of dressing both hair and beard may be seen more closely and with more precision in the angle sculptures of the long font in the north transept, the most interesting piece of work in the whole cathedral, in an antiquarian sense, and of much artistic value also. (See above, Chapter II.) – (Author's note.)

**275.** See in Mâle (p. 198 and following) the interpretation of the sculptures in the porch at Laon, representing Daniel receiving in the lions' den the basket that Habakkuk brought him. This porch is dedicated to the glorification of the holy Virgin. But according to Honorius of Autun, who has it from the sculptor of Laon, Habakkuk getting the basket of food to Daniel without breaking the seal which the king had impressed with his ring and, on the seventh day, the king finding the seal intact and Daniel alive, symbolised or rather prophesied Christ entering his mother's womb without breaking her virginity and coming out without touching the seal of the virginal home. – (Translator's note.)

**276.** At St Mark's: *Expecta me in die resurrectionis meae quoniam (judicium meum ut congregem gentes).* – (Translator's note.)

**277.** The medallion represents a small Gothic monument, a bird is perched on the lintel, and a hedgehog enters through the open door. One thinks of an Aesop's fable, and not of the terrible passage from *Zephaniah* that the artist has attempted to represent: 'The Lord will extend his hand over the north, he will destroy Assyria, and he will make a solitude of Nineveh, an arid land like the desert; flocks will lie down in her midst, animals of every kind, the pelican and the hedgehog, will live among the capitals of her columns, cries will be heard through the windows, devastation will be on the threshold, for the cedar panelling will be rent asunder.' (Émile Mâle, p. 217). – (Translator's note.)

**278.** In French (ornées de lambris) in the text. – (Translator's note.)

**279.** 'In another medallion on Zachariah, two winged women raise up another woman seated on a boiler forming an elegant composition; but what has become of the strangeness of the sacred text? (See verses 5 to 11 of Chapter V of *Zachariah*)' (Mâle, p. 217).

But compare particularly with *Unto This Last*:

Similarly also in the vision of women carrying a bushel, 'the wind was in their wings'; not the wings 'of a stork', as in our version, but 'milvi', of a kite, as in the vulgate; and perhaps still more precisely in the version of the seventy 'hoopoe', of a huppe, a bird that symbolises the power of wealth according to a large number of traditions, of which the wish to have a crest of gold is perhaps the most interesting. The *Birds* of Aristophanes in which she plays a major role is full of these traditions, etc. (*Unto This Last*, §74, p. 148, note). In *Unto This Last*, also (§68, p. 135), Ruskin interprets these verses from *Zachariah*. The bushel or large measure is the 'measure of their iniquity in the whole country'. And if this perversity is covered with a lid of lead, it is that it is always hidden under an act of foolishness. – (Translator's note.)

**280.** See above, Chapter I (§§7 & 8) for the history of St Firmin, and of St Honoré (p. 173, §8) in this chapter, with the reference which is given there.

**281.** On St Geoffroy, see Augustin Thierry, *Letters on the History of France*, *History of the Commune of Amiens*, pp. 271-281. – (Translator's note.)

**282.** At Rheims a portal is dedicated to the saints of the province equally; at Bourges, of five portals, two are dedicated to the saints of the country. At Chartres, all the saints of the diocese figure equally; at Le Mans, at Tours, at Soissons, at Lyon, windows retrace their lives. Thus each of our cathedrals records the religious history of a province. Everywhere the saints of the diocese take pride of place after the apostles (Mâle, pp. 390 and following). – (Translator's note.)

**283.** The study of the labours of the month represented in our different cathedrals constitutes one of the finest sections of Mr Mâle's book. 'These are really,' he says of these sculpted calendars, 'the works and the days.' After showing their Byzantine and Roman origins, he says of them: 'In these little panels, in these beautiful French georgics, man repeats his age-old labours.' Then he shows in spite of this the very realistic and local side of these works: 'Just outside the walls of the small mediaeval town begins the true countryside ... the beautiful rhythm of Virgilian labours. The two steeples of Chartres rise above the harvests of the Beauce and the cathedral of Rheims dominates the vineyards of the Champagne. In Paris, from the apse of Notre-Dame one could see meadows and woods; sculptors imagining scenes of rustic life could draw on immediate reality.' And further on: 'This is all so simple, so sober, so close to humanity. There is nothing of the somewhat insipid graces of the ancient frescoes, no grape-picking lover, no winged genius harvesting. These are not the charming Florentine goddesses of Botticelli who dance at the festival of Primavera. It is man alone in his conflict with nature; and so full of life that, after five centuries, it has kept its power to move.' One sees why after reading this, Mr Séailles, speaking of Mr Mâle's book, could say he knew no finer book of art criticism (Mâle, pp. 390 and following). – (Translator's note.)

**284.** These are the preparations for Christmas. – (Translator's note.)

**285.** Pagan reminder of Janus perpetuated at Amiens, at Notre-Dame de Paris, at Chartres, in many psalters. One of the faces looks at the year which has gone, the other to the coming year. At Saint-Denis in a window from Chartres, Janus closes a door behind which an old man disappears, and opens another to a young man (Mâle, p. 95). – (Translator's note.)

**286.** There are no longer any vineyards at Amiens, but there were in the Middle Ages. At Notre-Dame de Paris, the peasant goes to his vines, at Chartres, at Saumur, he prunes them, at Amiens he digs them. As the wind is cold, at Chartres (north door), the peasant keeps his hood and coat on (*ibid.*, p. 97). – (Translator's note.)

**287.** In August the harvest continues at the north gate of Chartres, at Paris and at Rheims. But at Senlis, at Semur, at Amiens, they have already started threshing (*ibid.*, p. 99) – (Translator's note.)

**288.** In other cathedrals they have already started the grape harvest. France of the Middle Ages appears to have been warmer than ours. (*ibid.*, p. 100). – (Translator's note.)

**289.** At Semur, at Rheims, wine country, work in the vineyards has finished. At Paris, at Chartres, it is sowing time. The peasant has already put his winter coat on again. (*ibid.*, p. 100). – (Translator's note.)

**290.** See the description of the Madonna of Murano in the second volume of *The Stones of Venice*. – (Author's note.)

**291.** On the manner 'in which Raphael thinks of the Madonna' and on Perugino's *Virgin Crowned*, 'falling to the rank of a simple Italian mother, Raphael's *Seated Virgin*', see Ruskin, *Modern Painters*, III, IV, 4, quoted by Mr Brunhes. – (Translator's note.)

**292.** Compare Mâle, pp. 209 and 210. 'Comparisons have been made not without reason at Chartres and at Amiens between the statues of Solomon and the Queen of Sheba. What was meant by that, consistent with ecclesiastical doctrine, was that Solomon represented Jesus Christ and the Queen of Sheba the church which brings the ends of the world closer together to hear the word of God. The visit of the Queen of Sheba was also considered in the Middle Ages as a representation of the adoration of the Magi. The Queen of Sheba who comes from the East symbolises the Magi, while King Solomon on his throne symbolises eternal wisdom sitting on Maria's knees (Ludolphus of Chartres, *Vita*

*Christi*, XI). This is why, on the front at Strasbourg, we see Solomon on his throne guarded by twelve lions and above the Virgin with the child on her knees.' – (Translator's note.)

**293.** Allusion to Chapter II of *Daniel*. The prophet describes to Nebuchadnezzar his own dream which he is going to interpret, and says in describing the dream: 'You are contemplating it (this statue) when a rock breaks off from the mountain, by accident, and hits the statue in its feet of iron and clay and breaks them. Then the iron, the clay, the bronze and the gold were broken' (*Daniel*, II, 34). – (Translator's note.)

**294.** *Exodus*, III, 3, 4. – (Translator's note.)

**295.** *Judges*, VI, 37, 38. – (Translator's note.)

**296.** 'Look, the rod of Aaron flourished for the house of Levi and it brought forth flowers, produced blossoms and yielded almonds' (*Numbers*, XVII, 8). – (Translator's note.)

These four subjects, apparently so far from the story of the Virgin, are brought together in the west porch of Laon and in a window of the collegiate of Saint-Quentin, both dedicated to the Virgin as the portal at Amiens. The connection between these subjects and the life of the Virgin can be found, according to Mr Mâle, in Honorius of Autun (sermon for the day of the Annunciation). According to Honorius of Autun, the Virgin had been predicted and her life symbolically represented in these episodes from the Old Testament. The bush that flames cannot consume is the Virgin carrying within her the Holy Spirit, without burning from the fire of sexual desire. The bush dripping with dew is the Virgin becoming fertile, and the area around that stays dry is her virginity remaining intact. The rock breaking away from the mountain without the help of an arm is Jesus Christ being born of a Virgin whom no hand has touched. Thus Honorius of Autun expresses himself in the *Speculum Ecclesiae*. Mr Mâle thinks that the artists of Laon, Saint-Quentin and Amiens had read this text and were inspired by it. – (Translator's note.)

**297.** *St Luke*, I, 13. – (Translator's note.)

**298.** *St Matthew*, I, 20. – (Translator's note.)

**299.** *St Luke*, I, 61. – (Translator's note.)

**300.** *St Luke*, I, 61 – (Translator's note.)

**301.** *St Luke*, I, 63. – (Translator's note.)

**302.** Performance of a legend reported by all the authors of the Middle Ages. Jesus arriving in the town of Solime made all the idols fall so that the words of Isaiah would come to pass. 'See the Lord arriving on a cloud and all the works by the hands of the Egyptians will tremble at his sight' (See Mâle, pp. 283 & 284). – (Translator's note.)

**303.** On the front of Amiens a rude figure whom two servants are placing in a bath is seen under the statue of Herod with the three Magi. This is Herod who when old tried to postpone death by taking baths of oil: 'And Herod was already seventy years old and he fell into a grievous malady; violent fever, rotting and swollen feet, continual torments, racking cough and worms which devoured him with a pestilential odour and he was badly tormented; on the advice of doctors he was put into oil from which he was taken half dead (*Golden Legend*). Herod lived long enough to learn that his son Antipater had not disguised his joy when he heard the story of his father's agony. Divine anger is manifested in Herod's death ... The sculptor of Amiens showed his ingenuity in foretelling the future and heralding the coming retribution of God when he placed Herod aged and broken beneath the feet of Herod triumphant' (Mâle, p. 283).

I have adopted Mr Mâle's milder version, not wishing to reproduce the crudeness of the original. The reader may refer to Mr Theodor de Wyzewa's fine translation of the *Golden Legend*, but he does not give the passage about the burning of the king's ship. – (Translator's note.)

**304.** 'As Herod was ordering the deaths of the innocents, he ... learned in passing at Tarsus that the three kings had set sail from that port, and in his anger ordered the burning of all the ships, according to what David had said: "He will burn the ships of Tarsus in his anger"' (Jacobus de Voragine, *Golden Legend*, on the day of the holy innocents, 28 December).

The Magi returning in a boat are visible, says Mr Mâle, on a section of the rose window at Soissons and on a window relating Christ's childhood that adorns the apsidal chapel at Tours. – (Translator's note.)

**305.** *St Matthew*, II, 12. – (Translator's note.)

**306.** *Isaiah*, IX, 5. – (Translator's note.)

**307.** Compare *Lectures on Art*: 'The influence of this realist art on the religious spirit of Europe has had more diverse forms than any other artistic influence, for in its highest branches, it touches the most sincerely religious minds whereas, in its lower branches, it addresses itself not only to the most common need for religious excitement, but to the simple thirst for feelings of horror which characterise the uneducated classes of partially civilised countries; not only just the thirst for horror, but a strange love of death which shows itself sometimes in catholic countries by doing their best, in the chapels of the sepulchre, to have powerful images taken literally for actual corpses.

'The same morbid instinct has often won over the minds of the most powerful artists, and the most imaginative, communicating a feverish sadness which distorts their most beautiful works; and finally, in the worst of its effects, the sensibility of Christian women has been universally exploited to lament over the sufferings of Christ instead of preventing those of his people.

'When you are travelling, make sure you study the meaning of sculptures and paintings which, in each chapel, cathedral and mountain path, recall the hours and represent the agonies of Christ's passion, and try to come to an appreciation of the efforts which have been made by the four arts: rhetoric, music, painting and sculpture, since the twelfth century, to tear from the hearts of the women the last drops of pity that his purely physical agony could still excite, for these works almost always insist on wounds or physical exhaustion, and degrade considerably more than they enliven the concept of grief.

'Then try to imagine the sum of time and fearful and shuddering emotion which has been wasted by tender and delicate Christian women during these last six hundred years. (This is somewhat reminiscent of the passage in Chapter II of *The Bible of Amiens* relating to St Genevieve on the subject of female martyrs.) As they thrashed themselves thus under the influence of similar imagery, these physical sufferings endured long ago which, since they were conceived as having been tolerated by a divine being, cannot for this reason have been more difficult to endure than the agonies of any human being under torture; and then try to appreciate what result would have been achieved for justice and human happiness if these same women had been taught the deep meaning of the last words that were said to them by their Lord: 'Girls of Jerusalem, do not cry for me, but cry for yourselves and your children,' if they had been taught to dole out their pity on the tortures of the fields of battle, the torments of the slow death of children succumbing to famine, better yet, in our own peaceful life, the agony of creatures who are not fed, nor taught, nor helped, who wake up on the edge of the grave to learn how they should have lived, and again the even more terrible suffering of those whose entire existence, and not its end, is death; those for whom the cradle was a curse, and for whom the words they cannot hear "ashes to ashes" are all they have ever received of blessing. Those, you who have so to speak wept at his feet where you are held near his cross, those you have always with you! And not him.

'You have always with you the unhappy in death. Yes, and you have always the brave and good in life. They also need to be helped, though you seem to believe they are only there to help others: those also ask that you think of them and that you remember them. And you will find, if you read history in this spirit that one of the principal reasons for the continual misery of humanity is that it is always shared between the cult of angels or saints who are out of its sight, and have no need of support, and proud and wicked men who are too much within its sight and should not have its support.

'And consider how the arts have thus served the cult of the mob. Of saints and angels you have innumerable paintings, of puny courtiers and haughty and cruel kings, innumerable also; what a small number you have (but note that those are almost always by great painters) of the best men and their acts. But consider what our history could have been; or rather, how history could have turned out differently for the whole of Europe if the aim of people had been to pick out, and their art to honour the great acts of the noblest of men. And if, instead of living as they always have up to now in an infernal cloud of discord and vengeance, lit by fantastic dreams of cloudy saintliness, they had sought to reward and punish according to justice, but above all to reward and at least bear witness to human acts deserving the wrath of God or his blessing, rather than seeking to discover the secrets of judgement and the bliss of eternity.'

It is after this sentence that the piece comes on idolatry which I have quoted in the postscript to my preface and which ends this long digression with these words:

'We serve some dear and sad image that we have created for ourselves, while we disobey the present call of the Lord who is not dead, who is not fainting at this moment before his cross, but orders us to lift up our own' (which corresponds exactly to the words from *The Bible of Amiens*): 'substitute the idea of past sufferings with that of our present duty.' (*Lectures on Art*, II, §§56, 57, 58 and 59). – (Translator's note.)

**308.** Jesus said to him: 'What is written in the law and what do you read there?' – He replied: 'You will love the Lord your God with all your heart, with all your soul, with all your strength and with all your mind, and your neighbour as yourself.' And Jesus said to him: 'You have responded well; *do that and you will live*' (*St Luke*, X, 26, 27, 28). – (Translator's note.)

**309.** The most authentic origin of the theory of purgatory in the teaching given through art is in the renderings subsequent to the thirteenth century, of the verse: 'by which also he went and preached among the souls in prison,' transforming gradually into the idea of the deliverance of the saints in waiting from the power of the grave.

In literature and tradition, the idea is originally, I believe, Platonic; certainly not Homeric. Egyptian possibly – but I have read nothing yet of the recent discoveries in Egypt. Not, however, quite liking to leave the matter in the complete destitution of my own resources, I have appealed to my general investigator Mr Anderson (James R) who writes to me as follows:

'There is no possible question about the doctrine or of its universal acceptance centuries before Dante. Curiously enough, though, the statement of it in the *Summa Theologiae* as we have it is a later insertion; but I find by references that St Thomas teaches it elsewhere. Albertus Magnus develops it at length. If you refer to the *Golden Legend* under All Souls' Day, you will see how the idea is assumed as a commonplace in a work meant for popular use in the thirteenth century. St Gregory (the Pope) argues for it (*Dial.*, IV, 38) in two scriptural quotations: (1) the sin that is not forgiven either "in hoc seculo" *or in that which is to come*, and (2) the fire that will try every man's work. I think Platonic philosophy and the Greek mysteries must have had a good deal to do with introducing the idea originally; but with them – as with Virgil – it was part of the Eastern vision of a circling stream of life from which only a few drops were at intervals tossed to a definitely permanent Elysium or a definitely permanent hell. It suits this theory better than it does the Christian one, which attaches ultimately in all cases infinite importance to the results of life "in hoc seculo".

'Do you know any representation of heaven or hell unconnected with the last Judgement? I do not remember any, and as purgatory is by that time past, this would account for the absence of pictures of it.

'Besides, purgatory precedes the resurrection – there is continual question among theologians what manner of purgatorial fire it may be that affects spirits separate from the body. – Perhaps heaven and hell, as opposed to purgatory, were felt to be an appropriate subject for painting because not only souls, but the risen bodies too are conceived in them.

'Bede's account of the Ayrshire prophet's vision gives purgatory in words very like Dante's description of the second stormy circle in hell; and the angel which ultimately saves the Scot from the fiends comes through hell, *quasi fulgor Sellae micantis inter tenebras – qual sul perss del mattino Per gli grossi vapor Marte rosseggia*. Bede's name was great in the Middle Ages. Dante meets him in heaven and, I like to hope, may have been helped by the vision of my fellow-countryman more than six hundred years before.'

– (Author's note.)

**310.** Compare with the literary, artistic and sweet Monastery of St Jerome, where the walls are painted with frescoes, in the quotation from *St Mark's Rest* which I have given in note 141 on pages 247 to 250. – (Translator's note.)

**311.** Ruskin says here *the stones of Amiens* as elsewhere he had said *the stones of Venice*. He also said in *Praeterita*: 'If on the day that I knocked on the door of the Scuola san Rocco the doorman had not opened it for me, I would have written *The Stones of Chamonix* instead of *The Stones of Venice*.' – (Translator's note.)

**312.** All the courageous acts. Ruskin does not think that war is less necessary to the arts than faith. See in *The Crown of Wild Olive* the third lecture on *The War.* – (Translator's note.)

**313.** I do not mean a*esthesis* – but *noūs*, if you must talk in Greek slang. – (Author's note.)

**314.** Every reader with a little metaphysical flair will find a certain relation between the idea expressed here (beginning with 'All human creatures') and the theory of divine inspiration in Chapter III: 'He is not gifted with higher ability, nor called into new offices, but enabled to use the natural powers granted him, he becomes inspired ... according to the capacities of his nature,' and this remark: 'The form which the monastic spirit took in later times depended far more ... than on any change brought about by Christianity in the ideal of human virtue and happiness.' Ruskin often insisted on this last idea, saying that the worship offered by a heathen to Jupiter was not very different from the one a Christian offered, etc. ... Moreover, in this same Chapter III of *The Bible of Amiens*, the College of Augurs and the institution of the Vestal Virgins are compared to the Christian monastic orders. Though this idea may seem to be, by the connection one sees, close to those that precede it and allied to them, it is nevertheless a new idea. In direct line it gives to Ruskin the idea of the faith of Horace and, in a general way, all similar developments. But above all it is closely related to an idea quite different from those we mentioned at the beginning of this note, the idea (analysed in note 164) of the permanence of an aesthetic feeling, which Christianity does not interrupt. And now that, from link to link, we have arrived at an idea so different from our starting point (though it is not new for us), we must ask ourselves whether it is not the idea of continuity of Greek art, for example, from the metopes of the Parthenon to the mosaics of St Mark's and the labyrinth of Amiens (an idea he probably believed to be true only because he found it beautiful), that led Ruskin, extending his primarily aesthetic view to religion and history, likewise to conceive of the College of Augurs as assimilable to the Benedictine institution, the devotion of Hercules as equivalent to the devotion of St Jerome, etc., etc.

But since the Christian religion differed little from the Greek religion (the idea: 'rather than on any change brought about by Christianity in the ideal of human virtue and happiness'), Ruskin did not need, from a logical point of view, to separate religion and ethics so strongly. Also, there is in this new idea, even if it is the first that led Ruskin to it, something more. And it is one of those views, rather particular to Ruskin, which properly speaking are not related to any system, and which in the eyes of purely logical reasoning may seem false, but which immediately strike anyone able, by the particular colouration of an idea, to guess its depth, as a fisherman would water's. Of these I shall mention among the ideas of Ruskin which may seem out of date to ordinary minds, incapable of understanding their true meaning and of feeling their truth, that idea which holds freedom as fatal for the artist, and obedience and respect as essential, the idea that makes memory the most useful intellectual organ of the artist, etc., etc.

If one wanted to try to find the hidden links, the common root of ideas so far apart from each other in the work of Ruskin, and perhaps as little connected in his mind, I need not say that the idea noted at paragraph 27, page 150, on 'I am alone, to my belief, in maintaining Herodotus's statement' is merely a different form of 'Horace was pious in the manner of Milton,' an idea which itself is but a counterpart of the aesthetic's ideas analysed in note 164. 'This dome is only a Greek vase, this Salome a canephora, this cherub a harpy,' etc. – (Translator's note.)

**315.** *Genesis*, XVIII, 23. – (Translator's note.)

**316.** Psalm LXV, 13. – (Translator's note.)

**317.** *St John*, *Revelation*, XI, 15. – (Translator's note.)

**318.** This is Appendix III in *The Bible of Amiens*, the second containing the list of photographs taken of the Cathedral of Amiens by Mr Kaltenbacher. – (Translator's note.)

**319.** Reprinted from the 'Advice', issued with Chapter III (March 1882). – (Author's note.)

**320.** No volume other than *The Bible of Amiens* has appeared in the collection *Our Fathers Have Told Us*. But *Verona and Other Lectures* contains two chapters from *Valle Crucis*: *Candida Casa* and *Mending the Riddle* (this chapter takes its title from something that happened to St Benoit in his childhood). – (Translator's note.)

**321.** On the beautiful sonority of the bells of Cluse, see *Deucalion*, I, V, §§7 and 8. – (Translator's note.)

Rouen – cathedral & S. Maclou / S. Ouen
Côte d'Albatre, Wlk fra Étretat / Fécamp
Modernist Le Havre
Caen (par Bla Bla Car)
Jumièges (Abbaye de)
Landg beaches (?)
Romanesque church at Manvilse (?)